PRAISE FOR
SIMPLE OBSESSION

Not only has Jamie started—and continued to pastor—one of the coolest churches I have ever encountered, she is a powerful author. I just finished reading her book *Simple Obsession*. I have read all the famous Christian authors and theologians of the past and present, yet never has a book been more powerfully used by the Holy Spirit in my life. It is a devotional, a theological treatise and a guide for practical ministry. This instant classic is for every Christian.

Rev. Jeff Roartet
Associate Pastor, Evergreen Fellowship
Evergreen, Colorado

Faith, doubt, betrayal, and renewed hope all intersect in this moving account of one young woman's simple obsession to follow Jesus regardless the cost. Jamie provides the reader with a window into her soul as she struggles with a God who permits abuse, is silent when we need to hear him the most and at times seems far away. In the process of walking away from religion, she discovers the tender heart of God. Jamie thinks like a theologian, writes like a novelist, and lives out her faith with abandonment. This book is filled with pearls of wisdom gained by a faith lived out loud. Readers will be able to relate to Jamie's journey and find hope and insight for their own.

Rev. Charles Bello
Founder, Coaching Saints
Author, *Prayer as a Place*

Jamie West Zumwalt has given the church a passionate wake-up call. In *Simple Obsession: Enjoying the Tender Heart of God*, she tells the story of her personal journey from performance-based "churchianity" to a grace-filled life of sitting at the feet of Jesus. Jamie calls for us to stop striving and start resting in the truth that we are God's simple obsession. The more we learn to sit at the feet of Jesus the more we learn God's heart. The more we learn God's heart the more we naturally bear the fruit of God's kingdom. I highly recommend Jamie's compelling story to all in the church who are broken down, worn out and ready to give up.

Rev. Eric Guthrie
Founder, Every Nation

Jamie is gutsy honest, not only about her own battles, but about her great God, whom she hears and with whom she walks. This page-turner, filled with stories of God's speaking and acting, will help readers better experience and serve God.

Rev. Hal Perkins
Senior Pastor, Church of the Nazarene
Grandview, Washington

I have heard Jamie speak several times and consider her to be one of the best speakers I have heard. After reading her book I realized that it was Jesus through her that was so life changing. In this simple book the great truths of God are available as the sweetest morsels. Like a spring of refreshing, this amazing book has given life to my spirit.

Dr. Thomas R. Sattler, Ph.D.
Professor of Philosophy, Retired
Morehead State University

I absolutely love this book, *Simple Obsession!* It has so blessed my heart to read all of the stories and testimonies of God's faithfulness and greatness in Jamie's life, as well as the others she has written about. Her life is a beautiful reflection of Jesus. Her faith, her love, her perseverance, her Simple Obsession has inspired me! Jamie, thank you for your obedience in taking on this challenge to write all of this down and compile it into a book so that those of us who need some nudging, a swift kick, an inspiration, can read it and seek HIM and desire HIM and trust HIM more.

Lynda Mote
Prison Ministry
Little Rock, Arkansas

I can't remember having ever read a book that has touched me more, other than the Bible. Jamie writes not just from her heart, but from God's. One of my favorite works of all is Tozer's *The Pursuit of God*. I truly believe *Simple Obsession* should rank right up there and should be required reading for every Christian. My fervent hope is that it will become a classic in Christian literature—I know it so rightly holds that place in my own heart.

Lawrence Cook
Attorney
Louisville, Kentucky

SIMPLE
OBSESSION

ENJOYING THE TENDER HEART OF GOD

by jamie west zumwalt

with a foreword by Floyd McClung

 **HGM Publishing**
a division of Heart of God Ministries
3720 S. Hiwassee Rd., Choctaw, OK 73020

2nd Edition
Copyright © 2010 by Jamie West Zumwalt

ISBN-13: 978-0-9679781-5-4

Printed in the United States of America
Published by HGM Publishing
3720 S. Hiwassee Rd.
Choctaw, OK 73020-6128

Cover art and design: Justin Falk

FOR EPHRAIM

"double fruit"

August 12, 2004 – November 17, 2004

whose brief life and sudden death has blessed and defined
my own journey in so many ways.

I pray that God will continue to bear abundant fruit
through this tiny seed that fell to the ground.

CONTENTS

A NOTE FROM THE AUTHOR

Throughout the text of this book, I have made many acknowledgments, as there have been so many who have contributed to me learning to enjoy the tender heart of God. Please do read the footnotes, as many of these acknowledgments are made there.

I would like to thank my editor, Audrey Falk, for helping to make sure that I have not made too big of a fool of myself. Thank you for finding my mistakes and for helping me think through how all of this is going to sound to someone outside my own head. Audrey, thank you for being so nice to me in this process.

Thank you, Justin Falk, for your beautiful cover design! You captured my heart in this cover and made it unbelievably special for me personally. See Justin's design work at: www.justincreates.com.

Most of all, I need to thank my family. John, thank you for being my biggest fan. Thank you for believing I could do this and for "locking me up" in the guest room to finally make it happen.

And my children, Jessi, Josiah, Jael, Jewel and James—thank you for giving me the hours away from you, and for picking up the extra chores and babysitting of the little ones. And thank you for letting me tell your stories. Each one of you are reflections of what God has done in me. I love you!

FOREWORD

Rarely does a book take us on a journey into a person's heart, and at the same time lead us to a new and deeper love for God and His redemptive plan for the world, but Jamie Zumwalt has pulled it off in *Simple Obsession*. Jamie does so by telling her story—warm, honest and straightforward. Jamie's journey is compelling because she is so real and down to earth. But don't let her modest style fool you: there is depth in this book.

Jamie has learned the ways of God and passes on what she has learned by inviting us to journey with her as she experiences God's gracious interventions in her life. Grace and tenderness pour off the pages of this book.

It's at once obvious that Jamie is not an armchair philosopher, but a real life practitioner. I was intrigued by Jamie's obvious depth with God. She is a deeply spiritual person, but her book does not reek of religiosity. There is tenderness, not arrogance.

Who then, is this book for?

There are many people who want to serve God, but are disqualified in their own eyes.

There are seekers and searchers after the heart of God.

There are those who want to live a life of passion.

There are those who have stopped growing.

There are those who want adventure, but don't know there is a price to pay.

There are some who are willing to rediscover Jesus.

Simple Obsession is for you if you are one of those people I describe above. Jamie has built her life on the simple truth of God's obsession to love us, to grace us with His goodness; she sees our obedience, therefore, as a response to the presence and love of God in our lives. There is no more profound way to live life and discover Jesus.

Floyd McClung
All Nations
Cape Town, South Africa

XVII

CHAPTER 1
A Simple Obsession Begins

I poured the large bottle of Advil into my coat pockets and walked out into the bitter cold. Wandering the college campus, I replayed, again and again, the shameful scenes that had caused my "condition." How could I have allowed this to happen? So stupid. Such a fool. With each memory, I swallowed a handful of pills. If the pills didn't kill me, maybe they would kill the baby, and I could start over—make some better decisions for my life.

My roommate discovered me lying on the floor of our dorm room— bloody vomit pooled on the floor near the phone, near the door. I had tried to call for help but lost consciousness and now lay in my own blood.

I'd grown up in a small tourist town in Washington State. In an attempt to save the failing economy, the town had been designed to look like the Bavarian Alps. Mountains encircled the quiet, peaceful village; German polka music played in the streets; shop owners wore lederhosen; the smell of bratwurst and schnitzel wafted on the breeze. It was a surreal, almost fantastic, life.

In this unique setting, my father was—what felt to me—like "the village pastor." There were other churches in town, but ours was situated right off the main highway through the center of town. If anyone needed help, ours was the church they could see. My dad knew everyone in town, and everyone knew him.

As a four-year-old little girl, I gave my heart to Jesus, kneeling at an altar after my grandpa had preached a fiery sermon about hell. I was raised attending Sunday School and memorizing verses for Bible quizzing competitions. I had a deep understanding of my own sin and need for Jesus' forgiveness. Every time the doors were open, I was there, immersed in church and the Bible.

Missionary services were especially interesting to me. I viewed their slide shows and heard their stories about far away places and people in other parts of the world. Sitting around our family dinner table, I heard their frightening tales of snakes and bizarre food and imagined that being a missionary was quite an adventure.

During a Sunday night service, we watched a film about some missionaries who had served in South America.[1] I remember their story as being very romantic. A young man and woman, who had fallen in love, shared the same calling and headed off together for that adventurous life of following Jesus to the mission field. I was enthralled as I watched their story. The romance ended abruptly, however, when the young woman and their baby died in childbirth.

The final scene of the movie showed the young man standing on a hillside, weeping as he looked down at the graves of his beautiful wife and baby daughter. He turned his gaze to the valley below him, to the villages of the people to whom God had called him to take the gospel. The movie ended with him rededicating his life to God and to stay — now alone — in this place and fulfill the call that God had given him.

I knew in that moment that God was calling me to be a missionary. When the lights came up, my dad announced that if anyone felt God was calling him or her to become a missionary, he would like us to come forward and let him pray for us. I went forward and knelt at that altar a second time, surrendering my life to God to serve him as a foreign missionary.

Revelation 12:12 says,

> "The devil has come down to you, having great wrath, because he knows he has a short time."

---

1. The film is called *The Calling*. It tells the story of Esther and Roger Winans, missionaries to the Aguaruna Indias of Peru. (Nazarene Publishing House, 1985). www.nazarenemissions.org.

Jesus said in Matthew 24:14 that the good news will be preached in the whole world, to every nation (ethnic group), and "then the end will come." Satan knows this verse very well. When every ethnic group on the planet has received the wonderful good news of Jesus, then Satan's time here on earth is finished. All the havoc that he is wreaking on the peoples of the planet will be put to an end! Satan will do everything he can to prevent us (God's people) from finishing the task that Jesus gave us 2000 years ago—getting the gospel to every ethnic group!

When I stood up from that altar, I had a target painted on me. Have you seen that *Far Side* cartoon where there are two deer talking in the woods? One has a bull's-eye on his chest. The caption underneath reads, "Bummer of a birthmark, Hal." That's what I believe happened to me. When people asked me, "What do you want to be when you grow up?" I would tell them, "I'm going to be a missionary," and the devil began doing everything he could to prevent me from ever fulfilling this call that God had placed upon my life.

All Hell Broke Loose

I was attending a Christian school that my parents had started—only about 50 kids. Such a safe place. I took piano lessons, rode my bike around our block, played with my friends in the barn down the street. It was a comfortable and predictable existence.

I might have stayed in this sweet Norman Rockwell picture my whole life. However, when I was fourteen years old, my parents took a new pastorate in a suburb of Seattle. My two little sisters and I were uprooted from our peaceful, easy life and thrust into an environment so unlike anything we had known.

I entered into a public junior high school that had 1500 students—the same size as my whole hometown! With all the normal insecurities of puberty, I now faced a crowd of kids that I knew nothing about. I had never heard the kinds of words these kids used. I had never known these topics of conversation. I had never seen such rebellious and confused young people.

Culture shock was overwhelming as I discovered that these kids were extremely wealthy. With Microsoft and Boeing money flooding the economy, these young people had more money than they knew what to do with. Many of my friends in high school received a Mercedes or a BMW as their sixteenth birthday present. I had friends who went to the senior prom in a helicopter, trying to outdo their peers who were just arriving in a limousine.

There was no way that I could keep up with the social pressure of this crowd. I was a preacher's kid! We didn't even have enough money for me to buy the seventy-five-dollar GUESS jeans that were so necessary to be popular. I never owned a car in high school—I walked.

I was terribly insecure, shy and embarrassed, so I tried to fit in with the more accessible crowd of musicians. I suffered from a bad case of acne, bad hair, out-of-style clothing and a small group of friends called "the band-tards." I actually did get a varsity letter for playing in the band!

Not So Shiny Armor
In the middle of this jumble of uncertainty, a young man visited our church. He was nineteen; I was fifteen. That Sunday, he took an interest in me. He invited me to come over to his house that afternoon and watch the football game with his family. That football "date" began a relationship that lasted for about two years.

It was a devastating relationship—abusive in every form. This young man was very intimidating in size and personality, and he used both to control me. He forced me to do things that I was ashamed of doing. His outbursts of anger often left me physically shaken and sometimes bruised. He kept me weak and insecure by verbally criticizing everything about me, from my personality to my clothing to my physique.

Once he was walking behind me and said, "Hey, you're starting to get a fat butt." I was only 98 pounds at the time! So I just quit eating. I didn't want to get fat, and I certainly didn't want him to think I was fat, so I just quit eating. My parents could tell that I was having emotional problems, and they began taking me to the doctor because of their concerns about my anorexia, but I would not tell them what I was experiencing in this relationship.

If I told them, they would end the relationship. I truly believed that this young man loved me, despite the abuse. There were moments of sweetness and romance. He was always apologetic, and I was "committed to making it work." I also enjoyed the status that he gave me among my friends—he was an older guy, already graduated from high school. I was *lucky* that he "loved" me.

I was the church youth group president. I read my Bible regularly, attended church, even was active in Bible quizzing competitions. As the preacher's daughter, parents looked to me to help with their wayward teenagers. On the outside, my religious life was all in order. No one would have guessed the shame that was eating me up on the inside.

Drowning Rat
When this relationship ended, he was the one who broke up with me. Now, not only was I abused, but I was rejected. He hadn't wanted me after all. I was devastated, lost and terrified that no one would ever want to marry me. I dated a couple of other guys in high school, but each relationship ended with rejection. I was an emotional wreck, they said. "Too much to handle."

I entered Northwest Nazarene College in Nampa, Idaho, as a music major. I had enjoyed my music classes and thought it might be a nice life to be a music teacher. I also entered college with a strong awareness that if I didn't find my husband in these next four years, I would die an old maid. Where else does the preacher's daughter find her husband but at the denominational college?

A young man asked me to some freshman mixer event, and I grabbed on to him with everything I had, afraid that I might never have another invitation. That began another relationship that was a carbon copy of the one I had experienced in high school.

I since have had counselors explain to me that this is a common theme. Those who have been victimized begin to see life through the lenses of their trauma. I truly did believe that this young man loved me. I believed that this was what all love relationships must look like. I expected to be abused and went along voluntarily with the things that he required of me.

In January of my freshman year, I became afraid I might be pregnant. I had good reason to be afraid of being pregnant. With this possibility, my mind was flooded with thoughts, my emotions became out of control. When I told the young man that I thought I might be pregnant, he said, "Well, I'll marry you," as though that would fix everything. I started thinking about what life with him would be like, and I was absolutely terrified. This was not the fairytale dream of true love—not by any stretch of the imagination.

I began meditating on my condition, and I was so ashamed. My parents had moved to Alaska at the same time I moved to college. They had taken a new church there, and all I could think was that I had ruined my dad's ministry. The one person that I wanted to please the most in my life was my dad, and now, all that the people in his new church would know about him was that his oldest daughter was a fornicator and had a baby outside of marriage. On my list, this was the worst sin I could have committed. The whole world would now know that I was a fake!

Ashamed, humiliated, guilt-ridden, overwhelmed and confused, I filled my coat pockets with Advil and took it, a few pills at a time, over the course of that whole evening. I didn't know if headache medicine could kill me or not (it was the hardest drug a good preacher's kid had in the medicine cabinet), but I do remember clearly thinking, "If this doesn't kill me, maybe it will kill the baby. Then I can start over. I can have another chance to do life better."

The paramedics, doctors and nurses saved my life. They rescued me from myself. I have very few memories of my time there in the hospital—mostly glimpses of faces, images of things they did to me. I do have one very clear memory though. It is of my dad, running through the door into my hospital room. Someone from the school had called him, and he had jumped on the first plane available from Alaska to Idaho.

The story that Jesus told of the prodigal son is the story of my life, only I was the prodigal daughter.[2] I had grown up in the Father's house. I had heard the gospel from the time I was a toddler. I had given my heart to Jesus as a young girl, even responded to a missionary call. But

---

2. Luke 15:11–32.

just like the son in that story, I now found myself face down in the mud, not knowing how to fix the mess I had made of my life.

My favorite part of that story is the homecoming scene. Jesus said that when the son "came to his senses," the father was waiting and watching for him.[3] It was not with tapping toe and crossed arms that the father stood, but with anxious anticipation. When he saw his son coming up the road, the father ran out into the road to meet his son and embraced him there, welcoming him back into the family.

Dad to the Rescue

I was so blessed to have a physical father who so represented what my heavenly Father is like. My dad ran through the door of my hospital room, ran straight over to my bed and threw his arms around me. He did not barrage me with a bunch of questions. He didn't really say anything. He just grabbed me and held me, while I sobbed. I began to tell him things that I had never told anyone—things that had been done to me, things I had also chosen to do.

I told my dad that I knew I hadn't been following Jesus. I told him that I wanted to, but I didn't know how to get there from here. I had messed things up so badly. Jesus seemed so far away. My dad reminded me of how simple the gospel really is—so simple that even a child can receive it.

> If we confess our sins, He is faithful and just to forgive us our sins and to cleanse us from all unrighteousness.[4]

It really is that simple. The clean, white slate that I had been hoping for was right there waiting for me. All I had to do was ask and receive. I did that there in the hospital with my dad. I told God that I was sorry for the mess I had made of my life. I told him that I wanted to follow him, and I asked him for help, because I didn't know how. I didn't know it yet, but the revelation of him as my Father welcoming me home was the beginning of him becoming my simple obsession.

---

3. Luke 15:17 (NIV).
4. 1 John 1:9.

Can You Trust Me?
When I got out of the hospital, my dad and I discussed my options. I could go to Alaska to be with my family, or I could stay there in school. I didn't want to go to a place with a bunch of new people, where all they would know about me was this story. I decided to stay there in school and begin seeing a counselor. My dad went back to Alaska.

One week later, I was walking around the campus again. It was Sunday afternoon, and I was feeling guilty about not going to church that morning. I hadn't been going to church in quite some time and thought it might be a good thing. So that Sunday evening, I walked into the very large church that stood right off of my campus.

I sat down in the back row, leaving many empty rows between the next pew of people and me. It was a huge church building and it was Sunday night—not a full house. The pastor stood up and announced that this evening's service was going to have a special missionary emphasis, and that we would be watching a film. It was the same missionary movie that I had watched as a young girl many years before!

I have since thought about the many details that God was putting into place, in order to get that film shown in that church on that Sunday night—for the one girl in the back row. I knew the moment it came on that it was for me, and I knew what God was asking of me.

He was not just calling me to be a missionary—though that was his desire for my life. He really was asking me, "Who will be on the throne of your life? Who will make the decisions for your life? Will you get off the throne and let me make the decisions? Or will you continue to make decisions for yourself?" It really was a question of who would be king.

As I watched that movie, I was absolutely terrified. I began thinking of what it might mean if I said, "Yes," to Jesus—if I told him I would do whatever he wants, go wherever he wants me to go. At the end of the film, the pastor said, "If anyone feels like God is calling you to be a missionary, please come down to the altar. I would like to pray for you."

I did not go down to the front. I stood in that back row, white-knuckled, gripping the pew in front of me, as I thought, "If I say I'll go wherever God wants me to go, he will surely send me to some place that has giant spiders! And I won't be able to stand it. I will be a basket case!" I told God over and over in my mind, "I can't do it! I know what you're asking of me, and I can't do it!"

Often our disobedience is not simply rebellion. Many times we do want to obey God, but we are terrified. Because we do not truly know him, we do not believe that he knows best, that he will take care of us, that he really has our best interests in mind. Because he is not our intimate friend, we have a trust problem.

That altar call seemed like it lasted forever. I'm sure it was just a few moments that I argued with God. Then I heard him speak to me—that precious, still small voice of the Holy Spirit that today has become my dearest, most intimate friend. He said, "Do you think you can do a better job with your life than I can?"

I knew the answer to that question. If I stayed in charge of my own life, for me it would mean death. I couldn't make the right decisions. I couldn't even decide what boys to date! Backed into a corner by a merciful God, I finally surrendered. I told him, "Okay, I will go wherever you want me to go. I'll do whatever you want me to do. But you're going to have to help me, because I am absolutely terrified!"

CHAPTER 2
We Can Rebuild Her

As a little girl, I loved to watch *The Bionic Woman*, a spin-off from *The Six Million Dollar Man*. Jaime Sommers, the main character, had nearly died in a skydiving accident but had been rescued and rebuilt by the same team of doctors who created *The Six Million Dollar Man*. Her surgical implants gave her extraordinary hearing, superhuman strength and the ability to run really fast. I tried my best not to miss weekly episodes of Jaime's adventures as a secret CIA agent fighting terrible villains.

My neighbor's name was actually Jaime Sommers. She was a friend of the writer of the show, and he had chosen to use her name. It was destiny. Jamie was not a popular name when I was a girl, and even though she spelled her name differently, I felt a connection with this fictional superhero. I thought she was beautiful, brave and altogether exciting.

I did not know it, but standing in that back row of church pews, God had begun to perform surgery. Not only had he brought me back from the brink of death, but now he intended to change me, to fix me, to equip me for the life that only he knew lay ahead.

Super Bowl
Excitement filled the air as noisy students began filling my dormitory lobby. The room had been divided in two, one side dominated by the color red, the other with orange and blue. It was Super Bowl Sunday, a week after my full surrender to Jesus, and the Washington Redskins were playing the Denver Broncos. Personally, I was an avid Seahawks fan, which by default made me anti-Broncos, so I chose the red side and found a place on the couch next to my roommate.

The rivalry increased with each Redskins score, the rowdy cheers being led by a vivacious and animated character. He was a long-haired, hippie-looking young man, wearing cotton Asian drawstring pants and canvas karate shoes—not your normal-looking college kid. Each time the Redskins scored, he ran around the room, high-fiving everyone, including me. His energetic personality, although slightly intimidating, was attractive and he appeared to be everyone's friend.

Many of the students had brought snacks and sodas, and shortly into the game, my roommate and I decided to order pizza. About halfway through my Canadian bacon, deep-dish deliciousness, the long-haired enigma bounced up to me and asked, "Can I have a piece of your pizza?" I hesitantly looked at the one piece left of my side of the pie and responded, "No. But you can have my crusts." Without a pause, he snatched them up, popped one into his mouth and said, "Hi. I'm John." Little did I know that was the first day of the rest of my life.

John was the missions fanatic on our college campus. God had sent him back from Taiwan, where he grew up, with a call to be "eyes and ears" for people here in the American church, many of whom have never seen the need of those around the world who have never heard about Jesus.[1] He had started a missions club on our campus, and following his charismatic leadership, I fully immersed myself in the creative and passionate club activities.

The purpose of the club was to raise awareness about those people on the planet who have yet to hear the good news of Jesus Christ and to mobilize a host of missionaries to take the gospel to them. We did everything we could dream up to call attention to the urgency of the need. We held missions events and prayer meetings. We hung large posters in conspicuous places. One such wall-sized poster was a picture of a giant whale, spitting Jonah up on the beach. The large caption simply read: "Don't Become Whale Vomit."

In February, we passed around a petition encouraging the student body to boycott the annual Valentine's banquet that was sponsored by the Student Senate. We purported that more student budget money was being spent on the insignificant banquet than all the money being

1. Much of John's own story is found in his book *Passion for the Heart of God* (HGM Publishing, 2000).

designated for student ministry clubs, so we called for the students to vote with their lack of attendance at the banquet. The petition worked — the Student Senate met and reallocated funds to the ministry clubs.

We got ourselves in trouble by writing editorials in the school paper that challenged some of the priorities of the religion department and large churches in the area. We were all around rabble-rousers. I admit our tactics were probably not the best, and perhaps they could be likened to missions moblization terrorism. However, everything we did was intended to call attention to those peoples on the planet who have never yet heard the good news of Jesus Christ.

That spring, John and I attended missions conferences together, we took missions classes that semester,[2] and we fell in love as we worked and ministered together in "God's cause." The God that I had just begun to know was putting into my life one piece after another of the things that I would need in order to obey this call that he had placed upon my life. It was a radical reordering, a new obsession: John, Jesus and the kingdom of God.

Sure Enough
John and I were married not quite one year after I got out of the hospital, and six months later, we went to Taiwan as missionaries. Now, John grew up in Taiwan, so going there was not going to the mission field for him. It was going home. For me, everything about Taiwan was foreign.

I am a country girl. I like nature. I like green (plants, trees, flowers, mountains). I like peace and quiet. Taiwan, where we lived anyway, was one large city — and John loved it. He loved the pollution. He loved the loud sounds of the traffic at all hours of the night. He loved the strong smells of cooking food mixed with running sewage. He loved the tall buildings and the busy streets. He loved the people, and he

---

2. Perspectives on the World Christian Movement is a dynamic — I would say life-changing — course that reveals God's heart for the nations in Scripture and history, and then examines the cultural and strategic complexities of accomplishing the task of delivering the good news of Jesus to every people group on the planet. I highly recommend that every Christian take this course: www.perspectives.org.

spoke their language! It was a homecoming for him. And I was mad at him for loving it!

Another missionary had arranged housing for us before we arrived, so we moved into this cute little house. It was a sweet little two-bedroom bungalow, down a back alley, away from traffic. It had a cute little walled-in yard and beautiful banana palm trees surrounding the house, providing shade from the hot summer heat.

However, in these banana trees live banana spiders! And that little house was infested with them. They are as large as John's hands. They're hairy and they're scary! They don't bite humans, but oh, they are terrifying to look at. It gives me the heebie-jeebies just remembering.

John's version of this story is a whole lot more humorous than mine. He includes charades and sound effects, but it is no laughing matter! There was many a day that he chased those spiders around the house with a broom. (What did you think? That you could use a Kleenex on them? No. Cats eat these things! They're the other white meat!)

I would make him go into the house before me, every time we returned from being out. I wanted him to search every room, to make sure there were no spiders showing themselves. I knew they were there, hiding in dark corners, but at least I wouldn't have to look at them.

These spiders are so big that you can't spray them with Raid. They just get drunk and scamper off behind the refrigerator or under the couch. Then, when you're sleeping at night, when you least expect it, they fall off the ceiling onto your bed! I don't care how hot it is, you always sleep with a sheet on you, so that you can fling them off!

Every day, I sat in the middle of that living room floor—I sat in the middle to be as far away from furniture and hidden spider enemies as possible—and I cried. I prayed, "God, I knew you would do this to me, and I told you up front that I can't do it!" I told him this every day.

Desires of My Heart

We landed in Taiwan in the middle of summer heat. It was over 100 degrees and near 100 percent humidity—tropical island, jungle conditions. It is the kind of heat that takes all your energy. We would lie on the floor in the living room under the ceiling fan, unable to move, barely able to breathe.

Every day, we went down the street to a shaved ice shop, where they served the most delicious treat called *bing*. It is much like a snow cone, only served on a plate and much tastier. The ice is very finely shaved, and then they put fresh fruit on top, with sweetened condensed milk— sometimes chocolate syrup. Sometimes we went twice a day, just trying to cool off, and God began to do something for me.

The family who owned this *bing* shop invited us to come and live with them. I got to move out of the spiderhouse! We still encountered them occasionally, but not many times a day. We became a part of this large extended Chinese family. We ate with them; we worked with them in their shop; we played games with them; we watched movies with them—and I watched them as they worshipped their idols.

This family knew nothing of Jesus. They had a room in their home that was dedicated to idol worship, and they also went daily to the village temple to worship the idols there. These are idols like you read about in the Old Testament—images carved out of wood and stone. Some of them look like humans; some of them like mythical creatures; some of them like pictures of dead ancestors.

I watched them teaching their little children, my new nieces and nephews, to bow down and pray to idols. They prayed about the same kinds of things that we pray to our God about—their grandmother who had cancer, their children's grades in school (so that they could have a good future), their business and finances (so that they could provide for their family).

I knew that these idols could not hear their prayers, much less answer them. Something began to happen in my heart. A desire to learn their language began to grow. I wanted to be able to talk to them about Jesus. I wanted to tell them how he saved my life. I wanted to introduce them

15

to the God who can hear and answer their prayers—who wants to live life together with them!

> Delight yourself in the Lord, and He will give you the desires of your heart.[3]

I found that verse does not mean that he is just going to give us whatever we want. He knows that, many times, the things we want are not the best things for us. But what that verse means is that, as we delight in him, allowing him to become our obsession, he actually takes his desires and places them in our hearts. He will *give* us the desires of our hearts. The tough conditions and emotional trials of Taiwan set the stage for getting to know Jesus—for beginning a life of walking with him, heart and soul.

Delighting in the Lord includes what I was doing, sitting in the middle of that living room floor. King David was called a man after God's own heart, and many of his psalms are like those prayers that I prayed there in that spiderhouse—honest, vulnerable, emotional, sometimes desperate, cries for God's help. This is true relationship with God. Delighting ourselves in him means true relationship.

Delighting in the Lord also includes obeying what he calls us to do. He is the King. He is the Lord. He is the one who decides what we will do with our lives. As we surrender to him, doing the things he asks of us, we discover that our hearts begin to change. I found that the spiders, the heat, the pollution, the noise—all those things about Taiwan that were difficult for me—began to diminish, and God's heart for those who had never heard about him began to increase in me. I began the transformation process—he began the work of changing me to look like my Jesus.

---

3. Psalm 37:4 (NIV).

WE CAN REBUILD HER

PART 1

Created for Relationship

This is eternal life, that they may know You, the only true God, and Jesus Christ whom You have sent.

Jesus

CHAPTER 3
Mystic Inclinations

To have found God is not an end in itself, but a beginning.

Franz Rosenzweig

When Brad Pitt left Jennifer Aniston for Angelina Jolie, newsstands were lined with magazines that highlighted the affair. Many Americans experienced great sadness as we watched the destruction of Hollywood's dream couple. I remember conversations in the grocery store checkout aisle as women discussed the pain and humiliation that Jennifer must be experiencing and their own personal outrage, as though she was their close personal friend—as though they had a "personal relationship" with Jennifer.

I grew up with the understanding that Christianity is about a personal relationship with Jesus. In fact, this is one of our evangelistic watchwords, as we attempt to introduce people to him. However, I wonder for how many of us this relationship is a reality. Is it merely a catch phrase, or do we actually experience intimate friendship with God?

> Then the Lord God took the man and put him in the garden of Eden to tend and keep it.[1]

When I met John, he was a long-haired, eclectic, hippie-ish fine arts major. As I became more acquainted with him and his circle of friends, I became immersed in a countercultural world of eccentric artists. He and his art buddies spent long hours, late into the night, down in

---

1. Genesis 2:15.

CHAPTER 3

ld boiler room that they had turned into a makeshift art studio affectionately named "Nirvana." I sometimes wondered how they could see their art pieces through the incense smoke and how they could concentrate through the thumping rhythms of the blasting music.

It was definitely a cool place to hang out, but I didn't really spend much time there, as it had an understood mystique of privacy about it. The artists there did not appreciate bystanders peering over their shoulders as they created. "It isn't finished yet." John spent countless hours working and reworking large oil paintings that were both artistically creative and powerful in the messages they contained. Sometimes, when I caught a brief glimpse, I was confused, because the piece had taken on a completely different look from the last peek I had taken. I was not often included in the creative process as the piece evolved.

Finally, the time for revealing would come. He would announce to me that he was finished. No more tinkering, no more adding or changing. I would descend those concrete steps to view the final piece, while John waited and watched my reaction. Sometimes, the beauty of the piece brought emotional response, and that was enough. Other times, he had to explain the metaphors of the piece to me, as John's pieces most often served to preach a sermon to the church. He would "walk me through" the piece, explaining what each part symbolized and why he had chosen the colors and the textures.

This is the very reason we were created. To burn incense? To paint? Well, maybe that too. But what I'm getting at is that God is an artist! In Genesis, we have the account of God creating every wonderful thing. He went to incredible lengths to make each piece of creation down to amazing detail.

I love flowers. I am not a gardener. In fact, I have the proverbial black thumb. Plants that are entrusted to my care inevitably die. However, when I was growing up, our family yard was always full of beautiful flowers. My dad loves to grow things. Even today, his yard is teeming with plants and flowers. In the middle of my busy life, Dad sometimes calls and asks me to come over. He wants to show me one of his prize flowers that is now blooming. With excitement, he points out the colors and the detail and the vitality of the plant. I love these moments with my dad, stopping and looking at the amazing detail of clematis or a bougainvillea that he picked up in Mexico.

Imagine the beginning. God has just finished creating the sky and the water, the trees, the flowers, the birds—oh, think of the details that birds have! The colors, the textures, the behaviors. He finished creating the fish, the animals. Each one of them is a work of art! A masterpiece.

But...there was no one to show them to. What is the point of a work of art if there is no one to view it? If no one responds, if no one reacts, if no one asks questions about it? You might think, "Well, there were the angels. He could show them." But think about it—they had to say it was great. He was God; they serve him. No, he wanted a friend to see what he had done!

God made for himself a friend. Genesis tell us:

> Out of the ground the Lord God formed every beast of the field and every bird of the air, and brought them to Adam to see what he would call them. And whatever Adam called each living creature, that was its name.[2]

Can you see the picture? God is bringing each one of his pieces of art to Adam to get his reaction.

> And they heard the voice of Jehovah God walking in the garden in the cool of the day.[3]

Can you imagine? I can just see him pointing out the details of the flowers. Even the different kinds of leaves. "Do you see how I did this one? Don't you like the purple here? Don't you like the lines of the veins? What do you think of this one?"

There was nothing else for Adam and Eve to do. They did not have jobs they had to go to. They did not have meals to cook. They didn't even have to work hard to get this garden to grow beautiful things. There were no church activities to be involved in. There was no ministry to be

---

2. Genesis 2:19.
3. Genesis 3:8 (ASV).

done. What did God create them to do? To enjoy his creation! We were created to be "tree-huggers"! Really, God desired friends who would enjoy and share with him this wonderful creation he had just made. We were made for relationship with him.

Mark and Patti Virkler describe it this way:

> "Adam! Adam, where are you?"
>
> When we hear those words we think of the sorrowful day when man's fellowship with God was broken. But let's think for a moment what it was like before that day. How many other days did the Father come to the garden in the cool of the day just to take a walk with the man and woman He loved so much. How often did He call, "Adam, Adam!" How many times did Adam respond joyfully, "Here I am, Lord!" Can you see the three of them perhaps hand in hand, slowly wandering through the lush flowers, sometimes stopping to pick a juicy fruit? ... As the sun set, they must have fallen into companionable silence, enjoying the brilliant display of colors, even more because they were enjoying it together.[4]

Walking with God

God created us to be with him. Throughout Scripture, we find individuals who were "with God."

> Enoch walked with God three hundred years...and he was not, for God took him.[5]

Not only did Enoch just disappear with God, but he had been walking with God for three hundred years. It was a way of life for him. It was so natural that when it came his time to die, he just continued as he had been. He just walked right into eternity with God.

> Noah was a just man, perfect in his generations. Noah walked with God.[6]

---

4. Virkler, Mark and Patti. *Dialogue With God* (Bridge-Logos, 1986) pp. 11–12.
5. Genesis 5:22–24.
6. Genesis 6:9.

We know that Noah was a righteous man. In fact, we know that there were no other righteous men in his whole generation. However, God wants us to know here that it was not just his goodness that caused him to be chosen by God. He walked with God. He was in fellowship with God.

> So the Lord spoke to Moses *face to face*, as a man speaks to his *friend*.[7]

What a thing for people to know about you! God spoke to Moses in a very intimate manner. Not as God afar, but God near. God considered Moses his *friend*.

Abraham had this distinctive title as well:

> "Are You not our God, who drove out the inhabitants of this land before Your people Israel, and gave it to the descendants of Abraham Your *friend* forever?"[8]

> "But you, Israel, are My servant, Jacob whom I have chosen, The descendants of Abraham My *friend*."[9]

> "Abraham believed God, and it was accounted to him for righteousness." And he was called the *friend* of God.[10]

What an amazing reputation! To be called God's friend—for others around us to know that we have a connection to God. That we're on the inside. That we have his ear. That he talks to us about all kinds of things. What an astounding reality—a friend of God.

God is still looking for friends. This is not a new concept for us. We often talk about having a "personal relationship" with Jesus. This is what it means to be a Christian, right? We know this. But the question is: Do we experience it? Do we have a connection to God? Are we on the inside? Do we have his ear? Does he talk to us about all kinds of things?

---

7. Exodus 33:11, emphasis mine.
8. 2 Chronicles 20:7, emphasis mine.
9. Isaiah 41:8, emphasis mine.
10. James 2:23, emphasis mine.

CHAPTER 3

Intimacy Issues

I was walking down the sidewalk with John, informing him of a
problem that was taking place within our ministry and trying to find out
how he wanted to handle it. I was in the middle of my long discourse,
when Jewel, our three-year-old daughter, came running up to us.

She had something to tell us and just began talking and talking, pulling
on my leg, trying to get my attention. I rather abruptly turned to her and
said, "Jewel, just a minute. I'm talking. Mama has issues."

Without a moment's hesitation, she responded, "Well, I have issues....
Tennis shoes." (I know, I know. She gets it from John.)

We all have issues! Don't we? Some more than others. Some have "ten
issues," as Jewel would say. As you might imagine from the painful
relationships in my past, I have intimacy issues.

What is intimacy? Over the years, I've found these definitions:

> **"marked by close acquaintance"**
> So we're not talking about that person that you run into in the
> bookstore and say, "Don't I know you from somewhere?" But
> rather the kind of person that you know very well.

> **"familiarity"**
> When I was a teenager, my dad would notice other teenage
> couples that were expressing more public display of affection
> than he felt was appropriate, and in concern, he would say,
> "Those two are too familiar." What he meant was that they
> obviously had more going on in private than what was
> happening in public. They were intimate with one another.

> **"of deepest nature, innermost"**
> Intimate friends know the deepest, innermost parts of one
> another's lives. Nothing is hidden.

> **"characterized by informality and privacy"**
> When you're with good friends, you can take off your shoes
> and put your feet up. You don't have to worry if your house
> isn't clean when they come over. You don't mind if they see
> you without your makeup.

26

There are things that take place in intimate friendships that never become public. Secrets are told; experiences are had together that no one else ever needs to know about, because it's just between the two of you.

"very personal"
Intimate relationships have inside jokes, common language that comes from experiences had together. There is a quality of relationship that exists from having been in friendship with one another for some time.

"sexual relations"
This, of course, is the most intimate expression of intimacy. In this book, I am not implying that we are to "have sex" with God. However, Paul tells us in Ephesians 5 that the marriage relationship is a picture of the intimacy that is available to us in our relationship with God.

Pain of Rejection
All of us receive rejection. It is part of life. Some of you have had similar painful experiences. Perhaps they were with men, as mine were. Perhaps they were with your parents. Perhaps your peers rejected you. Whatever its form, rejection is part of the consequences of living in a fallen world where sin exists and Satan rules.[11]

In response to rejection, we begin to put up walls to protect ourselves from pain. We distance ourselves from people. We begin to calculate the cost of new relationships. Are they worth the risk? We decide how much of our soul to open up to people.

And then we get married. True love! Aha! We've found the one person who will never leave us, never reject us—only to find that this person has the most potential of anyone to hurt us in the worst way possible. Why is that? It's because when we fall in love, we open our heart up wide. It is fully exposed. We love this one most. We care most what this one thinks about us. We want approval most from this one. We allow this one the greatest capacity to hurt us most!

---

11. 1 John 5:19.

Why am I reminding you of the pains of your past? Why do you have to relive them? Well, we are talking about intimate friendship with God, and we all have intimacy issues. We don't relate well with people, and our intimacy issues affect our relationship with God.

Sometimes we view him through our experiences with our earthly fathers, who were perhaps cold, distant, unfeeling or even abusive. Sometimes we see him as the friend who betrayed us, and we have a hard time trusting him. Perhaps we remember the pain of someone leaving us, and we don't believe that God really loves us or that he will take care of us or that he really has our best interests in mind.

God Is a Person

As we think about becoming friends with God, we must remember that God is a person.[12] He is a person with emotions, just like us. Maybe it's better said that we are people with emotions, just like him. I believe that the emotions we experience are really a part of us being created in his image.[13]

Think about the God you know from the Scriptures.[14]

> The Lord saw how evil humans had become on the earth. All day long their deepest thoughts were nothing but evil. The Lord was sorry that he had made humans on the earth, and *he was heartbroken.*[15]

> How often they rebelled against him in the wilderness! How often *they caused him grief* in the desert! Again and again they tested God, and they pushed the Holy One of Israel to the limit.[16]

---

12. I am not saying that God is a human, but rather I am affirming, with the creeds of old, that he is God in Three Persons.

13. Genesis 1:27.

14. These are merely a fraction of the Scriptures that reveal the myriad of emotions that God experiences in relationship with us. I have taken these quotations from God's Word translation, because I like the way they are informally worded. Other more traditional versions are no less obvious in their evidence of God's emotions.

15. Genesis 6:5–7 (GWD), emphasis mine.

16. Psalm 78:40, 41 (GWD), emphasis mine.

The Lord added, "I've seen these people, and they are impossible to deal with. Now leave me alone. *I am so angry with them* I am going to destroy them. Then I'll make you into a great nation."[17]

As a father has compassion for his children, so the Lord has *compassion* for those who fear him.[18]

As a bridegroom rejoices over his bride, so *your God will rejoice over you.*[19]

Some of the Old Testament prophets speak of God expressing amazement and disbelief that, after all he had done for them, the people of Israel would still choose to worship idols. Can God be bewildered? He knows everything. Nothing surprises him. Yes. But even while knowing everything, he expresses these emotions in relationship with human beings, just as we do—or more accurately, we do just as he does.[20]

As we are desiring friendship with God, we must be aware that he relates to us as a person. Just as we experience relationship with people, we do also with God.

Jesus said,

"No one comes to the Father except through Me."[21]

We can only relate to God through the person of Jesus Christ. Although there is a mystical awesomeness about God, the way that he has made for us to come into relationship with him is through relational interaction with the person—Jesus Christ—by his Holy Spirit.

This is what it means to have a "personal relationship" with Jesus—to relate with God as a person. We can expect that he will express

---

17. Exodus 32:9, 10 (GWD), emphasis mine.
18. Psalm 103:13 (GWD), emphasis mine.
19. Isaiah 62:5 (GWD), emphasis mine.
20. You can find some examples of this in Isaiah 5:4; Jeremiah 2 (the whole chapter); and Jeremiah 8:5, 19.
21. John 14:6.

CHAPTER 3

emotions with us, and we will experience emotions in relating with him. It will fit all of the definitions of intimacy that we examined in this chapter.

Why is this important to understand? Because friendships are emotional in nature. Friends share life together. They do things together. They tell one another secrets. They enjoy being together. They help one another. They cry together. They laugh together. This is what friendship looks like, and God—the most amazing, wonderful, exciting person ever—wants you to be his friend! And he wants to reveal himself as the Friend who fixes all our intimacy issues![22]

The married are those who have taken the terrible risk of intimacy, and having taken it, find life without intimacy to be impossible.

Carolyn Heilbrun

---

22. If you would like to further examine the emotional aspect of God's personality, I suggest listening to Gregory Boyd's sermon "The Compassion That Heals" from June 10, 2007. You can find this sermon online in the Woodland Hills Church sermon archives: www.whchurch.org.

30

CHAPTER 4
Between Best Friends

You love me for no other end
Than to become my confidant and friend;
As such I keep no secret from your sight.

Dryden

When I was in junior high, there was a girl in my class named Laura. Laura was passionate about the soap opera *General Hospital*. She watched it every day after school and knew all the storylines from years before. She talked about the characters as though they were her friends, and many times, I wondered if Laura realized that these people were not real.

However, not only was she an avid fan of the show, she was "in love" with Robert Scorpio, a dashing and debonair character played by Tristan Rogers. She really was not so deluded as to believe that this character was alive, but rather talked about her "love" by his real first name, Tristan. At lunch and during breaks between classes, often her conversation was peppered with the latest news of Tristan's life—who he had married, when his birthday was, how much he was being paid, what other roles he played. She acted as though she knew Tristan, although we all knew she was merely one of a multitude of loyal fans.

Hebrews 1:3 says that Jesus is the "brightness of God's glory and the express image of His *person*."[1] Colossians 2:9 tells us that "in Him dwells all the fullness of the Godhead bodily." That means that everything about God is shown in the person of Jesus Christ. Jesus

---

1. Emphasis mine.

himself said, "He who has seen me has seen the Father."[2] So, if we want to see what relationship with God is like, we need to look at how Jesus did relationships as he walked here on this earth.

Jesus was followed by multitudes of people. I am sure that many of them could have said that they "knew" Jesus. However, most of them knew him from afar. They knew the things he said to the crowds. They saw the miracles that he did, and they were attracted to him. But many did not even have any personal contact with Jesus. They were just members of the masses that swarmed around him.

There was a smaller group of followers. In Luke 10, Jesus sent out a group of seventy disciples. This was a group that he could clearly trust to multiply his ministry. He sent them to heal the sick, cast out demons and proclaim the good news of the kingdom. They must have been a group that had listened intently to many of his teachings, followed him for longer periods of time, and now they were being sent out to represent him. Interestingly, church planters are told that seventy is the maximum that one full-time person can pastor. Perhaps Jesus pastored, mentored and discipled these seventy, but most of them were not his intimate friends.

We know, then, that there were twelve who went with him everywhere during those three years of Jesus' public ministry. They heard all the teaching. He modeled for them how to do the ministry of the kingdom. Can you imagine what it must have been like to live with Jesus? They ate together around the campfire. They walked together for many dusty miles. They laughed together. They talked together. They saw every emotion that he expressed. These twelve truly were his friends.

Inner Circle

However, there were three of these disciples who had some experiences with Jesus that the others did not. When Jesus came to heal Jairus' daughter, he did not allow anyone in the room, except Peter, James and John.[3] These three were there to experience the resurrection power of God through Jesus! It is interesting to note that, later, Peter followed

---

2. John 14:9.
3. Luke 8:51.

everything the way that Jesus had modeled it when he raised Tabitha from the dead.[4] He learned well.

Peter, James and John were with Jesus on the mountain when he was transfigured before them. They got to see the amazing glory of God upon Jesus.[5] The other nine disciples were down below, unable to heal a demonized boy when he was brought to them.[6] I imagine the frustration that these other nine guys must have felt when they heard what the three had just seen. That's not fair!

The night of Jesus' arrest in the Garden of Gethsemane, the disciples were all there with him (except Judas). In fact, Jesus took them there. However, he asked eight of them to sit down, while he took Peter, James and John a little farther with him. Matthew 26:37 tells us that he became "sorrowful and deeply distressed." He fell on his face and began to pray.

This was the darkest moment in Jesus' emotional life. He was facing the greatest cost that could ever be paid—physically, emotionally, spiritually. When he found that his friends had been sleeping, he was hurt. There really was not anything they could do to help him in this distressing time, but Jesus just wanted them to be with him. Have you ever been in this condition? There's nothing anyone can do, but you just want your friends to be there. Jesus considered these three men his dear friends and longed for their companionship as he struggled, and he was hurt that they abandoned him. It was about relationship—friendship.

There was something nearer, or perhaps special, about these three friends. However, there was one of the disciples who had an even deeper, closer relationship with Jesus than any of the others. We need to examine that relationship to see its characteristics and what God desires in intimate relationship with us.[7]

---

4. Acts 9:39–42.

5. Matthew 17:1–13.

6. Matthew 17:16.

7. Thank you to Jack Deere for his article "Passion for Jesus" (Last Days Ministries) that introduced me to John the Beloved back in 1991. Your teachings contributed to the beginning of an amazing adventure of intimate relationship with Jesus for me.

Leaning on Jesus

John 13 holds the story of the Last Supper. It is a picture that you
probably have clearly fixed in your mind from the painting by
Leonardo da Vinci. There, seated and reclining around a low table,
are the twelve who have spent the last three full years with Jesus,
experiencing life together with him.

Jesus informs them that one of them is going to betray them. They
cannot believe this, because they are all friends of Jesus—they
love him. They had left their occupations to follow him. Why? He
was amazing! They saw him heal the sick, feed the poor, free the
demonized, bless little children, provide for them. They were enamored
with him—the way we are when we look at the amazing person of
Jesus!

The disciples begin to talk amongst themselves, confused about how
any of them could ever betray him. Then they look toward Jesus and
see "leaning on Jesus' chest one of His disciples, whom Jesus loved."[8]

Remember, John is the one who has written this biography that we call
the book of John. We must assume that he is being truthful, and more
than that, that he was inspired by the Holy Spirit. He unashamedly
writes it out clearly—that Jesus loved him. Not only did they (the
disciples) love Jesus, but John was so aware that this man, Jesus, loved
him in return. They were deep friends.

This picture of John leaning on the chest of Jesus is quite an intimate
picture. Now, I know that their culture was different from ours. Heart
of God Ministries[9] has some missionaries serving in the Middle East,
and I remember one of the young, single men on our team there relating
a story of going out on a boat ride with a group of men—some of his
Middle Eastern friends. As they were riding in the boat, the sun began
to set, and one of his friends came near and put an arm around his
shoulders while they stood watching the colorful picturesque scene.
Quite the intimate picture! Heterosexual men in our culture are not

8. John 13:23.
9. Heart of God Ministries is an interdenominational missionary training and sending
agency focused on taking the Good News of Jesus to the darkest parts of the world. You
can learn more about HGM at www.heartofgod.com.

often this physical with one another, but in Middle Eastern culture, this has been the norm for thousands of years.

Similarly, many of our Chinese friends of the same gender walk hand in hand down the street together—as good friends. In our culture, we rarely do this. However, despite the differences between our cultures, we can notice that none of the other disciples were leaning upon Jesus. There was something unique about John. We might say that he was Jesus' best friend—and the other disciples knew it.

In the midst of the discussion going on around the table, Simon Peter motions to John to ask Jesus who it is that is going to betray him. Peter knows that if there is anyone who can find out a secret from Jesus, it is John. John asks Jesus and receives an answer.

Last Will and Testament

In the scene of the crucifixion, we find Jesus on the cross, and there at his feet, a small group of people: Jesus' mother, Mary; his aunt (Mary's sister); Mary the wife of Clopas; and Mary Magdalene.[10]

Looking down from the cross, Jesus sees his mother standing there, grieving. He is concerned for her. Then he also sees another standing by. John says of himself that it was "the disciple whom Jesus loved." Jesus "said to His mother, 'Woman, behold your son!' Then He said to the disciple, 'Behold your mother!' And from that hour that disciple took her to his own home."

John and I travel a lot. Sometimes we travel together with our whole family. Many times, we leave the children with family or friends. We have written our last will and testament, and the most important component of our will is to whom our children will be given, if we die. We have chosen people who we know will raise our kids the way we want them to be raised, who will provide for them the way we would provide for them, who will love them the way that we love them. It must be people who know us very well.

---

10. John 19:25–27.

This is what Jesus was doing. He chose his best friend to take and care for his mother. He knew that John would comfort her in her grief, that he would provide for her, that he would love her the way Jesus loved her. The "one whom Jesus loved" became the adopted son. Jesus was not only calling him, "friend," but now he was becoming "brother."

Friendly Competition

John writes in Chapter 20 about the morning of Jesus' resurrection:

> Now on the first day of the week Mary Magdalene went to the tomb early, while it was still dark, and saw that the stone had been taken away from the tomb. Then she ran and came to Simon Peter, and to the other *disciple whom Jesus loved*, and said to them, "They have taken away the Lord out of the tomb, and we do not know where they have laid Him." Peter therefore went out and the other disciple, and were going to the tomb.[11]

Again, John calls himself "the disciple whom Jesus loved." He was unashamed of his friendship with Jesus. Perhaps it was even a title the other disciples used when talking about him. He was known by the others to be the nearest to Jesus.

The story continues:

> So they both ran together, and *the other disciple* outran Peter and came to the tomb first.[12]

Now why did he write that? Why did John want us to know that he beat Peter in the foot race to the tomb? Is there some sort of competition going on?

It goes on:

> And he [John], stooping down and looking in, saw the linen cloths lying there; yet he did not go in. Then Simon Peter

---

11. Verses 1–3, emphasis mine.
12. Verse 4, emphasis mine.

came, *following him,* and went into the tomb, and he saw the linen cloths lying there.[13]

Again he wants us to know that Peter was behind him.

And the handkerchief that had been around His head, not lying with the linen cloths, but folded together in a place by itself. Then the other disciple, *who came to the tomb first,* went in also; and he saw and believed.[14]

John points out to us three times that he beat Peter to the tomb! I do believe that there was some competition here. As we know from other passages, these men were not above pride and jealousy among one another. They even fought about which of them would be the greatest in the Kingdom.[15]

I want you to notice as well that when John saw the empty tomb, he immediately believed. He was the first one of the disciples to believe that Jesus was raised from the dead. It makes sense that if he was the one closest to Jesus, he would understand Jesus' heart, his mind, his intentions the best. He believed the moment that he saw that Jesus was not there.

Breakfast by the Sea

In their grief and confusion after Jesus' death, some of the disciples from Galilee had returned to fishing. When you don't know what to do, do what you know. Fishing was what they knew best. It was comfortable to them. It was home.

They had been out fishing on the sea all night and caught nothing:

In the morning, Jesus stood on the shore, yet the disciples did not know that it was Jesus. Then Jesus said to them, "Children, have you any food?" They answered Him, "No." And He said to them, "Cast the net on the right side of the boat, and you

---

13. Verses 5 and 6, emphasis mine.
14. Verses 7 and 8, emphasis mine.
15. Luke 22:24; Mark 9:34.

will find some." So they cast, and now they were not able to draw it in because of the multitude of fish.[16]

They had seen this miracle before, had they not? Jesus had done this same exact thing for them before, given them the same exact instructions, with the same exact result. And sure enough, John recognizes it—recognizes *him*!

> Therefore that *disciple whom Jesus loved* said to Peter, "It is the Lord!"[17]

Leave it to John to be the one to know him. They were best friends! Now watch what happens:

> Now when Simon Peter heard that it was the Lord, he put on his outer garment (for he had removed it), and plunged into the sea.[18]

He is not about to be beat by John this time!

The other disciples come to shore in the boat, and they find Jesus there with breakfast all prepared for them. They sit down, just like the old days, around the fire to eat and to enjoy one another, and once again, Jesus serves them.

Then the conversation turns to that wonderful, redeeming dialogue between Jesus and Peter. Jesus asks him three times (once for every time Peter had denied him) if Peter loves him. Peter responds that he does love Jesus, to which Jesus replies by commissioning Peter to feed his sheep.

Then Jesus speaks to Peter about his future:

> "Most assuredly, I say to you, when you were younger, you girded yourself and walked where you wished; but when you are old, you will stretch out your hands, and another will gird you and carry you where you do not wish." This He spoke,

---

16. John 21:4–6.
17. John 21:7, emphasis mine.
18. John 21:7.

> signifying by what death he would glorify God. And when He had spoken this, He said to him, "Follow Me."[19]

Basically, Jesus informs Peter that if he truly loves him and wants to follow him, Peter will be crucified. He will be martyred in the same way that Jesus was, and he calls Peter, with this new knowledge, to still follow him.

Now notice again the relationship between Peter and John:

> Then Peter, turning around, saw the disciple whom Jesus loved following, who also had leaned on His breast at the supper, and said, "Lord, who is the one who betrays You?" [All that to say "John"!] Peter seeing him, said to Jesus, "But Lord, what about this man?"[20]

I can just hear my little Jewel. She's six years old now. When I tell her that it's bedtime, she often asks about her younger brother, "Well, what about James? Does he have to go to bed?" We want life to be fair, don't we? Again it's that sense of competition. Peter is aware that in some way, John is extra special to Jesus.

But Jesus said to him:

> "If I will that he remain till I come, what is that to you? You follow Me."[21]

"Jewel, it's not your business when James goes to bed. You obey me."

I was talking with my children in home school one morning about becoming Jesus' best friend, and Jessi, my oldest daughter, got really upset. She was probably nine or ten years old at the time. She is a very black and white, Old-Testament-prophet-type personality, and she was concerned about my theology.

She interrupted me and said, "Mom, God does not have best friends. He loves everyone."

---

19. John 21:18, 19.
20. John 21:20, 21.
21. John 21:22.

There were tears in her eyes, and I felt a little bit of that competition coming from her that Peter must have felt. She was afraid that if God had a favorite, it might not be her.[22]

The glory of friendship is not the outstretched hand, nor the kindly smile, nor the joy of companionship; it is the spiritual inspiration that comes to one when he discovers that someone else believes in him and is willing to trust him.

Ralph Waldo Emerson

---

22. I first was introduced to the "best friends" of Jesus back in the 1990s through the article "Passion for Jesus" by Jack Deere (published by Last Days Ministries). His comments changed the nature of my walk with God, as he gave me vivid models that I could relate to and that challenged me to settle for nothing less.

CHAPTER 5
Abandoned to Love

Love anything and your heart will be wrung and possibly broken. If you want to make sure of keeping it intact you must give it to no one, not even an animal. Wrap it carefully round with hobbies and little luxuries; avoid all entanglements. Lock it up safe in the casket or coffin of your selfishness. But in that casket—safe, dark, motionless, airless—it will change. It will not be broken; it will become unbreakable, impenetrable, irredeemable. To love is to be vulnerable.

C. S. Lewis

A group of women followed and ministered to Jesus.[1] These women had first received ministry from him. He healed them, delivered them from demons, loved them as no one ever had. And now they took it upon themselves to take care of Jesus, to minister to him. We need to look closely at one of these women whose love for Jesus is a picture for us of the kind of intimate relationship that he desires with us. Let's start in Luke 10:

> Now it happened as they went that He entered a certain village; and a certain woman named Martha welcomed Him into her house. And she had a sister called Mary, who also sat at Jesus' feet and heard His word.[2]

There are some important things for us to understand here about these two sisters. Luke first tells us that one woman was *named* Martha and the other was *called* Mary. This is truly significant for "named" and

1. Matthew 27:55.
2. Luke 10:38, 39.

"called" are two different words in the Greek text.[3] Why does Luke emphasize the difference?

Martha was her given name—the name given to her by her parents. Martha had been called this name for her whole life. But Mary was what people had begun calling her. It was, in a sense, her nickname.

Chinese names have innate meaning. For example, when we chose a Chinese name for our oldest daughter, Jessica, we wanted to find one that sounds similar to her English name, but that has significant meaning, as each time it is said, the literal meaning of the name is heard. Her Chinese name is *Jye Shin*—"pure heart."

Similarly, Hebrew names were not merely syllables, as names sound to us in English, but they were packed with meaning. So what is significant about Mary's nickname? It means "rebellion" or "bitterness." Why would people have called her "rebellion" or "bitterness"?

Many Bible scholars believe that Mary of Bethany may have been a prostitute. If this is the case, it might explain the use of this nickname for her. We can only speculate as to why she would have entered into the business of prostitution. Perhaps her father died, leaving her unmarried with no way to provide for her physical needs. Perhaps she had willfully chosen a sinful lifestyle in rebellion against her father.

In Mandarin Chinese, when someone has lived a very hard life, or if tragedies have befallen them, we say that they *chi ku*—they "eat bitterness." We cannot know, but surely a life of prostitution would have provided many reasons to consider her a woman of bitterness.

Where You Belong

Mary was sitting at Jesus' feet. This word "sitting" means more than being seated on the ground. In Jewish culture, "to sit at the feet" of a rabbi means to be under his tutelage, to study under that particular rabbi. Jesus was considered a rabbi—even called by that title.

---

3. All of my Greek and Hebrew word meanings come from Strong's Concordance and the New American Standard Lexicon found online at www.biblestudytools.net.

Like many cultures today, in first-century Israel, women were not considered worthy of being taught, and they were not allowed to "sit under" the teaching of any rabbi. They were not permitted to even read the Scriptures. They were more than not allowed. Rabbi Eliezar said, "Let the words of the Torah be burned rather than entrusted to a woman."[4] There was discussion of whether or not women even had souls. Many rabbis even taught that women were of similar position to a work animal.

What Luke is telling us here is that Mary was a student of Jesus' teaching. She was listening—no, more than listening—she was soaking up everything that she could learn from him.

> But Martha was distracted with much serving, and she
> approached Him and said, "Lord, do You not care that my
> sister has left me to serve alone? Therefore tell her to help
> me." And Jesus answered and said to her, "Martha, Martha,
> you are worried and troubled about many things. But one thing
> is needed, and Mary has chosen that good part, which will not
> be taken away from her."[5]

Martha was trying to tell Jesus that Mary was not in her proper place. She was not even in the right room. Women were to be in the kitchen. They were to serve the men—not sit in the same room with them and listen to the rabbi. Mary was doing the culturally (and as many would have felt, spiritually) wrong thing!

One day I was reading this story, preparing to preach a message from it in our church, and I noticed that when I got to the end of the story, I sighed a big sigh. I stopped for a moment and realized that this story did not give me a good feeling. I began to look at that word, "good." Mary has chosen that *good* part.

That's right, I thought. *Mary's the good one. I'm the bad one. I have five children and a very full life of ministry. There is always something that needs to be done. I do not have time to just 'sit around.' Someone has to do all the practical things. It sounds like Jesus is saying that*

---

4. Jerusalem Talmud, Sotah 3:4, 19a7. As cited in Jeremias, Jerusalem in the Time, p. 373.
5. Luke 10:40–42.

we ought to just stop all the chores and sit down at his feet. Not gonna happen.

Well, I knew there must be something not right in my thinking here, because I know Jesus' character well enough to know that he does not belittle or condemn me. But what could he mean through this? So I looked it up—that word, "good," in the Greek—and it's not what I thought it meant at all!

The Greek word is *agathos*, and one of its meanings is: "agreeable, pleasant, joyful, happy."[6] Jesus did not mean good versus bad. He was not saying that Martha was the bad one, while Mary was the good one. He was not saying that that if you do your quiet time, if you sit at his feet and learn his Word, then you are doing the good thing—then you're a good Christian. No!

Jesus was saying that Mary had found her "happy place"! He defended Mary. He was quite aware of the privilege that Mary was experiencing—of how she was feeling. Leave it to Jesus to fly in the face of prejudice and oppression. Mary was so enjoying being with Jesus, listening to his teaching, that he was not about to make her leave—and she was not about to miss this experience!

Worshipping at Jesus' Feet
Mary's story continues in John 12:

> Then, six days before the Passover, Jesus came to Bethany, where Lazarus was who had been dead, whom He had raised from the dead. There they made Him a supper; and Martha served, but Lazarus was one of those who sat at the table with Him.

> Then Mary took a pound of very costly oil of spikenard, anointed the feet of Jesus, and wiped His feet with her hair. And the house was filled with the fragrance of the oil.

---

6. All of my Greek and Hebrew word meanings come from Strong's Concordance and the New American Standard Lexicon found online at www.biblestudytools.net.

Then one of His disciples, Judas Iscariot, Simon's son, who
would betray Him, said, "Why was this fragrant oil not sold
for three hundred denarii and given to the poor?" This he said,
not that he cared for the poor, but because he was a thief, and
had the money box; and he used to take what was put in it.

But Jesus said, "Let her alone; she has kept this for the day
of My burial. For the poor you have with you always, but Me
you do not have always."[7]

Six days before the Passover. Jesus knows that in six days he will be
arrested and executed. The religious rulers have made it very clear that
they are going to seize him, and Jesus is purposefully heading right for
it. But before he goes to Jerusalem, he stops at this home in Bethany.

We find Jesus visiting this home many times throughout his ministry. I
was privileged to sit under the teaching of David Smithers for over ten
years, and I often heard him teach about the significance of this home.[8]
Jesus recognized it as a place of hospitality. This was a home where
Jesus was welcome. He was made to feel comfortable. These people
were not just there to receive his ministry, to take from Jesus, but they
ministered to him. They served him. These people were Jesus' friends.

It's interesting to note that "Bethany" means "house of misery" or
"house of mourning."[9] It makes me wonder why a village would be
named something that has such a sad meaning. But it is fitting that
Jesus loved to hang out there. In Matthew 5:4, he says, "Blessed are
those who mourn, for they shall be comforted." Psalm 34:18 says, "The
Lord is near to those who have a broken heart." His heart is drawn to
the hurting, to the mourning.

Once again, Martha is serving the meal, and John tells us in verse 9 that
there were lots of people in her house!

---

7. John 12:1–8.

8. David Smithers presently serves on staff with Student Volunteer Movement 2 (SVM2)
as the National Prayer Track Director and is also the founder of Awake and Go Global
Prayer Network, which is designed to call this generation to watch, pray and prepare for
a genuine Christ-centered revival and global awakening. I am extremely grateful for the
teaching and influence that David has brought to my life.

9. All of my Greek and Hebrew word meanings come from Strong's Concordance and the
New American Standard Lexicon found online at www.biblestudytools.net.

CHAPTER 5

> Now a great many of the Jews knew that He was there; and
> they came, not for Jesus' sake only, but that they might also
> see Lazarus whom He had raised from the dead.[10]

Mary comes into this crowded dinner scene and kneels down at Jesus'
feet. She pours costly oil of spikenard upon them and begins to wipe
them with her hair. In the same manner as John, the disciple whom
Jesus loved, Mary places herself in a physically intimate position.

This scene is embarrassing in so many ways! Fragrant oil was a tool
of the trade for a prostitute—alluring, sensual. And her hair! A Hebrew
woman's hair was to be covered. Proper, righteous women would never
expose their hair in front of men, much less wipe a man's feet with it!
Long hair was part of the attractiveness of a woman. Exposing her hair
may have even been a tool of her trade. What a disgrace! Didn't Jesus
understand this behavior!

Yes, he did. If Mary really was a prostitute, then this scene is
overflowing with grace and mercy! She was ministering to him in
the only way she knew how. This was an amazing act of extravagant
worship. Why would she express her emotions in such an extreme way?

Think back to the last scene, when Mary was sitting at Jesus' feet. Here
was a man who was different. When she looked into his eyes, there
was no impure motive there. She saw no lust, no desire to use her, no
oppression—merely pure love and value and forgiveness. Never had
she encountered a man like this! We love him because he first loved us,
and her heart was filled with love for him. She was consumed with holy
passion for him! He was her simple obsession! Nothing else mattered,
including her reputation.

The great missionary, James Hudson Taylor, was once in a worship
service in England. During the song service, he had an overwhelming
desire to get closer to God, so he stood up on his chair. With his eyes
closed, he raised his hands as high as he could reach. When he finally
opened his eyes, he saw that everyone in the room now was standing
on his or her chair, having followed the great Hudson Taylor's example.
Passionate and obsessive perhaps.

---

10. John 12:9.

Years ago, I was in a worship service with some people who I didn't know very well. I was new to expressive worship, having grown up in a church where we kept the ceiling fans low.... These people I was with loved to raise their hands and whoop and holler in worship. I felt myself drawn to this open, demonstrative form of worship.

In the middle of one of the songs, a man who I did not know began to shout his praises at the top of his lungs. He became so overwhelmed that he took off running. He ran out the side door of the room, and we could hear him yelling his praises to God. He ran around the building and came charging back into the room through another door, all the while shouting, "Hallelujah!" and "Glory to God!"

I raised my eyebrows and thought to myself, *Okay, that's a little much. He has gone overboard now. A little out of control and disorderly.*

But, later, one of the women in the group told me the history of this man. Many years before, God had rescued him from a very destructive lifestyle of homosexuality that had threatened to ruin him emotionally, as well as physically. She was not apologetic for him, simply matter of fact, as she explained that whenever a worship song reminded him of what God had done for him, he became overwhelmed with gratitude. Jesus said that those who have been forgiven much, love much.[11]

Have you ever been in a worship service, and all of a sudden, your heart is filled with emotion toward God? You think of raising your hands, or you feel yourself begin to weep, but then you begin to consider what the people around you will think. I have done it many times!

Mary did not care what anyone in the room might think or say. He loved her. He valued her. He had forgiven her. Jesus had defended her once before. He was worth the risk. And wouldn't you know—the feeling was mutual. He defended her again.

---

11. Luke 7:47.

CHAPTER 5

Reality at His Feet

> Now a certain man was sick, Lazarus of Bethany, the town of
> Mary and her sister Martha. It was that Mary who anointed the
> Lord with fragrant oil and wiped His feet with her hair, whose
> brother Lazarus was sick. Therefore the sisters sent to Him,
> saying, "Lord, behold, he whom You love is sick." When Jesus
> heard that, He said, "This sickness is not unto death, but for
> the glory of God, that the Son of God may be glorified through
> it." Now Jesus loved Martha and her sister and Lazarus.[12]

Just as we saw with John the Beloved, Jesus has a love for them, a
relationship with them, that is unlike other relationships. We could call
them "the family that Jesus loved." It is very apparent to all that Jesus
loves them. I also like that Martha is first in this list, again showing that
Jesus did not consider her the "bad" one. He loved her.

> So, when He heard that he was sick, He stayed two more
> days in the place where He was. Then after this He said to the
> disciples, "Let us go to Judea again."[13]

We know also from the book of John that Jesus only did what he saw
the Father doing. He only said what the Father told him to say. He did
nothing of himself.[14] So we can know that his decision to not go to
Lazarus immediately was a Father-directed decision. He loved Lazarus
dearly, but he waited two days before he set off to Judea.

Let's skip down to Jesus' arrival in Bethany. Now, we are going to see
Jesus' interaction with Martha first, and then his interaction with Mary.
I want you to notice the difference, and I want you to be thinking about
your own relationship with Jesus. Which one does it reflect more?

> So when Jesus came, He found that he had already been in
> the tomb four days. Now Bethany was near Jerusalem, about
> two miles away. And many of the Jews had joined the women
> around Martha and Mary, to comfort them concerning their
> brother.

12. John 11:1–5.
13. John 11:6, 7.
14. John 5:19, 30.

Then Martha said to Jesus, "Lord, if You had been here,
my brother would not have died. But even now I know that
whatever You ask of God, God will give You."

Jesus said to her, "Your brother will rise again." Martha said to
Him, "I know that he will rise again in the resurrection at the
last day."

Jesus said to her, "I am the resurrection and the life. He who
believes in Me, though he may die, he shall live. And whoever
lives and believes in Me shall never die. Do you believe this?"

She said to Him, "Yes, Lord. I believe that You are the Christ,
the Son of God, who is to come into the world."[15]

This woman, Martha, has just lost her brother. It was not an expected
death. He had not been ill for a long time. It was a sudden tragedy. On
top of the suddenness, there was an unmet expectation that Martha had.
She truly believed that Jesus was going to come and heal her brother—
but he didn't.

Those of us who work at Heart of God Ministries have recently been
through this kind of experience. Our mission director, Orval Halley,
was diagnosed with pancreatic cancer in February of 2008. Orv was
John's and my pastor when we were in college in Nampa, Idaho. His
church was the church that all the radical young people attended. Those
who were involved in feeding the poor, inner city ministry, ministering
to AIDS victims, missions to unreached peoples, went to Orv's church.

We were attracted to this church because Orv was passionate about
Jesus and passionate about God's heart for people—hurting people and
those who have never heard of Jesus' love for them. He was determined
to see God's presence both in his own church and extended among
those on the planet who have never heard the gospel.

Orv was a giant of a man, standing at six feet four inches. He was the
pastor that married John and me. We opted to stand on the platform of

---

15. John 11:17–27.

the church, facing the congregation, while he stood down at the bottom of the steps. That put us at just about eye level.

Orv's passion was contagious. He longed to be one of those pioneers who would take the good news of Jesus to a people who did not yet know it. He had pastored for over forty years, and finally felt that God released him to go. He asked God for another twenty years of life, to serve in frontier missions. After spending a year in Kazakhstan, he agreed to oversee all the missionaries that serve through HGM.

Orv and his wife, Roberta, traveled to visit the missionaries, living with them in their huts in Africa, in the cities of the Middle East, on the grasslands of Tibet, in the poverty of India, in the spiritual oppression of Indonesia. At an age when most people are retiring, they braved malaria, dysentery, unusual food and extreme temperatures to bring guidance and encouragement to those younger pioneers who are living continually in such harsh conditions.

When Orv was diagnosed with cancer, none of us could believe that God would allow him to die. He was too important. He was invaluable in the kingdom of God. Many Scriptures came rolling in through emails and phone calls—promises of God's healing. All were believing that God would miraculously heal Orv and receive glory among the nations.

The cancer quickly progressed from his pancreas to his liver, and then treatment could not even be performed, as his liver could not process the chemotherapy or radiation. To the very last moment, we all believed that God would come through for Orv—for us. And then Orv died, only two-and-a-half months after the diagnoses. So fast!

I know what Martha must have been feeling inside. She believed that Jesus was going to show up! He didn't come. He could have come. Now, I want you to look again at the conversation that she has with Jesus:

> "Lord, if You had been here, my brother would not have died. But even now I know that whatever You ask of God, God will give You." Jesus said to her, "Your brother will rise again." Martha said to Him, "I know that he will rise again in the resurrection at the last day."

Jesus said to her, "I am the resurrection and the life. He who believes in Me, though he may die, he shall live. And whoever lives and believes in Me shall never die. Do you believe this?"

She said to Him, "Yes, Lord. I believe that You are the Christ, the Son of God, who is to come into the world."[16]

It is a theological discussion! She is in horrible pain and confusion, and she gets into a theological discussion with Jesus! He asks her if she believes these things...She says she does...He tells her who he is and asks if she believes that...She says she does...And that's that. Do you feel any better?

Do you realize that demons believe these very same things that Martha and Jesus are discussing? They believe that he is the Son of God. They know it. They believe that he is the resurrection and the life. They know it. Believing these things is not what God is after—it is not what he desires from us. Remember, we were made for relationship!

Let's look at Mary's interaction with Jesus:

And when she [Martha] had said these things, she went her way and secretly called Mary her sister, saying, "The Teacher has come and is calling for you."[17]

It's interesting that Martha uses that word "teacher," or rabbi. Maybe Martha only knew him for the theological information that he contained. Perhaps she is referring to that day when Mary sat at his feet. Perhaps she is acknowledging that Jesus was rightfully Mary's rabbi.

As soon as she [Mary] heard that, she arose quickly and came to Him. Now Jesus had not yet come into the town, but was in the place where Martha met Him. Then the Jews who were with her, when they saw that Mary rose up quickly and went out, followed her, saying, "She is going to the tomb to weep there."

16. John 11:21–27.
17. John 11:28.

> Then, when Mary came where Jesus was, and saw Him, she fell down at His feet, saying to Him, "Lord, if You had been here, my brother would not have died." Therefore, when Jesus saw her weeping, and the Jews who came with her weeping, He groaned in the spirit and was troubled.[18]

Mary says the same words to Jesus that Martha said: "Lord, if you had been here, my brother would not have died." Notice where Mary is though. She has fallen down at his feet. Every time we see her, she is somehow at his feet—in humility receiving, in worship, and this time, in all the emotions of grief. She is overwhelmed by her pain.

Heart Pain

My youngest sister, Joy, and her husband, Eric, have been missionaries in Asia for seven years. They came home for the delivery of their fourth son. Four boys! During their furlough, they came to our HGM Oakhill campus in Oklahoma. My parents live there on the campus in a remodeled barn, and we were living near the back of the campus in an apartment. Having them with us is always a treat, as my children love to play with their cousins. Great family times!

Wednesday night is usually "date night" for John and me, but this particular night, I wasn't feeling well. It was cold and rainy, and we decided to just stay in and watch a movie in our bedroom, rather than get out in the weather. In the middle of our movie, my cell phone rang. We decided not to answer, as we were having our date.

A moment later, we heard the siren of an ambulance. Now, we periodically will hear an ambulance drive down our street, but somehow John knew this time was different. He jumped up from the bed and said, "It's coming here!" He ran out the front door, with me following closely behind.

As we approached the front of the campus, my sister was running down the driveway toward the ambulance yelling, "My baby is dead! My baby is dead!" Little Ephraim was three months old. She had gone to

---

18. John 11:29–33.

wake and nurse him before letting him sleep the rest of the night, and she found him not breathing.

The paramedics lay him on a board on my parents' bed and began to work on him, trying to find some sign of life, while we prayed for resurrection. The policemen came and separated my sister and her husband to question them, when all they wanted was to be near their son. I held the other three little boys on the floor in the closet, trying to explain to them what was happening to their little brother.

The paramedics put little Ephraim in the ambulance to rush him to the hospital, hoping they could revive him there, while my parents and Joy and Eric followed in a car. John and I stayed with the little boys to try to bring comfort and rest to them.

In the middle of the night, they returned from the hospital with the news that little Ephraim was gone—that he wasn't coming back. As the words came out of their mouths, they both ran to the bathroom and began vomiting—too much emotion to carry.

As we sat in the living room in silence, my little sister turned to my dad and asked him to please go up to the bedroom and take down the baby bed. She said, "I can't look at it." My usually reserved dad rose and climbed the stairs to the bedroom. We could hear him sobbing, as he dismantled what had been a precious bassinet.

It has been three-and-a-half years since this event happened in my life, and I have told this story countless times, but I cannot write these words without weeping. Ephraim's death was the most painful experience of my life, and he wasn't even my own baby. This is what Mary was feeling.

Life stood still for us after that. For about six weeks, we did nothing but sit with Joy and Eric. Sometimes we played silly card games. Sometimes we watched stupid TV shows. Then something would remind one of us of Ephraim, and we would begin to cry.

We listened, and we cried with them, as they spouted their confusion, their anger, their questions. Why? Why would God allow such a thing?

Who is God anyway? Is He even good, as He says? Faith threatened to die with Ephraim.

This is what Mary was feeling! And where do we find her? Fallen down at Jesus' feet saying, "Lord, if you had been here my brother would not have died!" She was weeping. The Greek word here for "weeping" does not mean a few tears rolling down her cheeks. It is a word that connotes deep sobbing, gut-wrenching sobs.[19]

I remember bringing my grandma back to her home after standing around my grandpa's bedside with other family members, as he breathed his last breaths in the hospital. He was an old man and had been suffering from Alzheimer's for ten years. It was his time to die, and it was a very special celebration, as we sang his favorite hymns during those last minutes of his life.

We walked down the hall of Grandma's home with her. When she walked into the bedroom that had been theirs together for many years, she fell to the floor and began to sob. The sounds that came from her, I had never heard before. They were deep, gut-level moans and sobs. This is what John is describing. Mary was overcome with emotion.

The story goes on:

> Therefore, when Jesus saw her weeping, and the Jews who came with her weeping, He groaned in the spirit and was troubled. And He said, "Where have you laid him?" They said to Him, "Lord, come and see."[20]

And then, those most precious words of Scripture:

> Jesus wept.

Jesus, too, became overwhelmed with emotion. I have never yet seen one of the Jesus movies do it right. Usually they show a tear trickling down Jesus' face. But, no. Jesus began to sob with Mary! Can you see it?

---

19. All of my Greek and Hebrew word meanings come from Strong's Concordance and the New American Standard Lexicon found online at www.biblestudytools.net.
20. John 11:33.

Why? Why would he do that? He knows that he is going to raise Lazarus from the dead in just a few minutes. There is no reason to cry. There is reason to rejoice. Why didn't he just say, "Stop crying, Mary. It's going to be okay"?

Scripture tells us to rejoice with those who rejoice, and to weep with those who weep.[21] This is God's character. Jesus understood all that Mary was feeling—the grief, the confusion, the anger. He felt all of it with her. He loved her, and he hated seeing her in so much pain. He wept with her.

This is the kind of relationship that Jesus desires to have with us. Most of us have been conditioned to live in denial. We hide our emotions from ourselves, as well as others. We tell ourselves it's going to be okay. We even create theologies to make ourselves feel better. All the while, we are grieving, hurting, dying on the inside.

Life does not look like it did in the garden when God walked with Adam and Eve in the cool of the day. Life is not often a gentle garden experience. Because of sin and the devil, we often face the pains of rejection, loss, betrayal, persecution, sickness and death. God continues to desire to walk with us—through the experiences of this life. He is Emmanuel—*God with us*. Have you invited him into the painful places of your life?

---

21. Romans 12:15.

CHAPTER 6
The Indispensable

In true love the smallest distance is too great, and the greatest distance can be bridged.

Hans Nouwens

"Do I have to become charismatic and raise my hands and shout in worship?" "Do I have to become a blubbering idiot to be a good Christian?" "Is she asking us all to become totally run by our emotions!" "How essential is this to a Christian?"

When John Bunyan was imprisoned in Bedford jail, some of the men who had persecuted him received the report that the jailer often let Bunyan out of the prison. Frustrated by this news, they made a trip to the jail, planning to arrive in the middle of the night, in a surprise visit to investigate the accusation.

Bunyan was at home with his family, however he was restless and could not sleep. He explained to his wife that although the jailer had given him liberty to stay at home until morning, he just felt that he should return immediately to his cell. He did, and the jailer became angry with him for coming in at such an unreasonable hour.

Early in the morning, the persecutors arrived at the prison. They questioned the jailer: "Are all the prisoners safe?" "Yes." "Is John Bunyan safe?" "Yes." "Let me see him." He was summoned and all was well.

After the men had left, the jailer told Bunyan, "You may go in and out again, whenever you think proper, for you know when to return better than I can tell you."

As followers of Jesus, let's look at how he lived. We will discover how important intimate relationship with God really is. Jesus talked about his relationship with the Father many times.

> "Most assuredly, I say to you, the Son can do nothing of Himself, but what He sees the Father do; for whatever He does, the Son also does in like manner."[1]

> "I can of Myself do nothing. As I hear, I judge; and My judgment is righteous, because I do not seek My own will but the will of the Father who sent me."[2]

> "When you lift up the Son of Man, then you will know that I am He, and that I do nothing of Myself; but as My Father taught Me, I speak these things."[3]

Jesus lived in constant dialogue with the Father, only doing whatever he heard the Father telling him to do, only saying what he heard the Father telling him to say.[4]

> "He who has seen Me has seen the Father ... Do you not believe that I am in the Father, and the Father in Me? The words that I speak to you I do not speak on My own authority; but the Father who dwells in Me does the works."[5]

In fact, Jesus and the Father dwelt in such communion that he could say that they were one.

---

1. John 5:19.

2. John 5:30.

3. John 8:28.

4. As a young married couple, fresh from finishing two years as missionaries in Taiwan, we began attending a church where Hal Perkins, the pastor, introduced us to these verses—to this concept. He challenged us individually, but also corporately as a church body, to follow the example of Jesus and only do what we heard the Father doing. It was, and remains, an exciting adventure! Thank you, Hal.

5. John 14:9, 10.

Tuning In

Hal Perkins, my pastor during my early married years, related in a new way for me the story of the woman caught in adultery. When the Pharisees brought her to Jesus, they asked him what should be done. It was a trap. Would he follow and promote the Law of Moses, or would he give some new teaching that would prove him to be a heretic?

Jesus stooped down and began writing in the sand. Tradition tells us that he may have been writing out the sins of those in the crowd around him—perhaps even the sins of those Pharisees. We do not know from Scripture, and we can only speculate. But Hal suggested to us that perhaps Jesus was stalling for time! This was a difficult situation, without an easy answer. He needed wisdom, and he only did what the Father told him to do. Finally he rose with the brilliant, perfectly just answer:

> "He who is without sin among you, let him throw a stone at her first."[6]

Jesus was completely dependent upon the Holy Spirit—upon hearing from his Father. He is our model. Although we may not be in as critical of circumstances, if Jesus needed specific direction, how much more do we need it? We must grow in intimacy with God, in dependence upon God. Jesus showed us: Pause. Connect. Listen. Then act. The law gives stones; intimacy gives life!

Two young boy princes once, together, occupied the throne of Russia. Daily they sat in judgment on the most difficult of cases. The people marveled at their wisdom, as they were so young and inexperienced in matters of state. Their secret was that, behind the throne, hidden by a veil, their sister Princess Sophia sat listening to every case. She was the one who whispered decisions to them. Then they delivered her pronouncements.

In this way, the word of Christ should dwell in our hearts.[7] Just as Jesus did, we are to refer every matter to the Holy Spirit and listen for his decision. Whatever he tells us to do, we do. Whatever he tells us to say,

---

6. John 8:7.
7. Colossians 3:16.

we say. He will tell us not only the *what* to do, but the *how* to do it as well.

Wesley Duewel, missionary to India and author, tells of a time when he was seated on the platform during a church service. He was not the speaker for the event, but as the sermon closed and the invitation was given, he prayed that people would respond. As the hymn was being sung, he asked the Lord, "Is there someone that I am responsible to reach tonight?" This was not a usual prayer for him, but he felt led to pray that way. His eyes fell upon a young man in the back of the room.

None of the other ministers were going to individuals, but he felt impressed by the Holy Spirit, so he slipped off the platform and went back to that man. He asked, "Would you like to go forward to pray tonight?" Before he could even complete the question, the young man started forward.

Standing in the aisle, he prayed again, "Lord, is there anyone else?" He saw another person that he felt drawn to, so he went there. Again, immediately the person went forward. In the next few minutes, he went to five more people, all of whom went forward to make a commitment to Jesus that night. When he felt released that he had spoken to all whom the Lord wanted him to speak, he wondered in his heart, "What if I had not asked the question?"[8]

Perhaps we "have not, because we ask not."[9]

Knowing God

Jesus talked a lot about the importance of *knowing him*.

> "Not everyone who says to Me, 'Lord, Lord,' shall enter the kingdom of heaven, but he who does the will of My Father in heaven. Many will say to Me in that day, 'Lord, Lord, have we not prophesied in Your name, cast out demons in Your name and done many wonders in Your name?' And then I will

---

8. This story is told by Wesley L. Duewel in his book *Let God Guide You Daily* (Duewel Literature Trust, 1988) p. 41.

9. James 4:2.

declare to them, 'I never knew you; depart from Me, you who practice lawlessness!'"[10]

Okay, so maybe you haven't been doing these kinds of works. You haven't cast out any demons or prophesied lately. But you've been working and serving God in all sorts of capacities. You have been doing Christian activities. Is it possible that we can be doing many things that are not the *will* of the Father, because we do not *know* him?

We'd better stop and look at these words "to know." In the Greek language, there are two different words that mean "to know." *Oida* is the word that means to know about, to know information. *Ginosko* is the word that means to know in the sense of coming to know, learning, understanding, comprehending. It even includes the meaning of sexuality.[11]

The corresponding word in Hebrew is *yada*. Genesis 4:1 says that "Adam *knew* Eve his wife, and she conceived and bore Cain."[12] Again, I am not suggesting that we are to have sex with God. I am merely pointing out that the word that Scripture uses for knowing God is intimate in its meaning. It cannot mean to know from a distance or to know about. But rather, it is a kind of knowing that comes from experiencing relationship with him.

Jeremiah puts it this way:

> "Let not the wise man glory in his wisdom, let not the mighty man glory in his might, nor let the rich man glory in his riches; but let him who glories glory in this, that he understands and knows Me, that I am the Lord, exercising lovingkindness, justice and righteousness in the earth. For in these I delight," says the Lord.[13]

He wants us to understand him and *yada* (experience) him deeply. He wants us to experience him in all of his characteristics.

---

10. Matthew 7:21–23.
11. All of my Greek and Hebrew word meanings come from Strong's Concordance and the New American Standard Lexicon found online at www.biblestudytools.net.
12. Emphasis mine.
13. Jeremiah 9:23, 24.

CHAPTER 6

In Matthew 25, Jesus tells a story of ten virgins who had gone to meet
a bridegroom. There were five who had taken extra oil for their lamps
and were ready for the moment the bridegroom would come. The other
five of them had to leave while they were waiting, in order to go get
more oil. When the bridegroom arrived and invited the virgins into the
party, the five unprepared virgins were not there. They were left out.

The five who had been unprepared began calling to the bridegroom to
open the door and let them in, but he answered and said, "Assuredly, I
say to you, I do not *know* you."[14]

Jesus makes this issue of knowing him the central issue of Christianity:

> "And this is eternal life, that they may know You, the only true
> God, and Jesus Christ who You have sent."[15]

Eternal life is not a ticket that we get so that we can go to heaven after
we die. It is about right now, in this life, in this moment, *knowing* him.

> One day a happy Christian met an Irish peddler. He exclaimed,
> "It's a grand thing to be saved!"
>
> "Ah," said the peddler, "it is, but I know something better than
> that."
>
> "Better than being saved?" said he. "What can you possibly
> know better than that?"
>
> "The friendship of the man who has saved me!" was the
> unexpected reply.

Paul's prayer for the Ephesians was that "the God of our Lord Jesus
Christ, the Father of glory, may give to you the spirit of wisdom and
revelation in the *knowledge* of Him."[16] We are not after knowledge
about Jesus, but rather that we would experience knowledge of him. A
deep level of intimacy, *yada*, is possible and available to all believers
through the Holy Spirit.

---

14. Matthew 25:12, emphasis mine.
15. John 17:3.
16. Ephesians 1:17, emphasis mine.

Paul expresses that this deep level of intimacy is his greatest desire:

> Yet indeed I also count all things loss for the excellence of
> the *knowledge* of Christ Jesus my Lord, for whom I have
> suffered the loss of all things, and count them as rubbish, that
> I may gain Christ and be found in Him, not having my own
> righteousness, which is from the law, but that which is through
> faith in Christ, the righteousness which is from God by faith;
> that I may *know* Him and the power of His resurrection, and
> the fellowship of His sufferings, being conformed to His
> death, if by any means, I may attain to the resurrection from
> the dead.[17]

From a Distance

Like Martha, you may have all your intellectual beliefs in order. You
believe in the virgin birth. You believe in the Trinity. You believe that
Jesus came and died for your sin. You have even accepted his gift of
salvation for you. And you believe that you will go to heaven when you
die.

But let us remember that God created you for friendship with himself.
He still is looking for you as a friend. He loves you and wants to
experience life together with you — you sharing in his joys and sorrows,
him sharing in yours. That is what it means to truly *know* him. And that
is what it means to have eternal life!

> One ingenious teenager, tired of reading bedtime stories to his
> little sister, decided to record several of her favorite stories on
> tape. He told her, "Now you can hear your stories anytime you
> want. Isn't that great?"
>
> She looked at the machine for a moment and then replied,
> "No. It hasn't got a lap."

In John 5:39–42, Jesus rebuked the Pharisees:

---

17. Philippians 3:8–11, emphasis mine.

"You search the Scriptures, for in them you think you have
eternal life; and these are they which testify of Me. But you
are not willing to come to Me that you may have life. I do not
receive honor from men. But I know you, that you do not have
the love of God in you."

The Pharisees were not merely lacking in their love for other people.
They were not experiencing God's love for them. Their religion was
all about the Bible, but they did not have relationship with God. Now
Jesus, who looked exactly like the God of their Scriptures, was standing
in front of them, and they didn't even recognize him.

"I know all the things you do. I have seen your hard work and
your patient endurance. I know you don't tolerate evil people.
You have examined the claims of those who say they are
apostles but are not. You have discovered they are liars. You
have patiently suffered for me without quitting.

"But I have this complaint against you. You don't love me or
each other as you did at first! Look how far you have fallen
from your first love! Turn back to me again and work as
you did at first. If you don't, I will come and remove your
lampstand from its place among the churches.

"But there is this about you that is good: You hate the deeds of
the immoral Nicolaitans, just as I do. Anyone who is willing to
hear should listen to the Spirit and understand what the Spirit
is saying to the churches. Everyone who is victorious will eat
from the tree of life in the paradise of God."[18]

This church at Ephesus was characterized by diligence in working
hard for the Lord. They were especially concerned about sin in other
people's lives and careful about good doctrine. However, they were
missing the whole point of being a church at all. They had lost their
first love! They were lacking relationship with Jesus.

Now, I don't know exactly what "taking our lampstand away" means.
I'm not going to argue here the possibility of losing our salvation or

---

18. Revelations 2:2–7 (NLT).

eternal security. However, whatever it means, it cannot be good! Jesus is calling losers of their first love to repent.

I think the conditional promise attached to this call to repentance is amazing. He calls those who have lost their first love to return to relationship with him, and he promises that he will return us to the experience of the garden of Eden—eating from the tree of life, living in the midst of the paradise of God. We can return to the fellowship of walking with him in the cool of the evening.

The implication of some of the verses we have looked at here is frightening. It is possible for us to think that we are doing just fine. We've prayed the prayer. We're involved in Christian activities. We even serve God. However, the potential is that he could look at us and say, "I don't know you. I never knew you."

God did not create us just to serve him or even just to worship him. He had the angels for that. He created us for relationship with himself, because he desires relationship with us. Relationship goes beyond theoretical knowledge. It involves shared life—*yada*. He invites us into *yada*. Step into a shared life, a blended life. God and you. *God with us*.

CHAPTER 7
Prodigal's Dad

Muslims have 99 names for God, but among them all they have not "Our Father."

Anonymous

"And I will be a Father to you, and you shall be sons and daughters to Me," says the Lord Almighty.

2 Corinthians 6:18

An aged Quaker named Hartman had a son who enlisted in the army. The day came that he heard of a terrible battle, and he decided to go to the scene of the conflict himself, in order to ask about his son. The officer in charge told him that in calling roll, the son had not answered to his name. They feared that he must be dead.

This answer did not satisfy the father, so he hurried out into the battlefield himself to look for his beloved son. He bent over body after body, turning each face upward, with no success. When night fell, he took up a lantern to continue his search, but to no avail.

Suddenly the wind blew out his light, and he stood there in the dark, not knowing what to do. Finally, his love and concern prompted him to begin calling out his son's name. "John Hartman, your father is calling you!" All around him he heard the groans of the dying men. Someone said, "If only that were my father."

He continued shouting with more and more intensity until at last, off in the distance, he heard a trembling voice: "Here, Father." The old father rushed across the field, shouting, "Thank God! Thank God!" Carrying the son in his arms, the father bore him back to safety and nursed him back to health.

> See how very much our heavenly Father loves us, for he allows us to be called his children, and we really are![1]

The word that best describes my father's relationship with me as a young girl is probably: "teacher." I have many memories of listening to my dad explain concepts to me. He was usually responding to one of my many questions about life. Dad told me why the government doesn't just print more money in order to pay the national debt. As I watched Oliver North on the evening news, he was the one who explained to me the nuances of the Iran-Contra affair. Dad helped me understand the differences between my Mormon friends and me in what we believe about God.

When our family went to Disneyland—a "once in a lifetime trip," Mom and Dad explained to us kids—neither Dad nor I relished the idea of careening up and down, around and around, on thin rails of metal. So while my mom and two sisters enjoyed the Matador and Space Mountain, Dad and I sat on a park bench discussing fine points of theology. These are precious memories to me, as I saw my Dad as having all the answers. He knew everything.

> A devoted father came into the room where his eight-year-old was dying of an incurable disease. The child, sensing that he was not going to get well, asked his father, "Daddy, am I going to die?"
>
> "Why, son? Are you afraid to die?"
>
> The child looked up into the eyes of his father and replied, "Not if God is like you, Daddy!"

In thinking of God as our father, it is often difficult not to be reminded of our earthly fathers. If your memories are pleasant, this can be a benefit. However, if the relationship that you had with your earthly

---

1. 1 John 3:1 (NLT).

father was strained, distant or even abusive, it may be more difficult for you to even desire knowing God as father.

I have a friend who saw God through the emotionally painful experiences with his own dad. He remembers coming home from school one day to find his father exceedingly angry with him. That morning, he had ironed a shirt to wear for the day and had forgotten to turn off the iron. It sat dangerously on the ironing board all day, where his father found it when he came home from work. The beating he received for this mistake has stayed with him long into his adult life, creating an image of God as a harsh and angry taskmaster who scolds and severely punishes his children for their sins.

A Father's Love

John Dawson, in his wonderful article called "The Father Heart of God," talks about what kind of authority figure God is to us.[2] Every harsh or abusive experience that we have had with our earthly fathers has misrepresented to us the kind of authority that God is. He is always kind and gentle, longsuffering, and full of mercy and compassion toward us.

> "When Israel was a child, I loved him as a son, and I called my son out of Egypt. But the more I called to him, the more he rebelled, offering sacrifices to the images of Baal and burning incense to idols. It was I who taught Israel how to walk, leading him along by the hand. But he doesn't know or even care that it was I who took care of him. I led Israel along with my ropes of kindness and love. I lifted the yoke from his neck, and I myself stooped to feed him."[3]

Your earthly father may have been completely absent because of death or divorce. Maybe your parents were too busy with their own lives to pay attention to yours. Perhaps memories of broken promises haunt you.

---

2. John Dawson's article, "Father Heart of God," can be found online at: http://www. lastdaysministries.org.

3. Hosea 11:1–4 (NLT).

Tonight, between 40 and 50 percent of all American children will go to sleep in a house in which their father does not live. A generation ago, an American child could reasonably expect to grow up with a dad. Today, an American child can reasonably expect not to. Founder of the Institute for American Values, David Blankenhorn, cites fatherlessness as the most harmful demographic trend in this generation.[4]

A counselor who regularly ministers to our missionaries told me that she used to consider rejection the primary wound that people have suffered. However, in recent years, her counseling methods have changed, as the wound she most often encounters is that of neglect. She has found that to heal from rejection is somewhat easier than from being neglected. At least when you are abused or rejected, you have received some form of attention—even though it is negative. When you are neglected, there is nothing there at all—no relationship to heal.

God wants to be father to the fatherless.[5] To these pains of neglect God says:

"I will never leave you nor forsake you."[6]

John Dawson writes of the character of our father God:

Many children, particularly boys, have had no physical display of affection from their fathers, or no real compassion when they are hurt. Because of our false concept of masculinity, we are told, "Don't cry son, boys don't cry." Jesus is not like that. His compassion and understanding are measureless. He feels our hurts more deeply than we do because His sensitivity to suffering is so much greater.

I once had to hold my screaming two-year-old while a doctor stitched a large gash in his forehead. He quickly forgot his painful experience and fell asleep in my arms. But I was tormented by the experience and grieved for hours. You have forgotten most of your pains, but God has not. He has

---

4. Blankenhorn, David. *Fatherless America: Confronting Our Most Urgent Social Problem* (BasicBooks, 1995).

5. Psalm 68:5.

6. Hebrews 13:5.

perfect recall of every moment of your life. Your tears are still mingled with His at this very moment.

God was there when you experienced cruel teasing in the schoolyard and you walked alone avoiding the eyes of others. When you sat in a math class confused and dejected, He was with you. At the age of four when you got lost at the county fair and wandered terrified through the huge crowd, it was God who turned the heart of that kind lady who helped you find your mother. "*I led them with cords of human kindness, with ties of love.*" (Hosea 11:4 NIV)[7]

Terms of Endearment

Having spent his childhood in Taiwan, my husband John grew up speaking Mandarin Chinese. After we were married, John and I spent several years there as missionaries ourselves, overseeing the other HGM missionaries who served there. When our children were young, they were exposed to Chinese language and culture, so we chose for them to use the Chinese name, "*Baba*," instead of calling John, "Daddy."

When Jewel, our fourth child, was two years old, she began to call John by her own special name for him. She has the dimples and squeaky voice of a cherub, and he loves to hear her calling out for him: "Babi! Babi!"

This is what the Bible is talking about when it says:

> Because you are sons, God has sent forth the Spirit of His Son into your hearts, crying out, "Abba, Father!"[8]

"Abba" is an endearing name, like "Daddy," or like Jewel's "Babi." It is affectionate and close, tender and lighthearted. As a little girl, I remember my mother calling her father "Daddy"—all the way up until he died at the age of eighty-seven. It was attractive to me, a special thing. Many of us, as we have grown older, no longer call our fathers

---

7. John Dawson's article, "Father Heart of God," can be found online at: http://www. lastdaysministries.org.

8. Galatians 4:6.

"Daddy," but perhaps call him a more moderately affectionate term: "Dad."

Jesus experienced relationship with God in this way. As he came up out of the water of baptism, the heavens were opened to him, and he saw the Spirit of God descending like a dove. It landed on him. And then he heard the voice of his Father saying,

"This is My beloved Son, in whom I am well pleased."[9]

The next event of Jesus' life was being led by the Spirit of God out into the desert to be tempted by the devil. Look at it in Matthew 4:1. The Spirit of God *led* him straight into temptation! This was God's plan, and he knew it was going to happen. It is significant that God spoke loudly and clearly to Jesus before he went to face such a difficult test, reassuring Jesus of his love, care, provision and acceptance.

So you should not be like cowering, fearful slaves. You should behave instead like God's very own children, adopted into his family calling him "Father, dear Father."[10]

I spoke in our church in Oklahoma City on a Sunday during Valentine's Day season. John had asked me to share some things about intimate relationship with God, so I spoke about Jesus being the lover of our souls. At the end of that service, I did what you might think was a silly thing. I had filled the offering bags with Valentine's heart candies—you know, the ones with different phrases written on them. I had spoken of the many ways that God shows us his love, so I prayed over the bags and then had every person draw out a love message from God. I know it seems silly, but something as simple as hearing, "I love you," from God can be a life-changing experience.

After each person had taken their heart, I asked them to look at it and then meditate on God and his presence for just a few moments to see if the Holy Spirit might minister his love to them, and then we closed the service.

---

9. Matthew 3:17.
10. Romans 8:15 (NLT).

After the service, one of the young women from the community came forward. She wanted to ask me a question. I knew this girl and her story very well. She comes from a broken home where, as a little girl, she was passed back and forth between her mother and father. Whenever she stayed at her father's house, he abused her in ways that are almost impossible for my mind to imagine. When she finally told her mother about the abuse, she did not believe her and thought she was just trying to get attention. Because of this, she has been in and out of mental institutions much of her life.

She held out her pink Valentine's candy to me and said, "I don't understand this. Can you explain it to me?" Written on her heart were the words, "Good for you." I said, "Meghann, God is telling you, 'Good for you. You're doing a good job'—just like a father would." Tears began to form in her eyes, and she said, "My father never said that to me."

His baptism was not the only time that Jesus heard these words. On the Mount of Transfiguration, with Peter, James and John listening, a loud voice boomed from a cloud,

"This is my Beloved Son. Hear Him!"[11]

What validation. His father was proclaiming how much he loved Jesus. That is what that word "beloved" means—*loved*.

Trusting Dad to Catch You
We know that Jesus considered God to be his father, and that he was not the kind of distant or absent father that many of us have experienced. In the Garden of Gethsemane, when in the midst of the greatest struggle of his life, just before he faced torture and execution, Jesus called out to his father:

"Abba, Father, all things are possible for You. Take this cup away from Me; nevertheless, not what I will, but what You will."[12]

---

11. Mark 9:7.
12. Mark 14:36.

So much is packed into these two sentences. Jesus could intimately call out to his "babi," and remind him that he can do anything—that he is capable of any act. He could change the plan. He could do it another way if he wanted to. He is God—he can do anything. Sounds like the perspective of a little child, doesn't it? *My dad can do anything.*

Then we see that honest vulnerability that Mary showed to Jesus. *I don't want to do this. Is there any other way?* Jesus expresses his most true, most real emotions openly and honestly before his dad. Just like David in his psalms, Jesus pours his heart out to the one who knows him intimately.

And then in Jesus' prayer, we see the deep level of confidence that he had in his father. Why do we disobey God? Why do we fight him when he tells us to do something? It's because we do not trust him. We do not believe that he knows best. We do not believe that he has our best interests in mind.

Not so with Jesus. Although his honest emotions are that he really does not want to go to the cross, he trusts his father implicitly. *Whatever you see fit to do, I will do. You know best.* Jesus knew, with empowering assurance, how his dad felt about him. This prayer can only come out of our hearts when we know and experience the amazing love that our father God has for us.

> Karl Marx's daughter once confessed to her friend that she had not been raised in any religion and that she really was not religious at all. "But," she said, "the other day I came across a beautiful little prayer which I very much wish could be true." "And what was the prayer?" her friend asked. Slowly the daughter of Karl Marx began to recite in German, "Our Father, which art in heaven...."[13]

My Precious
There is a large gap in age between our older three children and our youngest two. When the little ones were born, Jessi, our oldest, claimed Jewel as her "precious," and Josiah, our second, claimed James as

13. Latham, Robert. "God for all Men."

his. James is now three years old. Everyone says that if you put a long goatee on him, he would be a "mini-me" of John. He has blond hair that, in the summer, turns almost white from the sun. His smile lights up the room, and his blue eyes always sparkle with mischief.

James has more energy than he knows what to do with, and he's always getting himself into trouble. He went through a phase in which he loved to pour liquid out of a bottle. Bottles of shampoo, soda pop, antacid and bleach are some of the ones that he has experimented with. He gets in trouble for using bad words—his favorite of which is "bootie." I don't know if you know that "bootie" is really a cuss word but if you heard him use it, you would recognize it as such, too. His latest adventure was climbing to the top of a bookshelf, which he then pulled down on top of himself and his two-year-old friend. Some days he nearly wears us out.

However, when James comes up close to you and begins to sing, "I got sunshine on a cloudy day…," your heart melts. He reaches up and begins to stroke your ear and lays his head on your shoulder, and you think that this may be the greatest moment you have ever experienced in your life. You wish it would never end.

This is how your heavenly father feels about you. He adores you. You are the apple of his eye. Do you know him? Do you experience his love for you?

> Have you ever heard Him chuckle, or congratulate you, or tell you He loves you? Has He ever comforted you, or given you miraculous and sudden bursts of insight— revealing knowledge otherwise unobtainable? Do you have conversations with your heavenly Father? Do you ask Him questions? Do you hear Him telling you "yes" or "no," or giving you timely words of counsel? Have you come to know Him as a warm, loving, all-wise and all-powerful "Dad"?[14]

Many years ago, there was a wealthy man who, together with his son, enjoyed a passion for collecting art. They traveled the world finding and purchasing treasures for their collection. Priceless works

14. Slagle, Charles. *From the Father's Heart* (Destiny Image, 1989) p. 131.

by Picasso, Van Gogh, Monet and others decorated the walls of their family home. The son developed a keen eye and business sense that made his father proud, as they dealt with art collectors around the world.

As winter approached, war broke out in their nation. The young man left to serve his country. After only a few weeks, the telegram arrived with the news that the beloved son had been killed in action while rushing a fellow soldier to the medic. Grieved and lonely, the father now faced a Christmas season without his dear son.

On Christmas morning, a knock came at the door. As he went to answer, his eyes caught the precious works of art on the walls of the hallway, reminding him that his son was not coming home. At the door, a soldier stood holding a large package. He introduced himself saying, "I was a friend of your son. I was with him when he died. May I come in?"

As the two sat and reminisced about their son and friend, the soldier told the father that his son had often talked of his love for fine art and of the fellowship he had with his father in their shared passion. Then, the soldier said, "I am an artist, and I want to give this to you."

Tearing the wrappings away from the package he had brought, he revealed a portrait of the son. Though the world would never consider it outstanding, the detail of the young man's face was striking, and the old man was overcome with emotion.

Pushing aside the expensive works of the masters, the old man hung the portrait above the fireplace in the center of the room. He sat in his chair that Christmas day, gazing at the face of his son.

Over the next weeks and months, stories of the son's bravery came to the old man. He learned that his son had rescued dozens of wounded soldiers before the bullet ended his courageous and caring deeds. Pride and satisfaction eased the father's grief, and the painting of his son became his most prized possession. He often told his friends that it was the greatest gift he had ever received.

The following spring, the man fell sick and passed away. The art world was electric with anticipation. The old man had left instructions that an auction would be held in honor of his son. The priceless pieces would be available for the highest bid! According to the will of the father, the auction was to take place on Christmas Day.

Excitement filled the air that day, as the crowd gathered with dreams of adding to their own art collections. The auctioneer stood and began the auction by asking for a bid on the portrait of the man's son. The room was silent. "Who will start the bidding with one hundred dollars?" he asked. From the back of the room, someone said, "Who cares about that painting? It's just a picture of his son. Let's get on with the good stuff." More voices echoed in agreement.

"No," the auctioneer responded. "We have to sell this one first. Now, who will take the son?" Finally, a friend of the old man said, "Will you take ten dollars? That's all I have. I knew the boy, so I'd like to have it."

"I have ten dollars. Will anyone bid higher?" called the auctioneer. "Going once. Going twice. Three times. Sold." And the gavel fell. Cheers erupted from the crowd, as now they could proceed to the treasures of the collection.

When he had quieted the crowd, the auctioneer firmly announced that the auction was over. In confusion and disbelief, someone asked, "What do you mean it's over? What about all these paintings? There are millions of dollars worth of art here. We have come to bid on them."

The auctioneer calmly replied, "According to the father, the one who takes the son takes it all."

> But as many as received Him, to them He gave the right to
> become children of God, to those who believe in His name.[15]

As Paul prayed for the Ephesians, I pray for you:

---

15. John 1:12.

That Christ may dwell in your hearts through faith; that you, being rooted and grounded in love, may be able to *comprehend* [to know experientially] with all the saints what is the width and length and depth and height to know the love of Christ which passes knowledge; that you may be filled with all the fullness of God.[16]

Pause with me at this chapter's end and ask God: *How do you feel about me?* Wait and see how he wants to show you his love.

---

16. Ephesians 3:17–19, emphasis mine.

CHAPTER 8
Time Well Spent

Friendship is a single soul dwelling in two bodies.

Aristotle

Friendship is born at that moment when one person says to another, "What! You too? I thought I was the only one."

C.S. Lewis

I have not been very good at friendships. When I was a little girl, I felt competition with other little girls. There was one girl in particular who seemed to copy everything I did. If I took up a new hobby, she decided she was interested in the same one. She gossiped about me, turning friends into enemies more than once. So, perhaps it was just my perception, but I decided that I did not need girlfriends. I decided that guys were much safer to befriend, nothing to compete over.

I worked hard to become admired by the guys—not as a girl, but as one of them. I learned to play football. I was pretty good on the offensive line. (We played two-hand touch.) Because I was small, I could "sack" the quarterback before he even saw me coming!

But my desire to fit in with the boys did not genuinely come to pass. I was not one of them. Instead, to my growing disappointment, I became the go-between. You know—I was the one that all the boys talked to when they wanted to communicate their interest in one of the other girls. I was the one the girls asked to let a boy know that she was interested in him.

I delivered notes back and forth between the boys and girls—"Do you like me? Check 'Yes' or 'No.'" You remember those notes, don't you? When conflicts arose between "couples" who were "going together" (My dad used to ask us, "Where are they going?"), I became the "couples' counselor." Never fitting into either world, I was left hanging somewhere in No-True-Friends Land. I had much to learn from Jesus about what a true friend is like.

> "No longer do I call you servants, for a servant does not know what his master is doing; but I have called you friends, for all things that I heard from My Father I have made known to you."[1]

J.O. Sanders writes:

> Friends are friends because they share common tastes, ideals and objectives. They share secrets with perfect confidence. Slaves do not share secrets with their masters, but friends do with their friends. Their relationship is relaxed and without inhibition. They find each other's company congenial. What a breathtaking conception of our relationship with our Lord![2]

How do we get to know Jesus? In the same way you get to know a new friend.

Kindred Spirit

Fourteen years ago, when I was pregnant with our son Josiah, God spoke to me very clearly about my need to have a friend. For most of my life, I had held true to the decision that I had made early on, never letting anyone into the deep or intimate places of my heart. God had begun to heal some of the wounding of my past, and according to him, it was time.

In church one Sunday morning, he pointed out a woman who I barely knew and told me that I was to make her my friend. Stumbling about in my socially awkward way, I went to her and reintroduced myself. Then,

---

1. John 15:15.
2. Sanders, J. Oswald. *Enjoying Intimacy With God* (Discovery House, 1980) p. 73.

I did something that was not only awkward, but that could have sent
her running the other way. I told her straight out that I did not have any
girlfriends, and that I believed that God wanted me to become friends
with her.

Tears filled her eyes, and she reached out her hand and began to stroke
my hair! She said, "Jamie, I will be your friend. Yes, I will be your
friend." It was the beginning of a friendship that formed my life over
the next ten years.

We began to spend time together, going out for coffee, taking our kids
to the park. In those early conversations, we shared bits and pieces of
our histories and began to discover our likes and dislikes, what kinds of
things we enjoyed, the books we read, what our husbands are like.

As I became more comfortable, I began to share with her some of the
deep secrets of my heart. She wept with me and prayed with me. Being
a few years down the road ahead of me, she gave me invaluable counsel
regarding marriage and child rearing. I cannot count the many things I
have learned from her.

This dear friend of mine is a lover of people, and I watched her heart
of compassion go out to the lady at the grocery store, the young man in
the park, the children who lived on her street. My own personality was
so much unlike hers, as I was often task-oriented and shy when meeting
new people. As I watched her life, I found myself longing to be like her.
She looked like Jesus, and I wanted to look like her.

Anne Shirley in *Anne of Green Gables* calls this kind of friend a
"bosom friend." Perhaps you could call her a bosom buddy or a kindred
spirit. It is the kind of friend who has all the characteristics of best
friendship. This is the kind of friendship that Jesus is looking for with
us. He longs to walk through life together with us, his bosom friends.

Developing friendship with Jesus is exactly the same process as it is
with human friends. Although he is God, he is also 100 percent human,
and as with any person, it will take time. You will have to make time to
get together with him. Just as it took many months for me to find out
the things that my new friend liked and disliked, it will take time for

discovery in your relationship with God. I had to ask questions. I had to listen to her.

When John was a young child, he would often lay his head in his mother's lap during church. He would take her left hand and hold her wedding ring close to his eye. When light hit the diamond, he would slowly turn the ring, catching the rainbow of bright colors. The pastor's sermon would pass quickly, as he enjoyed examining each one of the colors and patterns the refracted light made before his eyes.

The many characteristics of God's complex personality are like a diamond. It will take years to know him in all his fullness. Hold him up and turn him slowly around before your eyes. Examine his holiness, his mercy, his kindness, his patience, his creativity, his passions. You will find that as each facet is laid out in revelation to you, your heart will overflow with worship. You will fall deeper and deeper in love with your amazing God.

J.I. Packer writes:

> Why does God reveal Himself to us? Because He who made us rational beings wants, in His love, to have us as His friends; and He addresses His words to us—statements, commands, promises—as a means of sharing His thoughts with us, and so of making that personal self-disclosure which friendship presupposes, and without which it cannot exist.[3]

Quiet Times

Sitting in the lobby of a counselor's office, a waiting client noticed a round object plugged into the wall. It was making noise—not a loud sound, but a low constant droning. He asked the receptionist what it was, and she explained to him that it was called an ambient noise generator. In order to protect the privacy of people in the counseling room, the noise generator covered the sound of voices coming from the offices. Although the noise was not loud, the constancy tricked the ear, so that nothing being talked about in the offices could be distinguished.

---

3. *God Has Spoken* (Hodder & Stoughton, 1968) pp. 80-81, as quoted in *Enjoying Intimacy With God* by J. Oswald Sanders (The Moody Bible Institute of Chicago, 1980) p. 137.

This is what happens to us, when we are trying to hear God's voice. Many times, the "noise" of life around us blocks out the still, small voice of the Holy Spirit. Often, my own thoughts are full of conversations with other people, the list of things I must accomplish today, concerns about my children. It takes a purposeful quieting of my mind, my emotions and my spirit to be ready to hear what God is saying to me.

> One evening a speaker who was visiting the United States entered a telephone booth to make a call. The booth was different from those in his home country, but it looked simple enough to use. It was beginning to get dark outside, and so he was having some difficulty finding the number in the directory. He noticed the light in the ceiling, but could not figure out how to turn it on. A passerby noticed him looking around the booth and offered, "Sir, if you want to turn on the light, you have to close the door."[4]

Jesus encouraged us when we pray to go into our room and close the door.[5] In fact, he modeled this for us in his own time with his father. Luke 5:16 tells us that he often went away by himself. This is not because time alone is particularly religious or spiritual, but because in a very practical way, it helps us by removing external distractions that can keep us from connecting with the Holy Spirit.

Going Out for Coffee

Allow me to give you some practical recommendations for your "quiet time" with God. There are many great devotional books and other authors who can also help, so I will just mention a few things here from my experience.

Do not get hung up on one particular model. Most people do find that morning is the best time, because it focuses your day on living with him. However, sometimes accomplishing morning prayer is nearly impossible. As a mother, I have struggled with this over the years and, at times, felt condemnation because of my inability to "rise early in the

---

4. *Our Daily Bread.* Story told by hymn writer Wendell P. Loveless.
5. Matthew 6:6.

morning."[6] I set the alarm to get up before anyone in the family, only to find that the "mommy pheromones" have reached my children, and they are up asking for breakfast.

One of my dear friends has the nickname "Moonflower." We call her that because just like the flower, she blooms at night. Often her quiet time with God is spent after everyone else in the family has bedded down for the night. She finds the peaceful silence comforting, and as a "night person," she is ready to focus her attention on the Lord.

Find a time that works for you. If it's not working, make a change. My quiet times have varied during different seasons of my life. For a while, John would keep our little children, and I would steal away to a coffee shop for a couple of hours. I would take my Bible and journal, find a corner table and consider it a "date" with Jesus. Sometimes, I have had to steal a few minutes alone in the shower—which, if you have little children, you know is not even a private location!

It is helpful to develop a routine. Stopping the busyness of life as usual and focusing your attention solely on the presence of the Holy Spirit with you is important. My husband John used to light a candle at his desk every morning. There was nothing spiritually significant about the candle, but it was a little ritual that reminded his mind and emotions to get ready to spend some time with the Lord.

Worship
Take some time to quiet your heart and meditate on who God is. You might read through a psalm or sing a worship song. Allow your heart to focus on him and what he is like. When you have brought your attention toward him, you are ready to spend time fellowshipping together with him.

Bible
Spend some time in the Bible each day. You might have a devotional guide that walks you through portions of Scripture. Some people like to eat a "balanced diet" of Old Testament and New Testament passages

---

6. Proverbs 31:15.

every day. I recommend that regardless of other places you might read, always read something from the Gospels. Sadly, many Christians are more familiar with Paul than they are with Jesus. He is the one we follow. We must know what Jesus really said and how he lived. This is where we learn what God is really like![7]

As you read, be listening for the voice of the Holy Spirit. He may highlight a verse or passage for you. He may expound upon something you are reading. Charles Bello's book, *Prayer as a Place*, gives excellent instruction on how to meditate on Scripture and allow the Spirit of God to transform you.[8] I recommend you learn from the methods that he teaches and begin to seek what seems to help you connect with the active presence of God.

Prayer
Prayer is essential, of course. You may have your list of people to pray for, concerns and requests. But do not forget that prayer is a dialogue with God. Don't make it a monologue. None of us enjoys hanging out with someone who dominates the conversation, never letting us get a word in edgewise. That kind of person would not be a likely friend. Although Jesus' patience and tolerance is greater than ours, do take time to listen. Ask him questions and wait for his responses.

Love Languages
Over the years of teaching this material, I have had people come to me and say, "I just don't hear God. I wait. I sit quietly… And there's just nothing from him." It is a debilitating frustration for some. First, we must remember that he loves us and he is always communicating with us.[9] Perhaps we are just not recognizing his voice.

Gary Chapman has a wonderful book called *The Five Love Languages*.[10] In it, he explores the different ways that we give and receive love from one another. Just as we each have different personalities that make us unique, we all express love in different ways.

---

7. John 14:9.
8. HGM Publishing, 2008.
9. John 10:27.
10. Northfield Publishing, 1995.

He has identified five categories that seem to distinguish the more common ways that people love one another.

Some people love to give and receive words of affirmation. This is me! I want to hear John tell me how he feels about me. I want to hear that I have done a good job, that he likes what I am wearing, that the meal I prepared is fantastic. When I really like someone, I like to tell them the things I like about them.

Other people express their love by giving gifts. Usually the gifts they love to give are very personal, not just something picked up at the drug store, but something that has meaning and communicates that they know the heart of the one receiving the gift.

There are those who enjoy giving and receiving acts of service. When Jessica was a little baby, we did not have a washing machine or dryer. Babies make a lot of laundry! One of the women in our church showed up at my house one day and took away my piles of dirty clothes. She brought them back clean, pressed and folded like they fold them in the stores at the mall! She could never know what an amazing blessing her service was to me.

Quality time is another one of my favorites. The greatest desire that one of my children has is just to spend time with Mama. If I take her to the grocery store with me and we stop to have lunch together on the way, she feels my love for her. I enjoy a weekly date with John. Every Wednesday (if we are both in the same town) is our date night. We go out to eat and sometimes go to a movie. But my favorite dates are the ones when we go to Barnes and Noble, get magazines and coffee and spend the evening just talking with one another.

The fifth expression of love is physical touch. This is not just a sexual form of communicating love, but a broader arena of physical affection. Some people love to give and receive hugs. John has told me that holding his hand, touching his back or resting my hand on his knee fills up his "love tank," as Chapman calls it.

Just as God created us each with our own personality, he designed us with different languages of love. He is fluent in all of our languages! When listening for God to speak to you, remember that he knows you.

He wants you to experience his love for you. He will speak to you in the language that makes the most sense to you!

I often hear "words" from him, but others I know many times experience physical sensations in their bodies. They feel a mild electricity, a tingling, sometimes a warmth that comes over them. Some of the most amazing stories I have heard of God expressing his love to people have been those of individuals feeling a sense of God's arms around them, embracing them. What a privilege! To feel the very arms of God.

Don't forget to make time in your quiet time to wait and listen. He will speak to you in a "language" that the ears of your heart understand.

> A man working in an ice plant amid the ice, and the sawdust in which it was stored, lost a valuable watch. His fellow workmen searched with him for more than two hours, but were unable to find it. They left the plant for lunch and returned to find a little boy with the watch in his hand. "How ever did you find it?" they inquired. He replied, "I just lay down in the sawdust and heard it ticking." We, too, cannot find God by intensive, bustling search, but must "be still, and know that I am God."[11]

Wandering Thoughts

Attention deficit disorder is characterized by distractibility, inattention and hyperactivity. Many of us have a form of spiritual ADD. When we try to be still and hear from God, we have a hard time reeling in our thoughts. We mentally wander from topic to topic. Again, Charles Bello's book, *Prayer as a Place*, has valuable suggestions to help with this.

One thing that may help your mind not to wander to other subjects is to meditate on who it is you are listening to. Joy Dawson asks the question:

---

11. Travis, Rev. C. E. As reprinted in *Knight's Master Book of New Illustrations* (Wm. B. Eerdmans, 1956) p. 93.

> Can you imagine being in the Oval Office at the White House
> for a conversation with the President of the United States and
> asking him a question—and then letting your mind wander
> on to unrelated things?…Not concentrating on the President's
> reply would be unthinkable![12]

You are listening to the King of the Universe, and he is your personal
friend!

Journal

It is important to keep some kind of journal that records the things
that God is saying to you. Again, find a method that works well for
you. Some people like to write with different colors of ink, using one
for prayers and another to highlight the things that God is saying.
Journaling can be a great way to help your heart to focus and to release
the emotions that may be buried under the surface. Writing your
thoughts can be a place of vulnerability where, like Mary of Bethany,
you can express your deepest feelings.

One of my daughters loves to write poetry. Often her journaling takes
the form of a poem, as she releases her emotions to God. An artist
friend of mine writes his thoughts in his journal. Often the margins, and
sometimes whole pages, are filled with pictures that he has drawn to
express the things he feels.

Years ago, I used to write in a pretty journal, but as I have grown older,
my hands suffer from arthritic pain. It makes writing an unpleasant
experience for me. So I now use my computer. I like to type my prayers
in all lowercase letters. When God begins to speak to me, I hit the caps
lock button and write his words all in capital letters. That way I can go
back and review the things that he has said to me.

Be creative. Have fun. Make your journaling an activity that you enjoy,
and record the things that God is speaking to you. Regularly go back to
reread them. It is frustrating how short our memories are. We need to be
reminded of both the promises and the commands that he has given us.

---

12. *Forever Ruined for the Ordinary* (Thomas Nelson 2001) p. 41.

Just as it took time for me to develop trust in my new girlfriend, you will grow in truly believing God. We know that his Word tells us he loves us, that his ways are higher than our ways, his understanding greater than our own, but when it comes to entrusting our lives to him—this is where we get stuck. As you take time to get to know your new friend, Jesus, you will begin to experience what Scripture tells us is true. The walls of fear and mistrust will begin to crumble as you allow him to show you that he is really faithful and trustworthy.

As you spend time with your friend, you too will begin to desire to look like him. The personality traits that hold you back will begin to change, as you walk behind him into new situations and watch him work. The character that you are lacking will begin to develop as he takes you by the hand and shows you how he does things. Fears begin to fall away. Love and compassion begin to grow in your heart. Pretty soon, you find yourself looking like Jesus!

> "But let him who glories glory in this, That he understands and knows Me, That I am the Lord, exercising lovingkindness, judgment, and righteousness in the earth. For in these I delight," says the Lord.[13]

Get to know your friend.

**Alone with God, He speaks to me
As friend with friend;
He fills my heart with joy and peace
That has no end.
He tells me of His love for me,
And I rejoice.
Alone with God—to feel Him near;
To hear His voice!**

**Alone with God—the doors all shut—
I see His face;**

---

13. Jeremiah 9:24.

I feel His love, so strong and true;
I know His grace.
His comfort comes, in strength'ning power,
To fill my heart.
Alone with God—how blest it is
To come apart!

Alone with God—how sweet the sound
Of His dear voice!
To seek His face—in quiet place—
This is my choice!
'Tis good to know that He is there
My need to meet;
Alone with God—His presence near—
Ah yes, 'tis sweet!

Sylvia R. Lockwood

CHAPTER 9
Head Over Feet

A successful marriage requires falling in love many times, always with the same person.

Mignon McLaughlin

I hear God tell me, "I love you, Jewel." So I dance, and that's how I show him I love him too!

Jewel Wellspring Zumwalt

One of the most special weddings that I have attended was held in a Charismatic Episcopal church. It was a very formal, liturgical wedding in which the priest wore a robe and communion was served to all who approached the priest to receive a wafer and a drink. I generally have not appreciated liturgy and enjoy the informality of less traditional services. However, as this ceremony commenced, I was moved to tears repeatedly by the precious meanings that came through the symbolism.

We began with what seemed to be contemporary worship. In this formal, high-church setting, it felt incongruous to me. I looked around at the crowd and saw that there were a number of people with hands raised, genuinely worshipping God.

After the wedding party had come down the aisle, including several priests dressed in robes with a large cross being carried in front of them, there came a pause as the groom entered from the right. He stood facing the priest who then asked him, "Do you desire to be married today?" The groom answered in the affirmative.

The priest declared, "Then go get your bride!"

The groom turned and ran up the aisle and out the back of the sanctuary. We all waited in anticipation. In a few moments, the doors opened, and there stood the groom with his beaming bride. The music swelled, and we all rose to honor her as they walked together down the aisle.

The analogy of husband and wife—or bridegroom and bride—to our relationship with Jesus is probably best known from Ephesians 5:

> For we are members of His body, of His flesh and of His bones. "For this reason a man shall leave his father and mother and be joined to his wife, and the two shall become one flesh." This is a great mystery, but I speak concerning Christ and the church. Nevertheless let each one of you in particular so love his own wife as himself, and let the wife see that she respects her husband.[1]

Marriage is not merely a New Testament analogy. The book of Hosea is a timeless love story in which God commands the prophet Hosea to marry Gomer, a prostitute. She is unfaithful to Hosea, yet God calls him to forgive and welcome her back, even though she has borne children to other men.

God uses the lives of Hosea and Gomer as a testimony of his unfailing love for Israel, despite her unfaithfulness in idolatry. He calls Israel to return to loving and serving only him. He reminds Israel that he is a good and faithful husband.

In the book of Isaiah we find:

> "For your Maker is your husband, The Lord of hosts is His name; And your Redeemer is the Holy One of Israel; He is called the God of the whole earth."[2]

Jeremiah writes:

---

1. Ephesians 5:30–33.
2. Isaiah 54:5.

"Return, O backsliding children," says the Lord; "for I am married to you. I will take you, one from a city and two from a family, and I will bring you to Zion."[3]

The whole of Ezekiel 16 is a tragic and poetic story in which God likens Israel to a baby who was born in a field and left to die. He finds her and takes her as his own, cleans her up and gives her fine clothing. She grows up in his care. Then she goes and breaks his heart by prostituting herself to many other lovers, even though she has been raised to be a queen.

When Jesus came on the scene and began calling himself the bridegroom, this analogy was not foreign to the Jews.

> And Jesus answered and spoke to them again by parables and said: "The kingdom of heaven is like a certain king who arranged a marriage for his son."[4]

In this parable, Jesus describes a wedding day. He describes the guests, including one who was not a true guest, because he did not have on the wedding garment and was thrown out of the party.

Matthew 25 is the story of the ten virgins. This, too, is a story of a wedding day. And Jesus says that the kingdom of God is like this.

In Mark 2, as Jesus is explaining to the Pharisees why his disciples are not fasting, he clearly identifies himself as the bridegroom.

> "Can the friends of the bridegroom fast while the bridegroom is with them? As long as they have the bridegroom with them they cannot fast."[5]

In John 3, John the Baptist likens Jesus to the bridegroom and himself to the rejoicing friend of the bridegroom.

> "He who has the bride is the bridegroom; but the friend of the bridegroom, who stands and hears him, rejoices greatly

---

3. Jeremiah 3:14.
4. Matthew 22:1, 2.
5. Mark 2:19.

because of the bridegroom's voice. Therefore this joy of mine is fulfilled."[6]

Paul picked up this analogy when he wrote to the Corinthians:

> For I am jealous for you with godly jealousy. For I have betrothed you to one husband, that I may present you as a chaste virgin to Christ.[7]

Engaged to God

Betrothed is similar to engaged. When we get engaged in our culture, the girl receives a tangible promise—an engagement ring. Every time she looks at that ring, she remembers that the wedding day is coming, that soon she will be married to her betrothed.

> In Him you also trusted, after you heard the word of truth, the gospel of your salvation; in whom also, having believed, you were sealed with the Holy Spirit of promise, who is the guarantee of our inheritance until the redemption of the purchased possession, to the praise of His glory.[8]

The Holy Spirit is our engagement ring! Every time we interact with him, every time we hear his voice, feel his prompting, receive his comfort or encouragement, we are looking at our engagement ring. The wedding day is coming. We have been betrothed to Jesus!

Okay now, guys, I may have lost you. I hope not. I know that this analogy is hard for you to experience. You're a guy. How can you be a bride? But everyone adores a passionate and gallant storyline in a love story. According to Amazon.com, romance novels account for 53 percent of all mass-market paperback books sold in the U.S., reaching over a billion dollars in annual sales.

Years ago in Taiwan, a good Chinese friend of ours wanted to share with us his favorite kung fu series. So we watched at least an hour every evening with him for a whole month! It was a great way for me

---

6. John 3:29.
7. 2 Corinthians 11:2.
8. Ephesians 1:13, 14.

to learn Mandarin, as I could often guess what the characters were saying.

Now, every kung fu movie or television series has exactly the same plot. Maybe you have seen *Crouching Tiger, Hidden Dragon*. There is always a hero and a villain, good versus evil. Betrayal of a friendship always comes in there somewhere. And then there is the beautiful woman. Not only is she beautiful, but she is an amazing kung fu fighter as well. These films are full of hitting, kicking, flying and kissing. And there's always a tragic ending.

As we watched with our friend, we noticed that his attention never waned. He loved the whole thing. John teased him about his enjoyment of the romantic scenes, and he responded, "You've always got to have some vegetables with your meat." So stick with me, guys. I think you'll get blessed by this.

Many of these things that Jesus said do not have meaning for us in our culture, because he was referring to elements of a betrothal ceremony that we have never experienced. But as he told these parables, as he referred to different people and parts of the ceremony, every Jew in his hearing understood. He was describing an amazing romance story! A story that surpasses every romantic novel or movie that we have ever seen.

Look at this ceremony and see if you can recognize the romantic drama that they were watching unfold before them.[9]

In ancient Israel young people did not date they way we do in our culture. Fathers began thinking about marriage for their children when the kids were still young, as it would be the father's responsibility to find a spouse for them. When a son decided he wanted to get married, he would ask his father to arrange a marriage for him. They would discuss the options, who he liked, who he was interested in, but ultimately the father made the decision. The young man's father would then make an initial proposal to the girl's father.

---

9. This section is adapted from Lisa Bevere's description of the betrothal ceremony in *Kissed the Girls and Made Them Cry* (Thomas Nelson, 2002) p. 132–136.

The young man traveled to her home to meet with her father and her brothers. She was not in this meeting, but much like we see in the musical *Fiddler on the Roof*, young girls could be filled with a variety of emotions at the possibility of betrothal—excitement, dread, fear, anticipation. She would be waiting and wondering as the men discussed the proposal.

The main topic of the meeting was the bride price. This was a price that the young man must pay, in order to have her has his bride. In our culture, this may sound demeaning. However, in Middle Eastern culture, girls were often considered a financial loss. They did not bring revenue into the family, and so her father wanted to find a young man who will prove his commitment to take care of his daughter, who will see her as a privilege, not as a burden.

These meetings sometimes lasted for hours, as negotiations were made. If a price could not be agreed upon, the whole discussion ended, and the young man would leave. But if they agreed together upon a price, a document was then written that detailed the price, the promises of the bridegroom, and the rights of the bride. This became the marriage contract.

A goblet of wine was poured, and the young woman was invited into the room. It was now her time to make a decision. All the hours of negotiation would be for nothing if she did not consent to this marriage. She would be told about the agreement in detail, while the goblet of wine stood waiting. It represented the marriage covenant. She had two choices. Either she could refuse, turn around and leave the room, or she could say, "I do."

When she voiced her agreement, the cup would first be passed to the bridegroom, and then to her. When both had drunk of the wine, the marriage contract was sealed. The groom then gave a present to her to represent his promise to keep the covenant. They were "engaged" from this moment on.

The groom would stay at her home for a while, courting her so to speak. They spent time together, getting to know one another better, but always under the supervision of chaperones. They were never alone together During his stay, the bride would be baptized. It was a baptism of immersion, a ritual of cleansing and purification, symbolizing that her old life was over, and that she was preparing for a new life with her husband. It was even considered a form of spiritual rebirth for her. She was no longer single; she belonged to him.

After some time, the bridegroom would leave the bride's home and return to his father's house. He went to begin building a home for their future together. As he departed, he left her with this statement: "I go to prepare a place for you; if I go, I will return again unto you."[10] He left his bride with their covenant cup, the bride price paid in full, and a gift promising his return for her.

She began to make herself ready for marriage. In public, she always wore a veil to signify that she belonged to someone. Everyone who saw her in her veil would know that she was betrothed, that a price had already been paid for her. No one else was allowed to view the beauty of her face. As she went about preparing her linens, blankets and clothing that she would need as a married woman, she anticipated the day that he would return for her.

After returning to his father's house, the groom would begin work on a home for his new bride. It most often was a room or a new section added to the family house. His father watched and encouraged him, regularly inspecting his work. During the wait, the bride's family often sent envoys to make sure it was happening and to bring back reports. When the groom's father felt the place was completed and ready, he would tell his son to go and get his bride!

The bridegroom gathered his friends together and they would accompany him to go and retrieve his bride. They always planned this part of the ceremony to arrive at her home in the middle of the night. As they came near her city, they would blow a trumpet to notify the bride that her bridegroom was close.

Every betrothed bride would awaken, trembling and wondering if it was her turn. They would get their lamps ready, filling them with oil, trimming the wicks. Then they would listen for the announcement of the friends of the bridegroom, who would go before him and stand

---

10. John 14:2, 3.

outside her home, calling, "Here's the bridegroom. Come out to meet him!"[11]

The bride's father and brothers would go out first and check the identity of this groom to make sure he was really the right guy—the one they had agreed upon to marry their daughter and sister. When they were sure, then they would turn their backs to the whole scene. It almost felt like a kidnapping.

The bride would run, holding her lamp, with her handmaidens following, as the groom whisked her off to his father's house. He took her into the bridal chamber, where they would stay for seven days. While they were in there, the bridegroom's friends waited outside the door for the announcement that the marriage had been consummated. (I know, I know.) And when they heard his voice, they relayed his announcement to all the waiting guests, and the party started!

The bed sheet from their wedding bed was passed through a window and given to her father for examination. This shed blood finalized the sealing of the covenant, as she was declared virtuous and holy, worthy of union with this young man.

After seven days, she would take off her veil, and the couple would come out and join the marriage celebration. There was a great party, with much wine and food. Blessings were pronounced. Gifts were given, and all rejoiced with the new couple!

Isn't it romantic? Hopefully, you are seeing the symbolism in all of this. Jesus left his heavenly home to pursue the bride that his father had chosen for him. He sealed the agreement when he shared the cup with his disciples at the Last Supper. The price was negotiated in the Garden of Gethsemane, and he paid the most expensive price possible. In order to have us, his bride, he gave his life!

This is the story of redeeming love—the greatest love story of all time! This is the drama in which we find ourselves! Is this your experience in relationship with Jesus?

---

11. Matthew 25.

Missing Romance

I have often heard my husband John describe the different kinds of relationships with Jesus as those of fidelity and those of passion. Both of these are certainly necessary in a marriage. Most of us understand the fidelity part pretty well. We are faithful, loyal, moral Christians. In his book *Passion for the Heart of God*, John tells the story of my great uncle Tella. As a soldier in World War Two, he vowed to serve God the rest of his life if God would allow him to live. Faithfulness characterized this dear man's life, as he never turned from following his Savior.

However, if marriage were *merely* about fidelity, it would be a sad and lonely journey through the rest of life. If my marriage with John looked like many of our relationships with Jesus, I would be seeking marriage counseling. It would mean that we sleep in different beds, live separate lives, talk once a week on Sunday mornings, consult one another whenever there is a major decision to be made, and eat together in silence.

This is not the kind of relationship that John desires to have with me, nor is it the kind of relationship that Jesus desires. John and I both have embarrassed each other on occasion, as we forgot that other people were around and expressed our affection toward one another too openly for public arenas. That is passion!

Do you remember the first time you were in love? Maybe it was when you were in junior high, maybe high school. Maybe you remember clearly the season of courting your spouse.

Think about your five senses. What happens to them when you're in love? They are heightened, aren't they? Your sense of sight—all you see is the one you're in love with. In fact, they say that love is blind. His or her physical qualities are overwhelmingly attractive to you.

Your sense of hearing. When you pick up the phone and hear her voice on the other end of the line, your heart skips a beat. In a crowded room, you hear him call your name, and immediately, all your attention is focused on him.

Your sense of smell. *Oooh, that perfume is nice.* As she leans near, you can smell her hair—perhaps it's her shampoo or maybe she just naturally smells awesome. That's what all of us girls want you to think!

Your sense of touch. You pass the salt to him across the table. His hand lightly brushes yours in passing and electric shocks course up your arm. Love is not for the faint of heart.

Your sense of taste. Okay, maybe we'll leave that one out of this discussion. (I had to mention it or you would notice that I only mentioned four of the five senses!) You know what I'm saying, right? All your senses come alive when you're in love!

We call this "infatuation," or as Owl calls it in the movie *Bambi*, "twitterpated." That is exactly what it is—being overwhelmingly infatuated and twitterpated, passionately in love with another person to the point that only they exist. That person becomes our simple obsession.

When John and I were dating in college, we spent as much time together as possible. Both of us had a curfew, and we would be together right up until the last moment when they locked the doors to our dormitories. We made our plans in the evening for what the next day would look like. How soon could we meet? Could we have breakfast together? In between classes we looked for one another, planning out where we would find each other.

Is this what your relationship with Jesus looks like? What is the first thing that you think of in the morning? What is the last thing that you think of at night before you fall asleep? (If you're like me, it tends to be my to-do list.)

When you are alone with Jesus, what is it like? Do you do all the talking? Is it one request after another? Are you just checking off your list of spiritual disciplines that makes you a good Christian? Is he more of a short-order chef than your lover?

> "I will betroth you to Me forever; Yes, I will betroth you to Me
> In righteousness and justice, In lovingkindness and mercy; I

will betroth you to Me in faithfulness. And you shall know the Lord."[12]

The Wedding

> Then I heard what seemed to be the voice of a great multitude, like the roar of many waters and like the sound of mighty peals of thunder, crying out, "Hallelujah! For the Lord our God the Almighty reigns. Let us rejoice and exult and give him the glory, for the marriage of the Lamb has come, and his Bride has made herself ready;" it was granted her to clothe herself with fine linen, bright and pure, for the fine linen is the righteous deeds of the saints. And the angel said to me, Write this: Blessed are those who are invited to the marriage supper of the Lamb.[13]

When Jessica, our oldest daughter, was four years old, I took her to see a musical drama called *The Bride*.[14] It tells the story of the battle between God and Satan; Jesus' life, death and resurrection; and then his choosing of a bride. It follows a young girl—Jesus' bride-to-be—as she matures through childhood into her teenage years. She learns to bear the fruit and gifts of the Spirit and how to defeat Satan in her own life.

The drama was put on at a large church in Oklahoma City and had a cast of hundreds dressed in elaborate costumes. The stage covered the front of a large auditorium and was complete with lighting and sound effects. Scenes with Satan and his demons even included pyrotechnics. It was quite the production.

Jessi was dressed in one of her prettiest dresses, complete with tights and patent leather shoes. This was a special night out with Mama, and we had found a seat for her on the aisle where she could watch the whole event. She was transfixed by the drama. At one point, she even pulled the bow off of her shoe in a rush of adrenaline, as Satan and his minions jumped off the stage in a haze of fire and smoke.

---

12. Hosea 2:19, 20.
13. Revelation 19:6–9a.
14. McGuire, Dony and Reba Rambo (New Kingdom Music, 1983).

The production culminates with the bride finally ready for the wedding day. She was dressed in complete wedding gown and veil and waiting on the stage. To the sounds of cheers from the audience, Jesus came riding in on a huge, white horse, right down the aisle next to Jessi! I remember watching Jessi's beaming face, and I knew that she, too, was falling in love with this man, Jesus—her knight in shining armor.

> Then I saw heaven opened, and behold, a white horse! The one sitting on it is called Faithful and True, and in righteousness he judges and makes war. His eyes are like a flame of fire, and on his head are many diadems, and he has a name written that no one knows but himself. He is clothed in a robe dipped in blood, and the name by which he is called is The Word of God. And the armies of heaven, arrayed in fine linen, white and pure, were following him on white horses. From his mouth comes a sharp sword with which to strike down the nations, and he will rule them with a rod of iron. He will tread the winepress of the fury of the wrath of God the Almighty. On his robe and on his thigh he has a name written, King of kings and Lord of lords.[15]

The wedding scene commenced as Jesus took the hand of his bride and guided her to center stage. At the end of the dramatized ceremony, Jesus led his bride in a beautiful waltz around the stage, and Jessi turned to me and said, "Mama, all weddings should have dancing!"

This is the celebration that is soon to come! The great wedding feast of the Lamb when:

> We will dance on the streets that are golden,
> The glorious Bride and the great Son of Man
> From every tongue, and tribe and nation
> We join in the Song of the Lamb.[16]

---

15. Revelation 19:11–16.
16. Ruis, David. "We Will Dance" (Mercy/Vineyard Publishing, 1993).

Pleasing God

Hebrews 11:6 says that "without faith it is impossible to please God."
I was reading this one day and realized that what I heard in my mind
was, *It is impossible to please God*. Hmmm.... I knew that couldn't be
right. So I stopped to meditate on it a bit longer.

When I was growing up, my parents were both perfectionists. It came
out in their personalities in different ways. My mother had grown up
in a somewhat legalistic holiness denomination that focused on perfect
living. Added to her upbringing was a mother, my grandmother, who
was herself a perfectionist with only one way of doing everything—the
right way.

My father was a musician before he surrendered to God's call on his
life as a preacher. He had been studying for a degree in church music
and played a number of different instruments. He also had a beautiful
singing voice. It was his desire that all of his three girls learn to play at
least the piano.

We were each required to choose a second instrument after we had
adequately begun to master the piano. I chose the violin. Have you ever
heard a young child play the violin? It is something akin to fingernails
on a chalkboard. What made this life even more difficult for me was the
knowledge that my dad has perfect pitch!

My parents were good parents in so many ways, and yet I can honestly
say that their perfectionist tendencies raised me with the awareness
that I was always lacking—not quite perfect. So when I read, "It is
impossible to please God," emotionally, I only heard it affirming my
inadequacies.

I knew this could not be right, that God loves us dearly. So I decided to
look up the word "to *please*" God, and this is what I found. To "please"
means "to excite agreeable sensations or emotions in." We understand
the definition better when we see it as a noun: "pleasure," which means
"excitement, relish or happiness produced by enjoyment or expectation
of good—positive happiness."[17]

---

17. Definitions of "please" and "pleasure" as found on Dictionary.com. Webster's Re-
vised Unabridged Dictionary. MICRA, Inc. www.dictionary.reference.com.

Are you getting this? "Without faith it is impossible to please God." It does not mean that we are looking to gain his approval. This was my definition of "to please"—to gain approval, trying to please someone.

What the writer of Hebrews is telling us is that God wants to enjoy us! What liberating knowledge! We bring enjoyment and excitement and happiness to God. When? When we have faith. What does it mean to have faith? To believe him. To trust him.

Unclenched Hand

When John and I were first married, I was an emotional wreck, much of it the result of the abuses that I had suffered in my growing-up years. Those abuses had left me wounded, confused and defensive. John would tell me that he loved me, and I did not believe him. Down inside I believed that he had just married me because he wanted sex, and as a good Christian boy, that was the only right way for him to get it. I believed that he was using me—that our marriage was really just legalized prostitution.[18]

John knew I didn't believe him. He could feel it. He did everything he could to show me his love. He told me repeatedly. He complimented me often. But I was closed off from his love—and I could see that I was hurting him, but I didn't know what to do to fix myself.

There is a great old Tom Hanks and Meg Ryan movie called *Joe Versus the Volcano*. It is a silly little fairytale. Both Tom and Meg play characters that are socially awkward. Tom is an extreme hypochondriac, and Meg has an incapacitating fear of people.

They work together in the same office, and as time progresses, Tom's character falls madly in love with Meg's character. He decides to ask her out on a date. She merely is capable of a shy head nod in response to his invitation.

They go out to a lovely restaurant, where Tom does all the talking. When the meal is over, they begin to walk, and Tom extends his hand to her. There is a long pause, as Meg's character just stares at his

---

18. Marx, Karl. Private Property and Communism (1884).

outstretched hand, trying to muster up the courage to put her hand in his. You can tell that she likes him. She wants to hold his hand, but she is afraid. Finally, she slowly stretches out her fist and places it in his open palm. He looks down at her fist, gently closes his hand around it, and they walk off together into the sunset—hand in fist.

When John and I had been married for a couple of years, people around us began making noises about it being time to think about having children. I was terrified. I knew that I was an emotional mess. John and I were fighting a lot. I regularly had nightmares in which I relived the abuses that I had suffered. When we would attempt intimacy, I would hallucinate and think that John was one of these men who had abused me before—that he was attacking me. I cried a lot.

I knew that introducing a child into this family would be a disaster. I was incapable of being a wife, much less a mother. So I became desperate. I began to ask God for help. I began to beg him, really.

I was having a quiet time of devotions one morning, and I didn't know where to read in my Bible. I was not in the middle of a particular study, so I decided to follow my pastor's advice to just be quiet and wait and see if God would tell me what to read.

After a few moments of sitting quietly, I distinctly heard a voice inside of me say, "Song of Solomon." Now, I had never read the Song of Solomon. As my husband John has said, that was the book that the junior high boys used to peek through and giggle about in the back row at church. It was that sexual book. Hmmm....

I wondered what was there and thought I would just go with the idea, that maybe that had been the Holy Spirit leading me. So I began to read and what happened for me absolutely changed my life!

As you might know, the Song of Solomon is an allegory. Throughout church history, it has been used to illustrate God's love for Israel— Jesus' love for the church. It is a very romantic story of a king who falls in love with a country girl. In poetry form, throughout the book, the voice of the bridegroom can be heard speaking to and of his bride. And then it changes and becomes the voice of the bride declaring her love for him. It is wondrously beautiful.

As I read, I began to feel in my heart that there is a kind of love that is pure, that is tender, that is unselfish, that is without ugly motivation. I felt my heart desiring this kind of love—but knowing that it is really not available. It only exists in fairytales and dreams.

In college, my struggle with eating disorders had progressed to such an extreme that it was completely irrational. I was not only controlled by my thought life—seeing the image in the mirror as very different from reality—but I was so addicted that it no longer even made sense. I would buy several candy bars from the vending machine and take them with me to the bathroom. I ate them all, one after another, standing in the stall next to the toilet, and then I would immediately turn around and vomit them up.

When I met John, this behavior stopped, primarily as a result of accountability. Much like an addict receives in Alcoholics Anonymous, John became my "sponsor." He ate meals together with me and stayed with me after I had eaten to make sure I kept the food down. The bulimic behavior stopped, but for many years, I continued to be controlled in my thought life by food. I was overly aware of every bite I took, conscious of how many calories I had eaten each day. I fasted regularly to compensate for days I felt I had eaten too much, and that person in the mirror still did not look attractive to me!

As I came to a particularly graphic description in Song of Solomon— one in which the bridegroom speaks of the physical beauty of his bride—I began to hear the voice of Jesus. Hebrews 4:12 tells us that God's Word is *alive*! No longer were these just words on a page, no longer just a lovely story, but I could hear Jesus, my bridegroom, speaking of his love for me.

I could hear him telling me how beautiful he thinks I am. Not just in general, but down to the specific parts of my body that I hate. We all have them, right? Those parts that stand out to us in the mirror! He was telling me that he created me that way, and that he loves me that way— that I was overwhelmingly beautiful to him.

This did not seem right to me. We are supposed to praise him—because he is worthy of praise. But he is not supposed to praise us—me. I am not worthy to be praised!

Sometimes our little girl, Jewel, puts on her prettiest dress and then begins to spin around the room. She often will ask me, "Mama, am I pretty?" Yes! She is pretty, and I tell her so. Our son Josiah is an amazing drummer. Sometimes in the middle of worship at our church, I turn around from my position at the keyboard and just smile at him—because he is awesome! This is praise.

We are comfortable giving praise to our children, but somehow we have believed the devil's lie that there is nothing in us that is worthy of praise. Our heavenly father, our friend and our bridegroom wants to tell us differently.

There is a scene in which the bride has already gone to bed, but the bridegroom comes knocking on the door. He calls to her, but she hesitates. She has already gotten ready for bed, washed her feet even. They'll get dirty again if she goes to the door. He is so anxious to be with her that he puts his hand in through the latch, trying to unlock the door. When she finally decides to go to the door, he is gone.

I could hear the Lord calling me to spend time with him—not because it is my Christian duty, but because he wants to be with me. I could hear him calling me to prayer—again, not because it is a spiritual discipline that I need to do in order to be a good Christian, but because he loves to hear my voice.[19] He loves for us to talk together.

The whole thing came to a climax for me when I read chapter 4, verse 9:

> You have ravished my heart, My sister, my spouse; You have ravished my heart with one look of your eyes.

He feels this way about me! I was undone. The pain and anger of years past began to wash away in that moment. I lived in the Song of Solomon for the next few years, and God regularly takes me there to remind me how he feels about me.

---

19. Song of Solomon 2:14.

He feels the same about you. Perhaps you have just never heard him tell you so. Perhaps you have never felt him show you so. He wants you to know.

The Lord your God in your midst, The Mighty One, will save; He will rejoice over you with gladness, He will quiet you with His love, He will rejoice over you with singing.

Zephaniah 3:17

HEAD OVER FEET

PART 2
Hearing God's Voice

Man shall not live by bread alone; but by every word that proceeds from the mouth of God.

Jesus

CHAPTER 10
School for the Deaf

Note well that we must hear Jesus speak if we expect Him to hear us speak. If we have no ear for Christ, He will have no ear for us. In proportion as we hear we shall be heard.

C.H. Spurgeon

Margie Morton was a woman of wonderful faith. Over the years I had watched her exercise that faith in many different situations. She and her husband were committed members of the church from the very first day.

Margie suffered from brain tumors for a number of years. She had surgery that was somewhat successful, but continued on the long, long journey of this condition.

I was praying for her one day when I sensed the Lord speaking to me. It wasn't an audible voice. Rather, I felt that he gave me some guidelines for ministering to Margie while I sat before him quietly. He said, "You taught Margie how to live. Now you must teach her how to die."

I started sweating immediately. I was not happy to hear those words. I loved Margie greatly and did not want to see her life come to an end.

At the time, her doctors wanted to send her to a hospital in Los Angeles with no real prospect of being healed. They recommended a treatment that might prolong Margie's life but without much quality. She would suffer tremendously, even with the treatment. I shared with her that I thought her remaining weeks could be better spent at home with her children, husband, and loved ones. I told her to share her heart and life with them, and that I thought she would know when it was time to go be with the Lord. I didn't think that Margie would agree, because she was not one to give up without a fight.

However, the next eight weeks she chose to stay home, sharing her life with her family and friends while conscious of her impending death. She did not spend her energies simply fighting cancer.

When it was time, she told her husband that she needed to go to the hospital. When she was in the hospital, her children and husband gathered around the bed and prayed for her. As they left they said, "Well, we'll see you tomorrow, Mom." She responded by saying, "You won't find much."

As soon as they left, she took a shower and put on her brand new nightgown. The nurse happened to come in just as she was getting back in bed, and said, "My, how pretty you look! You're all dressed up to go someplace. Where are you going?"

"I'm going to meet my King," Margie replied. Then she died, and did meet her King. That's victory! That's death that has no sting![1]

Revealer of Mysteries
In the Old Testament, God showed Moses a plan for the tabernacle.[2] Later, we see David testifying that God had given him a detailed plan for building the temple:

> "All this," said David, "the Lord made me understand in writing, by His hand upon me, all the works of these plans."[3]

1. Wimber, John. *Living With Uncertainty*. As reprinted in Choice Contemporary Stories and Illustrations (Baker Books, 1998) p. 61.

2. Exodus 1:4.

3. 2 Chronicles 28:19.

Scripture contains some wonderful promises for us about receiving specific guidance from the Lord:

> "I am the Lord your God, who teaches you what is best for you, who directs you in the way you should go."[4]

> I will instruct you and teach you in the way you should go; I will counsel you and watch over you.[5]

> Trust in the Lord with all your heart, And lean not on your own understanding; In all your ways acknowledge Him, And He shall direct your paths.[6]

> Whether you turn to the right or to the left, your ears will hear a voice behind you, saying, "This is the way; walk in it."[7]

How much do we need to hear though? How specific does he want to be?

Loren Cunningham, founder of Youth With A Mission (YWAM), tells a story from when he was a young child. His mother sent him to the store to buy milk. She gave him a five-dollar bill and warned him to be very careful as he walked, not to lose the money. It was the only money they had for groceries.

As any young boy would do, Loren played along the way, kicking a can up the street. When he placed the milk on the counter at the store, he reached into his pocket and found that the five-dollar bill had fallen out somewhere along the way.

Devastated and ashamed, he raced back along the road, looking to the right and to the left, hoping to find the money. When he reached home, he was obliged to tell his mother that he had not been careful and that he had lost the five dollars.

---

4. Isaiah 48:17 (NIV).
5. Psalm 32:8 (NIV).
6. Proverbs 3:5, 6 (NIV).
7. Isaiah 30:21 (NIV).

Mrs. Cunningham, being a godly woman and accustomed to listening to the voice of God, placed her hand on Loren's shoulder. She said, "It's okay, son. God knows we need that money. He knows where it is. We'll just ask him to show us." And she began to pray.

She waited quietly for just a couple of minutes and then said, "Come on, Loren. The Lord has shown me that the money is lying under a bush." They headed off down the street together and began looking under every bush. Sure enough, the bill had blown up under a low bush, where they found it sitting just as Mrs. Cunningham had seen it in her mind's eye.[8]

As I read of the simple, experiential faith of this woman, I was provoked to jealousy. When I was growing up, my family prayed. We asked God for guidance, but usually it was regarding large decisions that we needed to make. For example, should we move to a new city? Should we attend public or private school? Should we buy a new car? I was intrigued by the idea that God might interact with me about everyday circumstances in a simple and natural way. This began an adventure for me!

> The humblest followers of Jesus may know the Divine will firsthand. "It is every man's privilege to be fully assured in the will of God." The Divine attention to detail is amazing. Nothing is too trivial for omniscience.[9]

Voice from Heaven
Jesus said:

> "My sheep hear My voice, and I know them, and they follow Me."[10]

---

8. Cunningham, Loren with Janice Rogers. *Is That Really You God?* (YWAM Publishing, 1984) p. 17.

9. Chadwich, Samuel. As quoted by Wesley Duewel in *Let God Guide You Daily* (Duewel Literature Trust, 1988) p. 23.

10. John 10:27.

If you are one of his sheep, then you have heard his voice. The Holy Spirit's job is to convict us of sin and to teach us all things.[11] It was the voice of the Shepherd that drew you to him in the first place. It may not have been as dramatic as Mrs. Cunningham's experience, but then again, your experience may make this story seem trite.

> "And I will pray the Father, and He will give you another Helper, that He may abide with you forever—the Spirit of truth, whom the world cannot receive, because it neither sees Him nor knows Him; but you know Him, for He dwells with you and will be in you. I will not leave you orphans; I will come to you."[12]

> "Now when they bring you to the synagogues and magistrates and authorities, do not worry about how or what you should answer, or what you should say. For the Holy Spirit will teach you in that very hour what you ought to say."[13]

Jesus' promise to us was that he would be with us—that he is not far off, but he walks with us and talks to us by the Holy Spirit. He is Emmanuel: God with us. What a comfort! Not only does he speak to us through his written Word, the Bible, but by his Spirit in everyday circumstances.

> For as many as are led by the Spirit of God, these are sons of God.[14]

> He who says he abides in Him ought himself also to walk just as He walked.[15]

If we are sons of God—if we say that we are his children, his followers—then we must be led by the Spirit. What does this mean? It means that our desire is to walk as Jesus walked—doing only what we see the Father doing, saying only what we hear the Father saying.

---

11. John 16:8; John 14:26.
12. John 14:16–18.
13. Luke 12:11, 12.
14. Romans 8:14.
15. 1 John 2:6.

Wow! Is this how life as a Christian was meant to look? Is it even possible?

Jesus said that his food was to do the will of the Father. Food is sustenance. We have to have it. If we are to do God's will, we—like Jesus—must be dependent upon the Holy Spirit's guidance—in every circumstance.

Let's look at some more:

> Without faith it is impossible to please Him [God].[16]

We've already talked about God's desire to enjoy us, and he cannot if we don't have faith—belief in him, trust in him. Well, how do we get faith? I have seen Christians trying to muster up faith. It looks something akin to spiritual aerobics. Prayers that are theological wranglings. Pep talks that pump up the jam so that we can all believe God to do great things.

These methods are not what the Bible tells us about getting faith. Faith is not something that we just dig down deep within ourselves to find. Romans 10:17 tells us clearly:

> So then faith comes by hearing, and hearing by the word of God.

How do we get faith? We get it by hearing from God! When we hear God say that he wants to do something, we can pray in full agreement, believing that we are praying his will. It's that simple.

Active Listening
I need to pause here and give a short Greek lesson. There are two words that we translate into English as: "word." One is the Greek word *logos*. *Logos* means "to collect, to count, intellect, rational, reasonable, spiritual." In Greek culture, this word was used to talk about written words on a page.[17]

---

16. Hebrews 11:6.
17. All of my Greek and Hebrew word meanings come from Strong's Concordance and the New American Standard Lexicon found online at www.biblestudytools.net.

The other "word" in Greek is *rhema*. It means "that which is stated intentionally, a word uttered by a living voice." This is hugely significant, as we need to know that what Romans is telling us here is not that we get faith from reading the Bible. Yes, that does happen. But what Romans is pointing out to us is that as we hear from God—from the Holy Spirit—faith begins to rise within us! When the *logos*, or written Word, becomes *rhema*, or spoken Word empowered by the Holy Spirit, that is when we receive faith. When we hear him speak to our spirits, we naturally believe him.

Paul Yonggi Cho, pastor of the world's largest church, tells of some of his elders who brought to him an article from the news. It was a story about ten African Christians who, upon reading the story of Peter walking on the water with Jesus, rowed their boat out into the deepest part of a lake. They believed the story they read and believed with their whole hearts that they too would be able to walk on water. The tragic news was that all ten of them had drowned. Cho's elders reminded him of his own teaching that they ought to believe God and his Word, and they wanted to know why it had not worked for these African Christians.

Cho's answer to them was that "Jesus commanded Peter to get out of the boat. He did not command the Africans."[18] They had trusted in the *logos*, not in the *rhema* word of God. We cannot rely upon formulas, even those extrapolated from Scripture, but rather, we must be filled with the faith that comes from hearing spoken confirmation from the Holy Spirit himself. When he speaks, it works.

How important is it for us to hear the voice of God? We cannot have true faith without it. It is everything to us. Without hearing from him, we cannot walk in fellowship with him. We can be a "good" Christian in the sense that we have prayed a prayer, we have decided that we believe some true things about Jesus, we begin to live a moral life. But what God desires is relationship! He wants us to walk together with him as friends, and friends talk with one another!

---

18. Dr. Paul Yonggi Cho video (The River Is Here Conference, 1998).

CHAPTER 10

Clear As Mud

My husband, John, has trouble with his hearing. Perhaps it is from listening to rock music too loudly as a young man. He especially has trouble when there is ambient noise in a room or if the frequency of a noise is too high. After watching *Pride and Prejudice* together, his comment was, "This movie must have been made for dogs to watch." I was totally offended, as my heart was caught up in the wonderful love story. I asked him what he meant, and he said, "Well, those girls' voices were so high and squeaky that only dogs could have understood them!"

There have been occasions when we've had a cricket in our bedroom. A chorus of them outside is beautiful, but one lonely chirp in a corner is quite annoying. John cannot hear the cricket! We have moved large furniture from place to place in our room, trying to track down that noise, as I call out to him, "There it is! Now it's over here! No, that way!"

There are entomologists (scientists who study bugs) who know cricket sounds. Not only can they hear them, but there are some who can distinguish between two hundred different crickets by their sound. How do they do that? They spend time listening—hours and hours—listening to the sound of crickets, studying their differences, putting the distinctions into their memory.[19] Perhaps we do not experience God's voice, because we are not accustomed to listening. Our ear is not trained to recognize the *rhema* word of the Holy Spirit.

Edge of My Seat

Duncan Campbell was used mightily by God in the Hebrides Revival of the early 1950's. He was seated on the platform after speaking for a service in Bangor, Northern Ireland, when he heard the Holy Spirit say to him, "Berneray!" A second time the name came to his mind, "Berneray." Praying silently, Duncan again heard the name a third time. He turned to the chairman and told him, "Brother, you will need to excuse me. The Holy Spirit has just told me that I am to go to Berneray."

---

19. This illustration came from Peter Lord in his book *Hearing God* (Baker Books, 1988), p. 27.

"Why, brother," the chairman replied, "you can't go there. You are the speaker again tomorrow."

"But what must I do? The Spirit says, 'Berneray,'" Duncan responded.

"I guess you'll just have to obey the Spirit."

Immediately, Duncan left the platform while the service still continued and went to the hotel to gather his things. He took a taxi to the airport and asked for a flight to Berneray. The ticket agent told him that they had no flights to this small island in the Outer Hebrides. "Well," Duncan said, "put me on the first plane to the nearest point."

He flew across the channel to the nearest airport and went down to the seashore. He asked a fisherman, "How can I get to Berneray?" The man told him that there were no regular boats, but that he would be willing to take him there for a price. The price he asked was almost exactly what Duncan had in his pocket.

When Duncan landed, he could not see over the bluff. He climbed up, dragging his heavy suitcases and found himself standing in a plowed field. Seeing a farmer up ahead, he approached him, and exhausted, he sat down on one of the suitcases.

"Please go to the nearest pastor," Duncan requested, "and tell him Duncan Campbell has arrived."

"Oh," said the farmer, "we don't have a minister for the church right now."

"Do you have elders?" Duncan asked.

"Yes," the farmer replied.

"All right," said Duncan, "go to the nearest elder and tell him, 'Duncan Campbell has arrived.'" The farmer looked confused and then started off across the field.

After a while, the farmer returned and told Duncan, "The elder was expecting you. He has a place ready for you. He has announced that the meetings begin at nine o'clock tonight! Here, let me carry your suitcases."

Three days before, while Duncan had been preaching in Bangor, this elder had been praying in his barn. He pled with God to send revival to his island, and God had given him Hosea 14:5 as a promise: "I will be as the dew unto Israel." He had prayed, "Lord, I don't know where he is, but you know, and with you all things are possible. You send him to the island." He knew in his heart that God would send Duncan Campbell, who God was using mightily in other parts of Scotland. He had been so sure that Duncan would be there in three days' time that he arranged to use the local church and had even announced the services.[20]

And this is only the beginning of the story! The account of how God sent revival to Berneray is filled with stories of people who fellowshipped in prayer with God, who knew how to recognize his voice and obeyed him immediately without question.

Walking by the Spirit is certainly exciting. Imagine what adventures Jesus might take you on, if you could hear him call you. Your life might look like the Book of Acts. Wouldn't you like to fellowship with him, to live the adventure of listening moment by moment to his still small voice, walking together in the things that he is doing?[21]

---

20. Woolse, Andrew. *Duncan Campbell* (Hodder and Stoughton, 1974).

21. Now you may have been told that God no longer works this way—that we now have the Bible, and we no longer need to hear the voice of God. Or perhaps you have been told that it is even dangerous for us to go around trying to hear God apart from Scripture. I recommend that you get your hands on *Surprised by the Voice of God* by Jack Deere. He is a brilliant theologian who, much like Saul, taught against these kinds of "charismatic" doctrines. And very much like Saul, he was amazed by the voice of God. His book will walk you through the history of the theologies that have caused us to disbelieve that God speaks to us in this way today, and you will discover that hearing God is not a charismatic doctrine, but the birthright of every Christian.

CHAPTER 11
Q-tips for Ears to Hear

Most people do not want to know the will of God in order to do it; they want to know it in order to consider it.

Dr. William L. Pettingill

President Franklin Roosevelt often endured long receiving lines at the White House. He complained that no one really paid any attention to what was said. One day, during a reception, he decided to try an experiment. To each person who passed down the line and shook his hand, he murmured, "I murdered my grandmother this morning." The guests responded with phrases like, "Marvelous! Keep up the good work. We are proud of you. God bless you, sir." It was not until the end of the line, while greeting the ambassador from Bolivia, that his words were actually heard. Unphased, the ambassador leaned over and whispered, "I'm sure she had it coming."

Our Chinese friend, Jack, once asked us about hearing God's voice. In response to his questions about why we were in Taiwan, we shared with him that God had told us to go there. He asked how we hear God. Do we hear with our ears? Do we have to sit in a certain position? Do we hold our hands any particular way? Does it have to be at a certain time of day?

People are often frustrated because they have been asking God for direction and he doesn't seem to be telling them anything. Unlike Buddhist prayer, there are no particular times of day or physical poses that we must use in order to hear God. However, in James 4:6–8 we find a prescription that we can follow to make sure that we are in a "posture" to hear his voice:

CHAPTER 11

> But He gives more grace. Therefore He says: "God resists the
> proud, But gives grace to the humble." Therefore submit to
> God. Resist the devil and he will flee from you. Draw near to
> God and He will draw near to you. Cleanse your hands, you
> sinners; and purify your hearts, you double-minded.

We first need to examine whether or not we are genuinely trying to hear
from God. Very simply, pride and self-sufficiency will hinder us from
hearing his voice. Many times it is in the arenas where we feel quite
competent that we do not even seek God's counsel. We move ahead
independently, because we feel pretty confident of our knowledge.

A report was made by a Royal Canadian Mounted Police officer who
said that most car accidents are not caused by faulty brakes, high speed
or even alcohol. His observation was that most drivers felt that they
were much better drivers than they really were. Because of a false
sense of their own skill, they take chances and make unwise or unsafe
moves.[1]

Jack Deere has said:

> Of all people, the proud have the most difficulty hearing
> the voice of God. They seldom seriously ask God's opinion
> because they are convinced they already know what God
> thinks. There is also a divine hindrance. God is repulsed by
> pride, and normally you don't talk to those who repulse you.
> One of the most sobering statements in the Bible is found in
> Psalm 138:6, "Though the LORD is on high, he looks upon
> the lowly, but the proud he knows from afar."[2]

We, like Jesus, must become completely dependent upon guidance
from the Holy Spirit. If we, in any way, think we do not need him, then
we most certainly will not hear his voice. He is a gentleman and will
not force himself upon us.

> Therefore submit to God.[3]

1. Mumford, Bob. *Take Another Look at Guidance* (Logos International, 1971) p. 63.
2. Deere, Jack. *Surprised by the Voice of God* (Zondervan, 1996) p. 243.
3. James 4:7.

Wesley Duewel says,

> The Lord will not cross the picket line of the will....
> Throughout the Bible...in almost every case it seems the
> person called was willing to do God's will before it was ever
> revealed.[4]

The first step in trying to hear God's voice is ensuring that we are
submitted to his lordship. Do we acknowledge Jesus as Lord? Is he
really our King? Are we prepared to do anything he tells us to do?

Joy Dawson says,

> Simply put, our level of abandonment to God determines
> God's level of directions to us.[5]

When we obey God, he blesses us. It is just natural. As we do the things
that God commands, they lead to a life of corresponding blessing.
However, when we do not obey God, he has to judge us, or you might
say that he disciplines us. Scripture is replete with examples of both
sides of this principle.[6] Hebrews 12:7 even speaks of God as our father,
disciplining us. No father enjoys disciplining his child, and yet he must,
if he is to train up his child in the way she should go. If we do not obey
God, then he must teach us by disciplining us.

I have observed that some who are frustrated about trying to hear God's
will for their lives are not in a posture of submission. They are not
ready and willing to obey absolutely any command given—whatever
the King might ask of them. And thus, they do not hear him speaking.

If God knows that we will not obey, and that he will then have to
punish us, sometimes in his great mercy, he withholds his will. He does
not tell us what he wants us to do. If you are discouraged because you
cannot seem to hear him speaking to you, first examine your heart, your

---

4. Duewel, Wesley. *Let God Guide You Daily* (Duewel Literature Trust, 1988) p. 66.

5. Dawson, Joy. *Forever Ruined for the Ordinary* (Thomas Nelson, 2001) p. 21.

6. Deuteronomy 28, the whole chapter, speaks of this principle. Jeremiah 7:23 also
clearly states this principle. An example of this principle in action is when Naaman was
healed after he obeyed God's command to wash in the Jordan River.

will. Are you fully submitted to him? Are you ready to obey whatever he says to you?

> "He who has My commandments and keeps them, it is he who loves Me. And he who loves Me will be loved by My Father, and I will love him and manifest Myself to him."[7]

I heard once of a preacher who was being interviewed to take a new pastorate. The church invited him to preach, and he preached a fine sermon that Sunday morning. When the congregation came back for the evening service, he preached the same sermon again. The deacons met and attributed the fact that he preached the same sermon to nervousness, and they extended a call to become the new pastor.

The preacher arrived the next Sunday to preach, and again he preached the same sermon. The people just shook their heads and came back that night to see what he would preach. Well, he preached the same sermon again. The deacons had had enough by this point and said among themselves, "If he preaches that sermon again, we will be forced to confront him."

Wednesday night rolled around and, you guessed it, he preached the same sermon again. The deacons met with the pastor after the service and said, "Now, Preacher, that is a fine sermon that you have been preaching, but when are you going to preach something new?" The preacher replied, "Well, I reckon when you do what I said in that sermon, we will go on to something else."

Forgetfulness
Bible teacher Joy Dawson tells of a time when she was trying to prepare a message that she was to preach. She was full of faith that God would speak to her, and she sat with her Bible and pen and paper, ready to begin writing. However, she heard nothing. God was not speaking.

She asked him, "Is there some unrepented sin in my life, so that you cannot speak to me?" The Holy Spirit convicted her that there was. Several days before, she and her husband had felt that God wanted

---

7. John 14:21.

them to give some money as an offering. They both independently felt directed by God to give to the same two missionaries, who were living entirely by trusting God to provide their finances. In the busyness of life, Joy and her husband had completely forgotten to send the money, and now the Holy Spirit was convicting her of it being a sin of disobedience.

Joy did not have the checkbook with her, so she called her husband, who had to stop what he was doing, sit down and write the checks, and put them in the mail. She then sat down again and asked the Lord what he would have her share in her message, and he said, "I want you to speak about hindrances to answered prayer"! And what was her big illustration?[8]

If you have been seeking an answer from God as to what his will is for you in your life, or in a particular circumstance, and you have not been able to get any direction from him, go back to the last thing that he told you to do. If you have not obeyed him in that, perhaps he is waiting before he will give you a new assignment.

Apologize and ask for forgiveness from him. Submit to God and complete that last command that he gave to you. Fellowship will be restored, and you can begin to seek him for the next step he has for your life.

Washing Up

> Cleanse your hands, you sinners; and purify your hearts, you double-minded.[9]

Our prescription for attaining the right "posture" for hearing speaks to us of the necessity of a pure heart. In Webster's dictionary, "pure" is defined as: "absence of contamination, elimination of evil." This

---

8. *School of Intercession, Worship and Warfare* video (Youth With A Mission with City Alive, 1994).

9. James 4:8. For those of you who noticed that I did not address resisting the devil, as it is mentioned in James 4:7, I am not avoiding that topic. It is just a larger subject than this book warrants. Perhaps I will address it in a future book.

part most of us understand. If we are to be pure, we must eliminate the negative, sinful practices from our lives.

However, the next part of the definition was a revelation to me. It says: "single mindedness, one purpose." James refers to this when he says, "Purify your hearts, you double-minded." Many times, I have felt this battle within my own nature. I want to do what Jesus wants for me, but then again I really don't. I want to do what I want. This is what purity means—that we would become single-minded, fully focused on intimate relationship with Jesus that leads to full obedience.

Living in Taiwan, John and I became good friends with a Chinese goldsmith on our street. He sold beautiful jewelry to people who lived there in the village, as well as those from other areas who had heard of his craftsmanship. He did beautiful work—necklaces, rings, earrings.

The 24-karat gold he used was much purer than the 14-karat gold that we are accustomed to in America, and because of that, it was much softer. Over time, these beautiful works of art would lose their shape, and customers would return their jewelry for our goldsmith friend to melt down and use to create something new.

The goldsmith would put the gold in a small crucible and aim a blowtorch at it. The beautiful yellow metal would quickly turn to liquid. He would heat it until it glowed red. Then removing the flame, he would take an instrument in his hand and begin carefully scooping the dross from the top of the puddle.

In becoming pure, we are to remove anything that is dirty. And yes, the dross contains dirt that the goldsmith wants to remove. However, my friend explained to me that not only was he removing dirt, but he also wanted to remove all other metals. Sometimes, mixed together with the gold would be silver or iron—things of value. But the purpose of refining the gold is to make it pure gold—only gold—single-minded, if you will. Simply fixed on him.

I have heard my husband, John, use this illustration: An Olympic sprinter does not wear a fur coat to run the one-hundred-meter race. Rather, she wears a small, thin racing suit that enables her to run as fast as she can. A fur coat might be appropriate for a dogsled race in Alaska, but if the runner is to win, she must be unencumbered by anything that will hold her back.

Many times, the things the Lord asks us to remove from our life are not sin—they are simply less than the best for us.

> Therefore we also, since we are surrounded by so great a cloud of witnesses, let us lay aside every weight, and the sin which so easily ensnares us, and let us run with endurance the race that is set before us.[10]

Weeds

James calls us to "cleanse our hands." I want to make a clear distinction here between forgiveness and cleansing.[11] This is extremely important, because many times, in our attempts to become pure before the Lord, we stop short at receiving his forgiveness without receiving cleansing.

When you have weeds growing in your garden, there are two different ways that you can get rid of them. One way is to get out your weed-eater and whack off those weeds. You no longer have to look at those weeds, but it is only a matter of time before the weeds will again overtake your garden.

The other way to deal with weeds is to get down on your hands and knees and pull the whole plant out by its roots. This definitely takes more time, and it obviously takes a lot more energy, but your garden will be free from that weed from now on. It cannot grow back, because there is nothing left of it.

Forgiveness can be likened to using the weed-eater. When you have sinned, you can always go to God for forgiveness—and he will always forgive you![12] But have you ever found yourself in a cycle of sin? You sin, confess, receive forgiveness. Then you commit the same sin, confess, receive forgiveness—repeatedly returning to the same sin again and again. You may have received forgiveness without cleansing.

---

10. Hebrews 12:1.

11. The difference between forgiveness and cleansing was first introduced to me by Peter Lord in his book *Hearing God* (Baker Books, 1988).

12. 1 John 1:9.

CHAPTER 11

Cleansing can be likened to pulling a weed out by its roots. Many times the sin that we are recognizing, the one that we keep confessing, is a behavioral sin. It is a sin of action. Those are the sins that are easiest for us to see. They are the most likely for us to recognize, because they often cause the most destruction, in our own lives and in damaging other people.

However, many times the root of our behavioral sin is different from the surface symptom, or the weed that we see growing in our life. For example, you find yourself repeatedly getting angry with your roommate. She annoys you. Her seemingly minor behaviors really get on your nerves, and before you know it, you say unkind things and hurt her feelings.

You feel terrible about this, and you confess your sin of outbursts of anger to the Lord. You ask her for forgiveness and commit in your heart to not do it again. But as time goes by, the pressure builds and once again you have wounded her.

You can repeatedly ask for forgiveness, or you can go for cleansing. Cleansing means that you ask God to show you what is underneath this sin of outbursts of anger. What is the root of it? In quiet meditation, allowing the Holy Spirit to search your heart, you may find that you are jealous of your roommate. Perhaps it is a sin that you were unaware of, but as it lay festering in your heart, the surface weed of outbursts of anger appeared above the ground.

In allowing the Holy Spirit to bring up the sin of jealousy, he also can bring healing to the wounds in your past that predispose you to that sin. You can not only get forgiveness, but also deep cleansing and healing that transforms your character.

Many years ago, when we were just getting started with our missionary training, one of our students became angry with his roommate and threatened him with a baseball bat. Obviously, this was unacceptable behavior for a missionary. You can't threaten to murder people. Anyway, in counseling with this young man about his anger, he finally confessed to a strong addiction to pornography. In fact, he had a stack of magazines under his bed in the dormitory on our campus.

As the Holy Spirit began to minister to him, a connection became clear. A festering sin of lust was brewing under the surface in his heart. Lust is an all-consuming hunger that cannot be satisfied. No matter how you attempt to feed it, it continues to ask for more. Living with this secret, driving desire caused him to carry an intense level of anger—never being able to satiate his desire for sex. It was coming out on the surface in hatred, anger and, ultimately, threats of murder.

Roots

John and I have been married almost twenty years. Those first few years of marriage were very difficult, as I was dealing with such deep emotional wounds. As I began to receive healing from the Lord, things began to improve between us. The nightmares ceased, intimacy improved to some degree, the arguments were less frequent.

However, although we argued less, each argument seemed much worse. I was extremely angry and could not stay on topic. Every argument was an opportunity for me to bring out my "list of offenses." Maybe you know what I'm talking about.

I would get frustrated with John about little things, like messes he would make and not clean up or not communicating with me when he was going to be late. I knew these were "small things," so I wouldn't make a big deal about them. In fact, I wouldn't even talk to him about them—but they went on my list!

My list of minor offenses would grow and grow, until some straw would break the camel's back, and I would start an argument. John would be completely blindsided. I would start out talking about the current offense, but before long, out would come my list, and I would describe for him how my frustration had built over each one of these items.

These arguments never stayed rational, as he did not understand the intensity of my emotions, and I could not keep to one topic. Eventually, and inevitably it seemed, the argument would descend to me talking about our sex life—and John would be thinking, "How did we get here?"

As I said, the arguments became worse and worse. I would be "fine," or so it seemed, for a week, maybe two, and then I would explode. I prayed, I confessed, I asked for forgiveness. I tried harder. I thought if I could just hold out longer, not explode as often, that it would be a sign that I was improving. But the wounding that happened within each argument became worse and worse.

Finally, the breaking argument came. I had jumped out of the car, as it was moving, yelling and cursing John as I fled. The things I said to him, I knew had caused potentially irreparable damage. I did not know if our marriage could survive—and I knew the problem was me.

I knew that I was full of the sin of bitterness. I honestly tried to forgive. I made choices in my mind every day to forgive these "little things." But somehow I could not keep from forming the list. It was an addiction to bitterness. I knew that I somehow enjoyed those seething feelings of anger and unforgiveness. I was controlled by them, and I did not know how to get free.

I called up my dear friend and asked her if I could come to her house. I knew that I could not do this alone. I had been trying to deal with it just between me and the Lord for years, and the problem had only gotten worse. She met me, weeping on her front porch, and ushered me into her bedroom, where she closed the door and sat down on the bed with me.

I told her the long story of our arguments and my despair about conquering this sin. For a few moments she just looked at me. Finally, she said, "I don't know what to do. I don't have any wisdom to give you. The Holy Spirit is going to have to help us." She leaned forward on the bed and began to weep with me. We began to cry out to the Lord for help. I confessed my sin openly to him, and I asked him to come and deliver me from the grip of bitterness. It was quite an emotional experience.

When the tears had subsided, we lay on the bed, desperate and waiting. She turned to me and said, "Jamie, I don't think this has anything to do with John. I think it is about your father." In that instant, my heart was flooded with pain. In a matter of moments, I relived the pain of the abuses I had suffered as a child, and my heart cried out that my father had not protected me.

My dad was a good father in so many ways. He loved me and was very supportive and encouraging. Never was he abusive in word or deed. However, my dad is a non-confrontational sort of person. He does not like conflict. Usually, he will do whatever he can to avoid it, and this was the way that he interacted with me as I dated abusive guys. He knew. He could see that these relationships were unhealthy. He did not like the way these guys treated me. But he did not step in to prevent them.

I have since had conversations with my parents about those events in my life, and they have explained their motives and their concerns that if they had interfered I might have rebelled completely—and perhaps I might have. I truly do believe that they did the best they knew how, but something in my heart had longed for my daddy to rescue me.

The root of my bitterness with John was really bitterness toward my father. I had to forgive him for not protecting me—and I had to forgive God, my father, as well. This prayer time was meaningful beyond description as I released my dad from the debt I had held him in for fifteen years.

This does not mean that John and I have never had another argument. But it does mean that my list is gone. Minor offenses are easy to let go. The sin is cleansed, and the garden is free from the weed of bitterness.

Sin separates us from God, and in order to clearly hear his voice, we must be cleansed. If you are aware of some potential sin roots in your life, and you want them to be pulled, I can guarantee you that God desires to free you from those sins. Your experience with him, as the Holy Spirit shines his light upon your heart, may look very different from mine. It may be dramatic; it may be quiet and simple. Don't settle for just forgiveness. Go for the deep work of root-level cleansing.[13]

---

13. I recommend that you get your hands on Charles Bello's book, *Prayer as a Place* (HGM Publishing, 2008). He will help you to learn some practical methods for quieting your heart and receiving the transforming work of the Holy Spirit's weeding in the garden of your heart.

CHAPTER 12
Loud and Clear

Never let good books take the place of the Bible. Drink from the Well, not from the streams that flow from the Well.

Amy Carmichael

When the famous missionary Dr. David Livingstone started his trek across Africa, he had 73 books in 3 packs, weighing 180 pounds. After the party had gone 300 miles, Livingstone was obliged to throw away some of the books because of the fatigue of those carrying his baggage. As he continued on his journey, his library grew less and less, until he had but one book left—his Bible.

The Bible is our most trustworthy and reliable method for hearing from God. Because of that, it is also the most comfortable method for most of us. Psalm 119 tells us that God's Word is a lamp unto our feet and a light unto our path. Through it, God gives direction to us.

Hebrews 4:12 also tells us that

> The word of God is living and powerful, and sharper than any two-edged sword, piercing even to the division of soul and spirit, and of joints and marrow, and is a discerner of the thoughts and intents of the heart.

The Bible is alive! I am sure that you have had this experience. You're reading along in your regular Bible study. Perhaps you read part of the Old Testament and part of the New each day. Maybe you like to spend time in the Psalms each day. But you're reading along, and all of a sudden, it is no longer just words on a page. It is as if the words leap off the page and penetrate your soul. You know that God is intending those words for you in that moment.

This should be our regular experience. It is through the Bible that we become accustomed to God's voice. Here is where we find out what he is like—what things matter to him, what he likes, what he doesn't like. The Bible is the beginning place of our relationship. Through it we discover God's personality.

My dad has done some construction work over the years. In fact, he did a lot of building on the dormitories and dining hall of our HGM campus. I have seen him use a tool called a plumb line. A plumb line is a string that has been covered in chalk. Sometimes the chalk is blue, sometimes it is red. At the end of this long string is a heavy weight.

A builder uses this plumb line to make a straight line. For instance, when determining where to place a window, he will hold the line up with the weight hanging down and place it near the wall that he has built. Holding it tight, he will snap the string, leaving a perfect blue or red line on the wall. From that point on, everything has to match up to that line. That line is what they call "square." If you match to it, you can be sure that you are straight.

Scripture serves as a plumb line for us. Every other method for hearing God's voice must be submitted to the Bible to see if it is "square." Now, the Bible does not talk about everything. It doesn't tell you who to marry or which college to attend, but it does have principles, and we do find God's character there. It is our starting and ending place for measuring whether or not we have heard from God.

> Studying the Bible is a lifetime project. In fact, the more mature we become as Christians the more we need to study it. Yet there are some Christians who either feel they've "arrived" or admit they are too busy doing "God's Work" and say they don't need to read it. We must read it and know it, for in the Bible is the key to our knowledge of the character and nature of God, as well as the key to understanding our own character and nature.[1]

---

1. Mumford, Bob. *Take Another Look at Guidance* (Logos International, 1971) p. 76.

As we come to know what the Bible says and who God really is, his
voice becomes clearer and clearer to us. So let's take a look at some of
the ways that God speaks to us, beginning with his use of Scripture.[2]

Memorization

Why are we taught to commit God's Word to memory? When we do
not have our Bible with us, God can speak to us by recalling Scripture
to our mind. I once read the moving story of Darlene Deibler Rose,
missionary in the Dutch East Indies (now Indonesia) from 1938–1942.
The Japanese captured her during World War Two, and in her book,
Evidence Not Seen, she tells of days and days of solitary confinement,
dysentery and depression. In those lonely weeks and months, she would
recite passages of Scripture that she had memorized, and through his
Word, the Holy Spirit brought her comfort and encouragement.

A Random Reference

Sometimes you may have a thought come into your mind that is
merely a Scripture reference. You have no idea what that verse even
says. I have had this happen to me most often when I am in a ministry
situation. Once I was in a group of people gathered around a young
man to pray for a need, and several of us prayed. When we had
exhausted the list of things to pray for and didn't know what else to
pray, a reference popped into my mind—"Zechariah 3:4."

I turned to that verse in my Bible and found the scene of God declaring
over Joshua:

> "Take away the filthy garments from him." And to him He
> said, "See, I have removed your iniquity from you, and I will
> clothe you with rich robes."

God wanted this young man to know that he was forgiven—that God
had taken his sin and made him righteous. As I read this verse, he
began to weep. It became a precious time of ministry, as he felt the love
and forgiveness of his Savior.

---

2. This is not an exhaustive list of the ways God speaks, but my hope is to introduce you
to some and to inspire you to pay closer attention to everything you are hearing!

Open-Page-and-Point Method

Another way that God sometimes uses the Bible to speak to us is what you might call the "flop-it-open-and-look" method. You open your Bible and read what your eyes fall upon. Now, this can definitely be dangerous and must not be abused. You very easily could read, "Judas hanged himself," and turn to another page where it says, "Go and do likewise."[3] However, God does use this method from time to time. Remember his Word is alive!

We were in Taiwan with a group of people that we were leading on a prayer walk. We had started in the northern part of Taiwan and were working our way to the south, visiting significant religious sites and praying together that God's kingdom would come to the people of Taiwan. Incidentally, there are some wonderful passages of Scripture to turn into prayers. Places in Isaiah and Jeremiah, where God promises that one day the names of the idols will no longer be remembered, but only the worship of the one true God will remain!

During this trip, John had spoken in several different Paiwanese churches.[4] God's Spirit was moving in miraculous ways, much like in the Book of Acts, bringing this former headhunting tribe to himself— but that's another story. John had spoken Sunday morning in a church, and we were riding in a minivan to a different location to hold another service that evening.

John turned to the driver of the van and asked him, "Will any of the people in attendance tonight have heard me in another service this week?" I knew the reason John was asking. He had spent many hours preparing his message in Mandarin. Using a second language meant that writing a sermon required a lot of study and preparation, seeking just the right words to use, the exact Biblical terminology. He had been preaching the same sermon in every location that week.

The driver responded, "Yes, about half of the people tonight will have been in one of the other services this week." Instantly, John began to sweat. Well, okay, he was already sweating, as it was over 100 degrees

---

3. Matthew 27:5; Luke 10:37.

4. The Paiwanese (not Taiwanese) are an indigenous people of Taiwan. Sometimes referred to as the aborigines of Taiwan, these indigenous peoples (of which there are ten tribes) were the earliest inhabitants of the island.

and 100 percent humidity! But the expression on his face told it all—he was panicked! What was he going to preach? He only had prepared the one sermon!

I remember John climbing over the seats of that minivan to sit by himself in the last row. In a panic, he began asking, "God, what am I going to do? What do you want me to say?" In desperation, he flopped open his Bible, and it fell open to the story of God calling Moses. His eyes fell on Exodus 4:12:

> "Now therefore, go, and I will be with your mouth and teach you what you shall say."

With a rush of peace and assurance, John's thoughts immediately became flooded with a new sermon, one that was full of story and testimony, one that would be comfortable for him to share. God's Word is alive!

Kevin and Sheryl and their two young children came with some friends to visit the Oakhill campus of Heart of God Ministries. They really were just tagging along with their friends who had an interest in missions and wanted to find out more about our ministry. Kevin had left his occupation, packed up his family and gone on the road, serving as a traveling evangelist.

The group of visitors received a tour of our facilities and a mini-sermon from John about God's heart for those peoples on the planet that have never even heard the name of Jesus. This was news to Kevin. He had never thought about becoming a missionary, but he was moved by the things that John shared.

He took some of our magazines and brochures as they left. And he took something else with him—a fire that began to burn within his heart. Over the next few days, Kevin read the articles and decided to fast and pray, seeking God's will for his life.

In the second day of the fast, Kevin opened up his Bible and his eyes fell on Matthew 24:14:

"And this gospel of the kingdom will be preached in all the world as a witness to all the nations, and then the end will come."

He closed it quickly and thought, "That's got to be a coincidence." He opened his Bible again, and his eyes landed on Mark 13:10:

"And the gospel must first be preached to all the nations."

Immediately Kevin picked up the phone and called our office. Weeping, he asked, "Is it too late to get into this next Boot Camp class? God has called me to be a missionary!"

Kevin and Sheryl arrived with fifty dollars in their pocket and no idea how they were going to pay for the training. This was not new to them, however, as they had been traveling all over the country, relying solely on the provision they received from God through his people. They could believe that God would pay the bill.

By the time they graduated, their bill was paid in full. They have been ministering to unreached people in Asia now for ten years. God's Word is alive!

Open and Closed Doors

"See, I have set before you an open door, and no one can shut it."[5]

One of the more common ways that I see people seeking God's will in their lives is through open and closed doors. This most definitely is a way that God shows us his will, as we pray that he will make a way for us in the right direction and will close opportunities that are not from him.

However, we must be careful to not rely solely upon this method, as coincidence and the devil himself can lead us down paths that are not

5. Revelation 3:8.

God's will for us at all. When God called Jonah to go to Ninevah, there was a boat waiting to go to Tarshish right there available to him.

I have seen Satan use this method many times to derail people who have heard a call from God to go as missionaries to the unreached. They begin talking about their call, making steps to get training, and then the most beautiful girl or handsome guy comes into their lives and is interested in them! It is inevitably someone who has no intention of going to the mission field. Many are the times that John and I have prayed with an elderly woman or man who, after hearing us speak, comes to us weeping and saying, "As a young person, I had a call to be a missionary, but I married So-and-So."

If it is not a new relationship that derails the call, it is a new job opportunity. One young man came to Boot Camp with a shaky sense of his calling. He felt that God had called him to be involved in missions, but was holding on to a dream of working for *National Geographic* magazine as a photographer. In the first week of his training, he received a call with an offer from National Geographic—the dream job! In a life and death struggle, he surrendered to God's call. He is now in Asia taking the gospel to Tibetan Buddhists!

Life Events

Cliff Barrows has been the worship leader for Billy Graham's crusades for many years. In 1945, before he had even met Billy Graham, Barrows had just gotten married. For the first night of their honeymoon, he and his new bride traveled to a city with a resort, only to find their intended hotel shut down.

They were stranded in a big city with only a little money and no idea what to do. They hitched a ride with a sympathetic driver who took them to stay in a room above his friend's grocery store.

The next day, the grocery store owner overheard Cliff playing Christian songs on his trombone, and she helped arrange for them to spend the rest of their honeymoon at a friend's house. The host invited them to attend a youth rally to hear a young evangelist speak.

When they got to the meeting, they found that the worship leader was sick, so Cliff was asked to help by leading worship for the service. The young evangelist, of course, was Billy Graham. The two have been partners in ministry ever since.[6]

Many of the circumstances we experience seem to be merely the everyday happenings of life. If we forget that God is speaking, that he is always teaching us, that he is walking together with us through this life, we may miss the things that he is saying.

Back when I had two small children, John would watch them for the evening and let me go away to get some time alone. Often I would go to Braum's, our local ice cream store. I would take my Bible and some devotional books, order a hot fudge sundae and a coffee, and sit down to have what I called a "date with Jesus."

One of these evenings I was studying a devotional book that was about the lives of women in Scripture. I was on the chapter that told the story of Deborah. It is found in Judges 4. Israel has been oppressed for many years by Canaanites. Deborah, who is a prophetess and the judge of Israel, calls for Barak, the general, and gives him instructions to fight against the Canaanites.

Barak appeals to Deborah to go with him. He will not lead the army into battle unless she agrees to go. So she does. The Israelites fight against the Canaanites, and the battle is going well. The Canaanite general, whose name is Sisera, runs away to the tent of a woman named Jael. She greets him and invites him to come into her tent for some milk. She covers him with a blanket and he goes to sleep. Then Jael quietly takes a tent spike and hammer and drives the spike through his temple into the ground, thus sealing the victory for Israel!

I was reading this story, expecting next to study the life of Deborah and learn from her, when I heard the Holy Spirit speak to me: "You are carrying Jael." I paused for a moment, because I didn't know what he meant. Suddenly, the thought came to my mind: *I must be pregnant!*

---

6. Larson, Craig Brian. *Contemporary Illustrations for Preachers, Teachers, & Writers* (Baker Books, 1996) p. 194.

I jumped up, gathered my books and drove to a nearby grocery store to purchase a pregnancy test. When I got home, I walked in our front door and went straight to the bathroom without a word to John as I passed him. In a couple of minutes, I emerged from the bathroom, holding the evidence, and announced, "John, we're having a baby, and her name is Jael."

God has not done this for me with all my children, but this began a season of nine months in which God used the story and symbolism of Jael to teach us many lessons.

We had just completed the first class of Beautiful Feet Boot Camp missionary training, and our graduates were in the process of figuring out where God wanted them to go as a team. A local Freewill Baptist college had offered dormitory and classroom space for us to use that first year. As the school began to prepare for the coming academic year, it became clear that they were going to need the space we had been occupying. They came to us and asked that we find another place to host our second class.

Our staff consisted of nine at that time, and we all agreed together that God wanted to provide for us a long-term campus that would belong to us, so we began exploring the different options. We also agreed that we would not try to purchase any property that we did not all agree upon. The search began. We were open to just about anything. We looked at old colleges, hotels, in Oklahoma City, outside the state even. None of us knew what God might direct.

In the meantime, we had to immediately move off the college campus. Friends from a local church in town took us into their homes. Different parts of the staff were living in different locations around the city. Some homes were available for a week or two at a time. Then we would move to another home to stay as long as they could stand us.

Homeless and Pregnant

John and I had our two little children, my exceedingly pregnant self, and all our personal items, as well as our computer. Another young married couple lived together with us in different locations. We would

143

temporarily set up sleeping arrangements and office space in a spare bedroom, a sunroom or, for several months, in a pool house.

We lived together with this other couple in a one-room pool house for four months, and God poured out his grace to do it. We never once had an argument. We laughed, we listened to each other sneeze in the shower, we forgot to turn off the music and it played Gregorian Chants all night... Many special, personal memories were made during those months.[7]

In Judges 5, Deborah sings a wonderful song about Jael, the hero of the battle. In her song, she says that Jael is the most blessed of women who live in tents.[8] God began to teach me how to live in tents—how to be mobile, to not have a lot of precious "stuff" that I had to carry, to be flexible—in a sense, to be a sojourner, this world not being my home. And he showed me that he could give me grace to do it.

Near the end of my pregnancy, my parents, who were on staff with HGM together with us, had gone to visit my aging grandparents. In searching for property, one of their concerns was for their parents and how to care for them as they were getting to a more needy stage of life. As they were leaving my grandparents' home, they noticed that the property next door was for sale.

This could be God's answer! We all went to view the five-acre plot of land with a house and large barn. The woman selling the home was in a hurry to leave, having just experienced a painful divorce, and was selling it all for only $85,000. We all agreed that here was our answer! The home could be turned into office space, and the barn would become our first dormitory. We began the process of purchasing it, and my parents moved into the remodeled barn on my grandparents' property right next door.

I have birthed all my babies at home with a midwife, so when the time came closer for me to deliver Jael, my concerns began to grow. As those of you who have experienced pregnancy know, there comes a

---

7. Tom and Rikki Manners—you are most precious friends, and I cannot thank you enough for your faithfulness, honesty, perseverance and just plain love for us over the years. I love growing old with you guys!
8. Verse 24.

time when a "nesting instinct" kicks in. I wanted to prepare a place to have my baby. I wanted to arrange her bed, her clothes, her dresser. But we had no such place. I doubted that the people who loaned us their pool house would appreciate me birthing a baby out behind their house!

Nearing the due date, I awoke one morning and John said, "The baby has dropped." I looked different. I went to visit my midwife and received the news that Jael was in breach position. I had already been experiencing contractions, so this was a great concern.

We went from the midwife appointment to a ministry staff meeting, where we asked everyone to pray. All committed to pray with us until we saw the baby turn over into the right position. One of the staff members even felt called to fast. That evening, we received a call from him. The Lord had assured him that his prayers were answered and had even told him to stop his fast. I awoke the next morning with the baby back in right position!

During the next couple of days, it crossed my mind several times that perhaps the umbilical cord was now wrapped around my baby's neck because of all that flipping and flopping. I mentioned my concern to my mother, and she responded that she had thought the same thing. Thinking that this could be the leading of the Holy Spirit, I called my midwife. The only way that we could find out for sure would be to have an ultrasound. However, we had no money for it. My midwife, who was a Christian, agreed that the Holy Spirit might be warning her to be particularly watchful for the cord when it came time for me to deliver the baby. All we could do was pray and trust the Lord.

I awoke in the early hours of the morning in the full swing of labor. We left the pool house and drove to the barn where my parents were now living, adjacent to our new property that was not yet ready for us to live in. My mother and several of my friends gathered to help me, as well as my midwife.

It was a very difficult labor. Without being too graphic, I will tell you that I pushed for three hours. This is uncommon for a third baby—at least I had been told that they're supposed to get easier with each one! It seemed that each time I pushed, she would move forward, only to retreat in between contractions.

In the middle of this struggle, one of my girlfriends went outside, where she began to walk around the barn. She felt that she needed to pray loudly, to fight against the enemy. God was leading her to battle on Jael's behalf. It was an intense time of physical effort, emotional turmoil and spiritual warfare.

When Jael finally appeared, the cord was wrapped tightly around her neck. Each time I had pushed, the cord was pulling her back in. Because the Holy Spirit had warned us, my midwife was watching and feeling for the cord. She began shouting at me to stop pushing. Quickly she cut the cord from around Jael's neck, and then I pushed her the rest of the way out. She began to rub Jael vigorously, and then she quickly fed a tube down her throat to clean out her airway. The baby coughed and wheezed and then began to turn pink.

She was all right! We had a keen sense that the devil had tried to kill our baby, but the victory was won! God spoke to us through the story of Jael's decisive killing of Sisera about how to deal with our enemy, the devil. We learned a lot about prayer, about depending on the body of Christ, about spiritual warfare.

The barn where my parents live is affectionately called "The Victory Barn." Sometimes we tease Jael by asking her if she was born in a barn. We gave her Wisdom for her middle name, as we decided that she probably would need some wisdom to go along with that holy violence. She feels called to take the gospel to the Tibetan Buddhists who have been held tightly in the grip of Satan for thousands of years. You can pray for her.

God Shouts
A man was caught in a flood and ended up floating on the roof of his destroyed home. He prayed desperately for God's help. In time a rescue team came by in a boat. "We've come to help you," they shouted. "Get in our boat and you'll be safe." "No," the man shouted back. "God's going to save me."

It grew dark and scary and the man prayed harder. The beat of helicopter blades could be heard coming from the distance, growing louder and louder, until they were thumping overhead. A bright light framed the house wreckage and the man. The loudspeaker boomed, "Take the rope, and you'll be safe." "No, thanks," the man shouted as he waved the helicopter away. "God's going to save me."

Shortly thereafter, the roof disintegrated and the man drowned. He was grateful to arrive in heaven, but irritated that God hadn't answered his prayers. When he stood before Jesus, he complained. "Why didn't you save me as you promised that you would?"

"Whatever do you mean?" the Lord said. "I sent a boat and a helicopter!"

Many times, God is shouting to us in our experiences, but we are so intent on just one option that we fail to hear him. Many of the daily experiences of our lives seem merely to be regular, normal events. Occupations that we have. Conflicts that arise. Births. Deaths. Vacations that we take. And yet, God is speaking all the time. If we are aware of his presence, he will walk with us through the course of everyday circumstances and turn them into mighty spiritual lessons.

Preaching

Preaching is an obvious method that God uses to speak to his people. I remember going to church every week anticipating that God was going to say something directly to me. Our pastor, who was committed to only saying what he heard the Father saying, would not just prepare a good teaching from Scripture. Rather, every week, we knew that what he would share was a message straight from God himself. It was absolutely exciting!

I believe this is the difference between preaching and teaching. A teacher can teach a lesson that is full of biblical guidance and practical helps. But true preaching comes from the heart of God and is anointed by his Holy Spirit. God can use both, of course, but it's quite the adventure when we tap into what God is saying to us now.

I mentioned that my parents, Jim and LaVina West, are on staff with us at Heart of God Ministries. My father was a pastor in the Church of the Nazarene for over twenty years—first in Washington State and then in Alaska. When they moved to Oklahoma City to help us in the formation of HGM, my dad took a position as a part-time associate pastor at a local Nazarene church, so that he could help us part-time as well.

It came time for the annual Pastors Retreat, which several hundred Nazarene pastors from the region attend. It was held in Oklahoma City, and Dad decided to attend the services. During an evening convocation, the speaker was attempting to encourage these local pastors. He was very aware of the trials and pains that pastors endure, and he called them to persevere.

In his message, the speaker told of his flight to Oklahoma City. During the flight, he was seated next to a man who told him the story of his life. He had been a pastor, but due to struggles with church members, betrayals and conflicts, he had burned out and now had gone back to school to become a lawyer.

The speaker cautioned the preachers against burnout, reminded them of their calling and challenged them to get renewed grace from God. He sent them back to their hotel rooms to spend the evening in silence, listening and responding to whatever the Holy Spirit said to them. Because Dad lived in the same city, he went home and explained to my mother that he would be spending the evening in silent prayer.

As the evening wore on, Dad began experiencing the symptoms of a cold. His head filled up, his eyes began to water, his head hurt. He took some cold medicine and lay down to go to sleep. But sleep would not come. He lay there in bed, staring up at the ceiling fan, wondering if he could ever fall asleep, and not feeling all that near to God.

Suddenly Dad heard the Holy Spirit speak to him. He said, "Jim, I want you to be a lawyer." Immediately, Dad knew that God was not calling him to a career as an attorney, but that God was using this illustration to penetrate his heart with the need of the unreached. 2.1 billion people on the planet have not yet heard the name of Jesus even once, and God was calling my dad to represent them. To give his life in making their cause known to the church. To preach on their behalf, to raise money on their behalf, and to call missionaries to take the gospel to them. He was to be a lawyer—an advocate for the unreached!

The next morning, he awoke and announced with determination to my mother that he would be quitting his job as associate pastor at the church and coming on full time to work for Heart of God Ministries. He gave up a regular paycheck to trust God to supply every need. He turned in his retirement fund to invest instead in raising up a multitude of missionaries to take the gospel where it is not yet known.

That preacher did not intend for Dad to hear his sermon the way God used it, but it was anointed by the Holy Spirit. If preachers will allow him, God will speak through them, and if we will listen with anticipating ears, we will hear the very voice of God coming through the mouths of his ministers.

Peace

> And let the peace of God rule in your hearts, to which also you were called in one body; and be thankful.[9]

This may be the simplest and most widely used method for hearing God's voice. When I was a little girl, my dad preached a series of sermons on the book of Colossians. These sermons are now put together in his book entitled *Complete in Him to Complete the Task*.[10]

Dad points out that the Greek word for "rule" really means "to umpire." In a baseball game, the umpire is the one who stands behind home plate and determines whether each pitch is a strike or a ball—whether it's a good or bad one. This is what Paul is trying to tell us here in Colossians. He says, "Let the peace of God rule in your hearts." If something is of God, there will be peace in your heart. If it is not of God, there will be no peace.

One of our Boot Camp students told the story of his decision to come to missionary training. He had received the opportunity to go to Taiwan to teach English and had heard about Boot Camp during the same short period of time. He very much wanted to go to Taiwan.

---

9. Colossians 3:15.
10. West, James L. *Complete in Him to Complete the Task* (HGM Publishing, 2002).

He said that sitting in a restaurant, he began thinking of Taiwan and suddenly he felt that he was going to vomit. Every time he thought of making that decision, nausea would overwhelm him. After much thinking and wrestling in his mind, he finally decided that he would come to Boot Camp for training. His testimony was that immediately his heart was flooded with peace. Turmoil, anxiety, nausea as you're making a decision—these are obviously not from God! Look for the peace.

I read a story of a man who was driving at night. Suddenly he experienced a feeling in his spirit that he described as a "disturbance of the peace"—a caution. He asked the Lord what was wrong, and he heard God say, "Watch out for deer." Being accustomed to recognizing the Holy Spirit's promptings, he immediately slowed down. Rounding a corner, his headlights caught the form of a large doe standing in the middle of the road. He was able to stop without hitting it, because he had been warned by the "disturbance of the peace."[11]

I was teaching this material in Mexico and the Spanish translation of this verb, "to rule," really struck me. In Spanish the verb is *gobernar*. It means "to govern"—the same thing as "to umpire"! We are to let peace be the governor, the decision-maker in our life. My dad so loves this verse that he has written a song from it:

> Let the peace of Christ rule in your hearts.
> He calls the balls and strikes,
> Puts an end to our strife.
> He made us one Body,
> And He will be our Umpire.
> So I will let the peace of Christ rule in my heart.

The Body of Christ

People love to give advice. Many times advice is good. Sometimes we even say to one another, "I believe this is from the Lord for you," or perhaps, "I feel that God would want you to...." Maybe it is even stated, "I have a 'word' from the Lord for you." Some will even claim to be prophets.

---

11. Mumford, Bob. *Take Another Look At Guidance* (Logos International, 1971) p. 99.

God will speak to us through one another. We can expect that as we love, encourage, teach and correct each other that his voice will come through. It will happen in our daily interaction, and it will happen in more purposeful messages that we deliver to one another. I want to give you some guidelines for receiving from another believer.

First, we need to pay attention to the person's character. Is this person submitted to the lordship of Jesus? Do they have a pure and trustworthy walk with the Lord? I am not suggesting that they must be perfect, for none of us are. However, as we have talked about, in order to hear correctly from the Lord, we must have a pure and submitted heart before God. If this is not evident in a "counselor's" life, then be cautious to receive from them overt declarations of "words from the Lord."

Every one of us has the capacity to become deceived. Safety exists only as we walk with other believers who have permission to speak into our lives, to bring cautions and corrections if we have gotten off the beaten track of following Jesus. Without accountability, we are all in danger of coming up with all kinds of crazy ideas.

Paul encouraged this kind of accountability. He said, "The spirits of the prophets are subject to the prophets."[12] So notice whether a "prophet," or even just another believer who has "heard God for you," is submitted to friends and authorities who can bring correction to him or her. If not, then use caution in receiving his or her words as the voice of God. Seek confirmation within your own spirit and through other methods that God uses to speak to you.

Another red flag in receiving from prophets is whether or not they are willing to have their "word" tested. If a person were to walk up to you and tell you that they believe that God is calling you to start a home for unwed mothers in Dallas, what would you think? What if you have never even considered this kind of ministry before, and yet they want you to pack up your things and move tomorrow? To your knowledge, God has not been speaking to you about it. This is the first you've heard of it. It could be the Lord leading you, but you would want to seek confirmation first, right?

---

12. 1 Corinthians 14:32.

We no longer must go through a priest to speak to God or to hear from him. Each of us has access, through the Holy Spirit, to direct relationship with him. Therefore, if God wants to tell you something, he will speak to you himself. There are times when he uses other people to get our attention, but even so, he will bring confirmation. Ask him, seek him—you will find out what he desires. Don't be afraid that you are of little faith. He is happy to confirm his direction.

> If you need wisdom—if you want to know what God wants you to do—ask him, and he will gladly tell you. He will not resent your asking.[13]

God is speaking to us all the time. As you see beautiful flowers, a butterfly, a rainbow, people interacting with one another, a baby born—God is speaking. Remember to listen for him in unlikely places as well.

Our family was in Taiwan where our young missionary team was disintegrating. There had been confusing conflicts between team members, misunderstandings, pride, rebellion. It was a mess. And now, some of our dearest friends were leaving the ministry—leaving us is what it felt like—and the team was crumbling.

John and I had been careful to protect our children from hearing us talk about the conflicts that were happening because they were very close to many of the people involved and we were hoping for reconciliation. One afternoon, I was sitting on the couch in the living room of our base in Taiwan. The children were playing on the floor at my feet.

I was overcome with emotion about the situation we were in and sat there crying. I could not stop the tears. It felt to me as though everything we had been building toward in ministry was crashing down around us. I was hurt, angry and confused.

My son Josiah, who was six years old, got up from the floor where he was playing with a truck. He came over and laid his hand on my knee. He said, "Mama, the apple tree will flourish and not die." Then he immediately turned around and went back to playing with his truck on the floor, while I sat in stunned silence!

---

13. James 1:5 (NLT).

Jo was a normal six-year-old. He had never used that word, "flourish," before (and, I'm quite sure, never since). God had just spoken to me through my little boy, and what a beautiful picture he gave to me. An apple tree, a fruitful apple tree. I could see it in my mind's eye.

In that moment, although nothing had changed, hope filled my heart. I did not know how he was going to do it, but I knew that God would not allow the complete destruction of our ministry—of the fruit that would come from our lives. He would grow it, and one day, it would be a fruitful tree, bearing fruit among the many tongues, tribes and nations that had finally received the good news of Jesus Christ!

Casting Lots

One young man had heard what he thought was God leading him to come to Boot Camp for training. God had spoken through several means, and yet he still was not quite sure. He was looking for one last confirmation. The decision needed to be made, as the application was due, so in faith he prayed over an ordinary quarter and asked God to speak. He decided that tails would mean he was not to apply, and heads (which has the words "In God We Trust") would represent God saying, "Yes." He flipped the coin and turned in his application the next day.

What? Is this an acceptable way to hear from God? Although strange and maybe dangerous, it is in the Bible:

> "Therefore, of these men who have accompanied us all the time that the Lord Jesus went in and out among us, beginning from the baptism of John to that day when He was taken up from us, one of these must become a witness with us of His resurrection." And they proposed two: Joseph called Barnabas, who was surnamed Justus, and Matthias. And they prayed and said, "You, O Lord, who know the hearts of all, show which of these two You have chosen to take part in this ministry and apostleship from which Judas by transgression fell, that he might go to his own place." And they cast their lots, and the lot fell on Matthias. And he was numbered with the eleven apostles.[14]

---

14. Acts 21:26.

This was certainly a more serious decision than whether or not to go to a training program! We are talking about who would be the twelfth apostle! What is it that makes this method work? It is faith. In both of these examples, those who are casting the lots are fully submitted to follow God's leading, whatever the decision may be. They fully believe that he will lead through the lot and are committed to take it as an answer from God. That is faith.

> The lot is cast into the lap, but its every decision is from the Lord.[15]

Fleece

You know the story of Gideon. God calls Gideon to lead an army against the Midianites, and Gideon is terrified. He feels weak and unqualified. He needs confirmation. He wants to know that this really is God's word to him.

So he lays out a fleece of wool upon the threshing floor in the evening. He tells God that if there is dew on the fleece in the morning, but the ground all around is dry, then he will know that God has been speaking to him. And it was so. In the morning, the fleece was soaked, and nothing else was wet.

This was not yet enough for Gideon though. It could have been coincidence, so he asks God for another confirmation. He puts out the fleece again, but this time tells God that if the fleece is dry in the morning, but the ground all around is wet, then he would be sure. God did it for him.

What I love about this story is that God is not angry with Gideon for his doubts. He is not angry that Gideon wants more confirmation. Gideon truly wants to obey God. He just wants to be sure that he is hearing the instructions correctly.[16]

God is not hiding from us. He really wants us to know and do his will, not just for his kingdom's sake, but because he knows what will be best

---

15. Proverbs 16:33.
16. Judges 6:36–40.

for us! He does not mind us seeking confirmation when our heart is set upon following him, no matter what his will is for us.

Nearing the end of our first Boot Camp class, Tom and Rikki Manners, who had been colleagues and friends of ours for quite a while, felt that God might be calling them to come and join the staff of HGM. John had given a seminar at their local church in Tulsa, Oklahoma, where Tom was a youth pastor, and from that day they had begun praying about joining us.

One morning, as John was working on his computer, the hard drive crashed—right in the middle of laying out our magazine, *Frontlines*. Frustrated and not knowing what to do, we began thinking about who we could call for help. We are users of computers, but technically, rather challenged. After fretting for some time, John said, "I'll call Tom. He might know what I should do."

When Tom answered the phone and heard John's voice on the other end, Tom began to weep and then told John with excitement that he had just prayed that morning, "God, if this is really something that you want us to do—if you are calling us to join Heart of God Ministries— would you have John call me?" He and John had not communicated in a couple of months, and he could think of no reason that John would have for calling him. To this day, John blames Tom for his hard drive crashing!

CHAPTER 13

Gentle Whispers

But the Lord was not in the wind; and after the wind an earthquake, but the Lord was not in the earthquake; and after the earthquake a fire, but the Lord was not in the fire; and after the fire a still small voice.

2 Kings 19:11, 12

I was sitting in a coffee shop, preparing a lesson to teach in the evening, when a young man at a nearby table asked me what I was studying. He, too, had a pile of books on his table, and we began talking together about our lives. I was working on a lesson for a missions class and began to talk to him about missionaries. He had never heard of missionaries.

Knowing that he would probably not understand why missionaries take the gospel to other countries, I told him of the 100,000 children living on the streets around the train station in Mumbai, India. Some of them have run away from the countryside to the city to find a "better life." Some of them have been brought there by parents who, as they walked through the crowds, let go of their child's hand, leaving these kids to fend for themselves on the street.

I told him of the little girls who are scooped up by the sex industry and made to live in cages, servicing men around the clock, until they are used up by the age of twelve and die from tuberculosis or AIDS. I told him of the gangs that swallow up little boys and make them thieves and criminals. And then I told him of our missionaries who serve in India, ministering to the needs of these children.

He was amazed that anyone would go to another country and live there
for the purpose of caring for kids who are not their own. He said, "I
am a terrible person. I would never think of doing anything like that."
He asked me many questions that afternoon, and I was able to tell him
of the love and compassion of Jesus that compels Christians to act on
behalf of the poor and needy.

A week later, I visited that same coffee shop, hoping that I might
see this young man and have another conversation with him. As I
sat reading my book, he came through the front door with a large
Life Application Bible, still in the box, under his right arm, his face
beaming. I asked him, "What happened to you?"

Over that week the Holy Spirit had drawn him to Jesus. He had
experienced disappointments and difficult circumstances and found
himself in the pit of despair, when he heard a voice tell him, "Go to that
coffee shop. God is there." The owner of the coffee shop is a Christian
friend of mine, and this young man asked him if he knew of a church
he might be able to visit. My friend took him to church that Sunday,
where the young man gave his life to Jesus.

I was thrilled! He sat down and began to ask me questions. He was
planning to start reading the Bible, but it is such a big book. He wanted
to know if he should just start at the beginning. I suggested he read
the book of John. His next question was, "What is this voice I keep
hearing?"

"My sheep hear my voice, I know them, and they follow me."[1]

Provision

My grandpa was a pastor for forty years, and my grandma still
remembers the early days when there was often no salary given. They
had a young family with little children and sometimes the cupboards
went bare, as they had to rely upon God to provide through the
parishioners in their church. Sometimes it came in the form of food
items; sometimes someone would give them cash.

1. John 10:27.

My grandpa was headed out the door to spend the day visiting the homes of his church members. As he turned the handle on the front door, my grandma said to him, "I must have milk for this baby, and we cannot go another day. Surely God will provide. Do not come back until you have some food." He looked at her and knew that she was serious.

He visited many homes that day. Some were the homes of invalids, some the faithful members of his church. He checked on them, prayed for them, counseled them and invited those he hadn't seen for a while to come back to church. However, as evening drew near, no one had offered him any gift or "blessing" that he could take home. With a heavy heart, he turned in the direction of his house.

The closer he got to home, the louder my grandma's words rang in his ears. He could see the look on her face so clearly in his mind, and he knew there was no way he could show up empty-handed. He turned up the road to the church building and went inside to pray. Without even taking the time to turn on the lights, Grandpa hurried to the altar and knelt. He began laying out his complaint to God. "I have been serving you diligently. Why are you not taking care of my family? I cannot go home without food. My children are hungry. My wife is not happy. Please help me. What can I do?"

As he knelt there praying, a knock came at the front door of the church. Thinking it strange that someone would be knocking at this hour, he went to see who it was. There at the door stood a man who he did not recognize. The man said, "Oh, I wasn't sure that anyone was here."

He told my grandpa that he had been walking down the street and had clearly heard the voice of the Holy Spirit tell him to go to the church and knock on the door. Seeing no lights, he thought he must be mistaken. No one was there. He had continued on down the street, but the impression had come again, this time with greater strength. So he had turned around and made his way back to the church.

He thrust out his hand and said, "God told me to give you this." In his hand were two twenty-dollar bills. My grandpa took the money and just stood there, mouth open in awe. The man smiled and wished him a good evening, turned around and walked away. My grandpa walked through the door of their home that evening carrying bags of groceries and shouting, "Glory!"

If you are one of his sheep, you have heard God's voice. You may not have heard him in one of these more dramatic ways. Perhaps you did not recognize him, but most assuredly you have heard him. Jesus promised us:

> "I tell you the truth. It is to your advantage that I go away; for if I do not go away, the Helper will not come to you; but if I depart, I will send Him to you.... When He, the Spirit of truth, has come, He will guide you into all truth; for He will not speak on His own authority, but whatever He hears He will speak; and He will tell you things to come."[2]

Many times, we hear that still small voice of the Holy Spirit somewhere deep inside. It may be words, it may be just an impression. Paul reminds us,

> It is God who works in you to will and to act according to his good purpose.[3]

How can we know if the voice we are hearing really is the voice of the Holy Spirit and not just our own thoughts or, even worse, the voice of a demon?

1 John 4:1 tells us that we are not to "believe every spirit, but test the spirits, whether they are of God." What kind of test? How do we do it?

When your mother calls you on the phone, she does not have to begin the conversation by saying, "This is your mom." She can just begin talking to you. You know her voice because you spent eighteen or more years with her. You knew her voice before you were even born. Studies have shown that newborn babies turn their faces toward their mothers when they hear their voices. It is a voice that is familiar and comforting.

---

2. John 16:7, 13.
3. Philippians 2:13 (NIV).

How do we recognize God's voice? We have to become familiar with it.
Just like we do with our mother, we must spend time living life together
with him, fellowshipping with him, learning what his voice sounds
like. Our most basic way of doing this is taking quiet time to spend in
his Word, finding out the kinds of things he says, the topics he speaks
about and the tone of his voice, as found in his character.[4]

Approach

First, we can recognize God's voice by his approach. In this, we must
know him personally. We must experience the tender, compassionate,
loving character that is his nature. Even in discipline, God is gentle
and kind. The fruit of the Spirit is the character of the Holy Spirit's
voice. He will always exhibit in his dealings with you love, joy, peace,
patience, kindness, goodness, gentleness, faithfulness and self-control.

> But the wisdom that is from above is first pure, then peaceable,
> gentle, willing to yield, full of mercy and good fruits, without
> partiality and without hypocrisy.[5]

You can expect that he will call you his child, his beloved, his son, his
daughter; he will use your name, perhaps even a special name that he
chooses for you himself.

I once sat down to pen a letter to a young man in our Boot Camp
training. It was a letter from the Lord to him. The Holy Spirit prompted
me to do this, so I simply wrote what I felt that God wanted to say to
him. Instead of starting the letter with "Dear, Jeff..." I heard the Lord
call him, "My Boy." The letter went on to give him encouragement and
affirmation.

Later, Jeff came to me with tears in his eyes to explain that he, as a
young father with a new son, had been calling his own son, "my boy."
Only God could have known that greeting would have such a personal
nature. Expect your interactions with him to be the same—intimately
designed for you.

---

4. Peter Lord's book, *Hearing God* (Baker Books, 1988), has influenced much of the material in this chapter. In fact, I have used much of his outline, as it has been very helpful
to me over the years in testing and discerning the voice of God.
5. James 3:17.

There are a number of things to which God's voice will be relevant.
Jesus' emphasis was always on today. Remember, he told us not to
worry about tomorrow.[6] Usually, God does not give us the plan for
many days or months or years in the future. He may give us a calling to
last our whole life, but his guidance is for the decisions in front of us.
He tells us what his will is for us today, what the very next step is.

Resources

He will also speak to us in a way that's relevant to our resources.
If someone asks you for twenty dollars, but you don't have twenty
dollars, God is not asking you to give something that you do not have.
However, we must remember that God's view of our resources may be
very different from our own. He may see that we really do have more
money or time or energy than we think we do.

John and I returned from Taiwan for me to finish a degree in linguistics.
We came to Oklahoma on a scholarship at Southern Nazarene
University, so my tuition bills were paid for. My uncle let us live for
free in a little rental house, just off of campus, but we needed to pay for
the utilities, as well as our own food and living expenses.

John was working, without pay, on our college campus through an
organization called Student Frontier Missions Fellowship. It was the
remains of what was once called the Student Volunteer Movement. His
desire was to mobilize college students to consider the needs of those
on the planet that have never yet heard the good news of Jesus and to
ask the Holy Spirit whether they might be called to go as missionaries
to them. We held prayer meetings and missions events on the campus to
raise awareness.

John began looking for a part-time job to pay our bills. The economy
was so poor in Oklahoma at that time that finding a job at McDonald's
was not even easy. He applied for a number of jobs that would pay
the bills, but they seemed completely incongruous with what God had
called us here to do. None of these places offered him a job. He began
pulling weeds in the yards of the old women in our neighborhood for
five dollars an hour. It was discouraging and confusing.

---

6. Matthew 6:34.

Finally, one morning, as John and I were separately having our own quiet times with the Lord, we both felt that God was saying, "If you will just do what I tell you to do, I will provide all your needs." This seemed consistent with "Seek first the kingdom of God...and all these things shall be added to you."[7] So we decided to give all our energy to mobilizing college students, have no paying jobs, and wait and see if God would provide our needs.

The day after we made this decision a knock came at our door. There stood an old friend of ours who had just come to Oklahoma to finish her college degree. Sarah Jane felt that God was calling her to become a missionary. She had one year left of school and did not want to go into debt to pay her tuition bills, so she was asking if she could live with us.

Now, I have to tell you that our little house was truly little. The kitchen and living room made up the front half, and the bedroom with a tiny bathroom made up the back. We had no place to put her but the couch and, being a tall volleyball player, she was longer than it was!

John and I looked at one another, reading each other's thoughts. We knew that there was only one bag of dry beans and one bag of rice in the cupboard, and that she had no money to contribute for food. Our electric bill was due, and we didn't know how we were going to pay it. We told her we would pray about it and get back to her.

In prayer and discussion, both of us felt that God was telling us to let her come. I had heard the Holy Spirit simply say, "Yes." John felt an impression that this was what God wanted, and though it made no sense, there was a peace in our hearts that passed all understanding. We told her she could move in the next day.

In the morning, after Sarah Jane's first night on our couch, I got ready to go to class. I opened the door and stepped out on our front porch to find that the whole porch was covered with sacks of groceries! This began an adventure of watching God provide for us for the last eighteen years. I say it is an adventure because that is what it truly feels like. I often think, "Okay, God, how are you going to do it this time?" and then I sit back to watch the show!

---

7. Matthew 6:33.

During that same semester, we were invited to attend a party with
the International Students Club. When we arrived, the hosts quickly
ushered us into the kitchen and quietly asked, "Do you know how to
cook Chinese food?" Those who were to prepare the food had called
at the last minute saying they were unable to come, and now there was
a mountain of ingredients, but no one to cook the food. We happily
jumped in.

At the end of the party, there was a huge amount of leftovers—
ingredients that had not even been cooked—as the crowd was much
smaller than they had anticipated. They told us to take it all home with
us. We were thrilled, and it was much better than rice and beans. There
was chicken, shrimp, fresh vegetables. We decided to save it all for a
rainy day or a special occasion and put it in our freezer to keep.

Several days later, I returned from classes in the afternoon to find a
puddle of water on the kitchen floor. The refrigerator had died and, in
the summer heat, all our special meat had spoiled. We had to throw it
all away. God taught us that the things that he gives to us are for today.
When we need something tomorrow, he will provide it tomorrow. "Do
not store up for yourselves treasures on earth"—including chicken and
shrimp![8]

Comprehension

When John was a child in Taiwan, his mother was concerned about
him learning to speak English properly. She worked regularly with
him on developing his vocabulary. Every Sunday, before he could eat
his dinner, he had to fill out and pass the Word Power Challenge that
his mother had pulled from old copies of *Reader's Digest* that church
members had sent to them in care packages. Consequently, John often
has to "dumb down" his vocabulary when speaking to the rest of us
normal people, so that we can understand what he is saying.

God wants you to understand him. He will speak to you in vocabulary
that makes sense to you. Husbands and wives who have been together
for many years can communicate with one another with a look of the
eye, an expression of the face. Parents can do this with their children

---

8. Matthew 6:19 (NIV).

as well As we walk in fellowship with God, we too will become sensitive to his gentle prodding or the impressions of his Spirit giving us instruction.

A strong riptide separated a father and his autistic son, Christopher, and carried them out into the Atlantic Ocean. Christopher's malady seemed to be a blessing, as he had no fear of the water. In fact, water had often been a comfort to him, and as they bobbed up and down, Christopher seemed to even enjoy the swim.

Darkness fell, and the sound of the helicopters and boats grew faint as they gave up their search. Christopher's verbal communication skills were almost nonexistent, but his father knew his favorite Disney movie. Through the night, he called out to his son, "To infinity!" to which Christopher would respond, "And beyond!" It was twelve hours before they were finally rescued.[9]

It has been my experience that, over the years of your life, you will develop between you and God a language of symbols that are all your own. Ten years ago, I was part of a women's prayer group that was very significant to me. We enjoyed our times of prayer together and often heard from God with one another.

On one occasion, the leader of the group presented a short object lesson to us about the ladybug. Ladybugs have a unique purpose in the insect world. They eat the aphids that live on plants. Aphids do have the potential to kill a plant, but often they merely suck the life out of it, leaving it withered and unfruitful. She likened the aphids to the little sins in our lives that keep us from fulfilling God's desires for us and exhorted us to allow the Holy Spirit, like a ladybug to eat those aphids, so that we might bear large fruit from the tree of our life.

Okay, I know it's really girly, but go with me on this. The ladybug has come to represent a very special symbol of fruitfulness for me, and each time I see one, the meaning of that lesson comes back to my mind.

The night that my little sister's baby, Ephraim, died, we all were thinking of fruit. Ephraim's name means "doubly fruitful," and God

---

9. You can find the original version of this news story, "To Infinity and Beyond: A Sparkling Survival Story" by Mallory Simon (September 11, 2008) at www.cnn.com.

had encouraged us through his birth. As he lay on my parents' bed, receiving CPR from the paramedics, some of the ladies on our staff, noticed that above the bed, on the ceiling, were a bunch of ladybugs. They caught their eye because it was winter. Ladybugs usually hibernate in winter.

As Ephraim lay there, the Holy Spirit brought to mind Jesus' words in John 12, "Unless a grain of wheat falls into the ground and dies, it remains alone; but if it dies, it produces much grain."[10] We could not imagine how the death of this little baby could possibly bear any fruit in the Kingdom of God! All we could see was death, grief, sorrow, pain.

Later that night, John and I returned to our home to try and get some rest. When we walked through our front door, ladybugs fell from the ceiling and landed on us! My other sister, Julie, and her family who live in Dallas, Texas, came the next day to be with the family, and we gave them one of the dormitory rooms to stay in. The walls in that room were covered with ladybugs!

One of the staff ladies ran all over campus looking in all the rooms. The only rooms that had ladybug colonies were the places where my family was staying. The Holy Spirit prompted her to write a long letter to Joy and Eric. It was about the meaning of Ephraim's name, his death, and the fruit that God was promising would come from this little one's life—even though they would probably never comprehend it.

The HGM staff decided to plant an apple tree in the center of our campus in remembrance of baby Ephraim. An apple tree! This was a symbol that God had many years before used to encourage my heart that from our ministry much fruit of people from many tribes, tongues and languages would be brought into the kingdom! Double fruit!

The next spring, God called us to begin an annual conference at our Oakhill base. We call it Nomads. Hundreds of people bring their tents and camp out under the stars. We meet together for worship under the beautiful trees and listen to the challenge of the needs of the unreached.

---

10. John 12:24.

As we were preparing to begin that first Nomads conference, I was especially nervous. I had been practicing to sing and play with the worship band, but earlier in the week, our practice had not gone so well, and I was embarrassed and worried that I might wreck the whole worship experience with my mistakes. People were already gathering in the outdoor sanctuary and my anxiety mounted.

I grabbed a few of the ladies on staff and asked them to pray for me. First, they gently rebuked me for my pride and reminded me that leading worship is not about me, but that it is about God—to which I nodded knowingly. Then they prayed for me. They prayed everything you might imagine they would pray, but nothing was helping. I felt just the same. My stomach was in knots. When they finished, I opened my eyes to sort of begrudgingly thank them, and there on my shirt was a ladybug!

Instantly, my heart was at peace. I knew that God was with me. I began to walk across the sanctuary, heading for the stage, and came face to face with Ephraim's tree. That weekend 150 young people pledged their lives to take the good news of Jesus to those peoples who have never heard! Big fruit! Double fruit!

God's Rules

God will speak to you within his already self-established ways. This is, again, the reason that we need to know what Scripture says. What are the principles that he has already laid out for us? The Ten Commandments tell us not to steal. So God will not ask you to rob from the rich, in order to give to the poor. That would violate a principle that he has already given to us to follow.

When we pray for guidance regarding something we already know about God's will, we open ourselves up to deception. I have known people who walked headlong into sin, all the while thinking that God was leading them there. For example, you find a wallet lying on the floor at the grocery store. It contains five hundred dollars! You don't need to ask God, "Should I return this money? Or is it your will that I keep it."

One woman I knew believed with her whole heart that God was leading her to divorce her husband and marry another man. She felt that she no longer loved her husband, and this new man was meeting her emotional needs. When she had asked God about it, she believed he had told her the new man was his blessing to her. The voice that she was hearing could not have been God's voice because his Word already tells us that he hates divorce and that we are not to commit adultery.[11]

Proverbs is replete with principles that are merely natural consequences of action or inaction.

> A man who has friends must himself be friendly.

> A soft answer turns away wrath.

> Anxiety in the heart of man causes depression, but a good word makes it glad.

> He who blesses his friend with a loud voice, rising early in the morning, it will be counted a curse to him.[12]

What are the laws of nature that he has already put into place? If you step off the top of a tall building, you will fall to the ground. Gravity is a law that God has already put into place. When Satan tempted Jesus to throw himself down from the pinnacle of the temple, this was not God's will. Yes, God could do it; he could prevent Jesus from falling, but that would be a miracle. It would be an act that overrides or counteracts the God-set laws of nature. Satan's temptation was a challenge against an already established principle.

This topic might be a bit controversial, but I'm going to risk stepping on a few toes here. There are Christians who believe that they should not use any form of birth control, but instead rely on the conviction that God opens and closes the womb. They just "trust God" to give them however many children he wants them to have.

11. Malachi 2:16; Exodus 20:14; Matthew 5:27–32.
12. Proverbs 18:24; 15:1; 12:25; 27:14.

I have heard a number of women say, "God will not give me more than I can handle," as though that is a Scripture verse. The only thing that resembles this idea in Scripture is,

> No temptation has overtaken you except such as is common to man; but God is faithful, who will not allow you to be tempted beyond what you are able, but with the temptation will also make the way of escape, that you may be able to bear it.[13]

It is in the context of temptation, not children! I have seen a number of women suffer nervous breakdowns due to the load they are under. Sometimes, God allows us to experience much more than we are able to handle, in order to get us to come and abide in him.

God has already established a law of nature regarding having babies. If everything is working normally, women monthly release at least one egg. If sperm is introduced to that egg, she *will* get pregnant. It is a principle that God has put into place.

I must say here that Scripture says that children are a blessing from the Lord, and I have five blessings![14] However, we must never take verses out of the context of the whole of Scripture and the whole of the principles that God has already ordained. When God "closed" a womb in Scripture, it was an unusual circumstance. This woman then was considered barren.[15] When he opened a womb, it was always a miracle—a healing of a barren woman.[16]

God does not mean for isolated incidents in Scripture to define formulas for us. We all gravitate to formulas. It seems much simpler to live by laws that say, "Do it this way every time, and God will respond this way every time." For example, some believe that God wants to heal sickness every time—if a person is not healed, it is because they do not have enough faith. Jesus didn't even heal every sick person that he encountered![17] He only did what he saw the Father doing.

---

13. 1 Corinthians 10:13.
14. Psalm 127:3.
15. 1 Samuel 1:5.
16. Genesis 19:31; 30:32.
17. John 5:1–9.

God has designed us for relationship with him! He wants to walk with us. If we hear his voice telling us that he is going to heal, how much easier is it to have faith then! Faith comes by hearing him.[18] If he tells us to have another baby, or to stop having babies, this too is living by the Spirit, in relationship with him. He knows what is best for the life that he has planned for us. Walk in fellowship with the living God!

Topics

Peter Lord identifies a list of topics about which God will speak. The first is *himself*. He wants us to know him. He wants us to know how he acts and how he thinks. He wants us to know the things he cares about, the things that are a priority to him. He will speak to you about his character in balance and entirety.

If you are always hearing the wrath and judgment of God, and rarely the mercy of God, then the voice you hear may very well be your own thoughts. Scripture tells us that his mercy always triumphs over judgment.[19] But if you always hear the tender love of God without his discipline or correction in your life, you are missing some of what he is saying as well.

God will speak *guidance* that we are seeking from him. We need to know what decision he wants us to make or what action he wants us to take. Again, God will speak within the principles that he has already outlined in Scripture. However, many specifics are not found in the Bible—for example, whether or not to buy a new car or to marry a particular person. It is important that we have spent a great deal of time learning what the still, small voice of the Holy Spirit sounds like. Remember to look for the fruit of the Spirit.

Seeking counsel from godly advisors will also protect us from mistaking our own thoughts and desires for God's voice.[20] This can be a tricky task, as our hearts can easily deceive us. Often when seeking counsel, we only go to those who we know will give a desirable answer. Or when we ask, we only reveal part of the truth, in order to more likely receive a favorable direction. We must be very careful to

---

18. Romans 10:17.
19. James 2:13.
20. Proverbs 11:14.

be honest with ourselves, as well as with those we are seeking counsel from.

A principle that we must know when seeking guidance from God about his will for our lives is that God is often more interested in developing our character than he is in changing our circumstances. Many times, we hope that God will allow us to leave difficult or challenging situations or relationships, when his plan is for those trials to develop our character as we respond to his leading inside the circumstance.

God will speak to us about our *sin*. This issue of conviction can be a tricky subject. How are we to know when we are being convicted by the Holy Spirit, which we desire to receive, and when we are being condemned by the devil, which we want to resist?[21] Peter Lord has provided a little chart that I have found to be incredibly helpful.[22]

Conviction by the Holy Spirit	Condemnation by the Enemy
1. definite and specific The Lord will tell you what you have done wrong.	**1. indefinite and vague** You feel guilty, but you cannot identify any specific sin.
2. recognizable It will be something unconfessed and unforgiven, and you will recognize it. Usually it will be something from your immediate past.	**2. imaginary** You have a hard time putting your finger on any sin, unless it is something in the past that has already been forgiven. (Satan loves to do this one to us!)
3. definite solution The Holy Spirit will tell you how to take care of the sin. When you obey, you immediately get relief from the soul-pain of regret.	**3. usually no solution** If any solution is offered, it is irrational and unscriptural. Even if you try to fix it, the soul-pain only intensifies. You can get no relief from the guilt.

---

21. Romans 8:1.
22. Lord, Peter. *Hearing God* (Baker Books, 1988) p. 130.

About Us

God wants very much to speak to us about ourselves. Because we all have experienced rejection, we all are wounded and suffer from poor self-images. We do not see ourselves the way that God sees us. We do not value ourselves the way that he does. He wants to tell us what he thinks about us.

> Johnny Lingo is known throughout the islands for his skills, intelligence, and savvy. If you hire him as a guide, he will show you the best fishing spots and the best places to get pearls. Johnny is also one of the sharpest traders in the islands. He can get you the best possible deals. The people of Kiniwata all speak highly of Johnny Lingo. Yet, when they speak of him, they always smile just a little mockingly.

> A couple days after my arrival to Kiniwata, I went to the manager of the guesthouse to see who he thought would be a good fishing guide. "Johnny Lingo," said the manager. "He's the best around. When you go shopping, let him do the bargaining. Johnny knows how to make a deal."

> "Johnny Lingo!" hooted a nearby boy. The boy rocked with laughter as he said, "Yea, Johnny can make a deal alright!"

> "What's going on?" I demanded. "Everybody tells me to get in touch with Johnny Lingo and then they start laughing. Please, let me in on the joke."

> "Oh, the people like to laugh," the manager said, shrugging. "Johnny's the brightest and strongest young man in the islands. He's also the richest for his age."

> "But..." I protested. "...if he's all you say he is, why does everyone laugh at him behind his back?"

> "Well, there is one thing. Five months ago, at fall festival, Johnny came to Kiniwata and found himself a wife. He gave her father eight cows!"

I knew enough about island customs to be impressed. A dowry of two or three cows would net a fair wife and four or five cows would net a very nice wife.

"Wow!" I said. "Eight cows! She must have beauty that takes your breath away."

"She's not ugly…" he conceded with a little smile, "…but calling her 'plain' would definitely be a compliment. Sam Karoo, her father, was afraid he wouldn't be able to marry her off. Instead of being stuck with her, he got eight cows for her. Isn't that extraordinary? This price has never been paid before."

"Yet, you called Johnny's wife 'plain'?"

"I said it would be a compliment to call her plain. She was skinny and she walked with her shoulders hunched and her head ducked. She was scared of her own shadow."

"Well," I said, "I guess there's just no accounting for love."

"True enough," agreed the man. "That's why the villagers grin when they talk about Johnny. They get special satisfaction from the fact that the sharpest trader in the islands was bested by dull old Sam Karoo."

"But how?"

"No one knows and everyone wonders. All of the cousins urged Sam to ask for three cows and hold out for two until he was sure Johnny would pay only one. To their surprise, Johnny came to Sam Karoo and said, 'Father of Sarita, I offer eight cows for your daughter.'"

"Eight cows," I murmured. "I'd like to meet this Johnny Lingo."

I wanted fish and pearls, so the next afternoon I went to the island of Nurabandi. As I asked directions to Johnny's house,

I noticed Johnny's neighbors were also amused at the mention of his name. When I met the slim, serious young man I could see immediately why everyone respected his skills. However, this only reinforced my confusion over him.

As we sat in his house, he asked me, "You come here from Kiniwata?"

"Yes."

"They speak of me on that island?"

"Yes. They say you can provide me anything I need. They say you're intelligent, resourceful, and the sharpest trader in the islands."

He smiled gently. "My wife is from Kiniwata."

"Yes, I know."

"They speak of her?"

"A little."

"What do they say?"

"Why, just...." The question caught me off balance. "They told me you were married at festival time."

"Nothing more?" The curve of his eyebrows told me he knew there had to be more.

"They also say the marriage settlement was eight cows." I paused. "They wonder why."

"They ask that?" His eyes lighted with pleasure. "Everyone in Kiniwata knows about the eight cows?"

I nodded.

"And in Nurabandi, everyone knows it too." His chest expanded with satisfaction. "Always and forever, when they speak of marriage settlements, it will be remembered that Johnny Lingo paid eight cows for Sarita."

So that's the answer, I thought: Vanity.

Just then Sarita entered the room to place flowers on the table. She stood still for a moment to smile at her husband and then left. She was the most beautiful woman I have ever seen. The lift of her shoulders, the tilt of her chin, and the sparkle in her eyes all spelled self-confidence and pride. Not an arrogant and haughty pride, but a confident inner beauty that radiated in her every movement.

I turned back to Johnny and found him looking at me.

"You admire her?" he murmured.

"She... she's gorgeous." I said. "Obviously, this is not the one everyone is talking about. She can't be the Sarita you married on Kiniwata."

"There's only one Sarita. Perhaps, she doesn't look the way you expected."

"She doesn't. I heard she was homely. They all make fun of you because you let yourself be cheated by Sam Karoo."

"You think eight cows was too many?" A smile slid over his lips.

"No, but how can she be so different from the way they described her?"

Johnny said, "Think about how it must make a girl feel to know her husband paid a very low dowry for her? It must be insulting to her to know he places such little value on her. Think about how she must feel when the other women boast about the high prices their husbands paid for them. It must be embarrassing for her. I would not let this happen to my Sarita."

"So, you paid eight cows just to make your wife happy?"

"Well, of course I wanted Sarita to be happy, but there's more to it than that. You say she is different from what you expected. This is true. Many things can change a woman. There are things that happen on the inside and things that happen on the outside. However, the thing that matters most is how she views herself. In Kiniwata, Sarita believed she was worth nothing. As a result, that's the value she projected. Now, she knows she is worth more than any other woman in the islands. It shows, doesn't it?"

"Then you wanted…"

"I wanted to marry Sarita. She is the only woman I love."

"But…" I was close to understanding.

"But," he finished softly, "I wanted an eight-cow wife."[23]

Judgment

Just as we have not seen our own value, we tend to devalue others around us. In a great attempt to make ourselves feel better, we often criticize and judge others, lowering their value in our own minds, so that we can feel superior to them.

The enemy puts degrading thoughts into our minds about other people. We see certain behavior and because of that behavior, we assign a character judgment to it. For example, you know that at your house, there is a rule that everyone who uses dishes must wash them. You see that one of your kids has left his dishes in the sink for you to wash. Immediately, your mind begins to meditate on how lazy he is or perhaps how rebellious he is toward your authority. These may not be

---

23. Bronson, Michael. "Johnny Lingo's Eight-Cow Wife." As reprinted at BibleHelp.org. Based on a Reader's Digest article (February 1988).

accurate judgments at all. Perhaps the phone rang and he fully intends to return and finish his chore.

Perhaps your friend is late. You have been waiting for fifteen minutes, and you begin to think about another time he made you wait. You start meditating on how inconsiderate and selfish your friend is when, in reality, he may have had some mitigating circumstance that was completely out of his control. When we make these kinds of character judgments, we are cooperating with the "accuser of the brethren"—the devil himself.[24]

God will speak to us about how to relate to *other people*. He will show you the value he sees in them. He will speak mercy and forgiveness for them. He will show you good things in them—the things that are of him. He will show you your role in helping them. He will show you how you can work together with them. He will even gently remind you of your own failings in the past, in order to promote humility within your own heart.

Mistakes!

A woman stood at the kitchen counter preparing dinner, while her husband sat at the table reading the newspaper. Filling him in on the latest gossip, she said, "Carla got a new horse." He mumbled in response to her, "Who got a divorce?"

Many in the church are uncomfortable with this idea of hearing from God apart from Scripture. It is dangerous. Terrible mistakes can be made. Misinterpretations can be embraced. Heresies can be formed. Damage can be done.

One safeguard that we must have in place is an awareness that we cannot help but hear God through the paradigm—or grid—of our own understanding. We have our ideas about God, how he works, what he does and doesn't do, and so on. These form our own personal theology. If God decides to say or do something outside the box of our understanding, sometimes we miss his voice entirely.

---

24. Revelation 12:10.

Years ago, I got into a heated discussion with a friend of mine who asked his wife to carry a handgun in her purse when she drove to ladies' prayer meeting. I asked him how he would feel if his wife shot someone, even in self-defense. He explained to me that if someone broke into his home in the middle of the night, he felt that it was entirely within his rights to shoot the person and that the law of the state would back him up in this.

I was appalled and questioned him about his reasoning. Jesus clearly taught that we are to turn the other cheek. I could not imagine Jesus carrying a handgun on his way to a prayer meeting. It was a frustrating conversation that ended with us agreeing to disagree on the matter.

Several days later, this man testified in church that he had grown up in Texas in a home where his father believed strongly in the right to bear arms. He had been raised to not only value his guns, but to value his "government-given right" to use them to protect himself, his family and his stuff. He testified that God had used our conversation to convict him that his ways of thinking were not godly, and he wanted to publicly declare that he was now entrusting his wife to God's protection, rather than the protection of a gun.

In Acts 21, Paul was on his way to Jerusalem. He stopped to stay at the home of Phillip the Evangelist. While there, a prophet named Agabus delivered a "word from God" to Paul. He bound Paul's hands and feet and declared to him that if he went to Jerusalem, this is what would happen to him. Basically, he told him that going to Jerusalem would mean that he would be imprisoned.

Immediately, everyone in the room began to plead with Paul not to go, and "Paul answered them by saying, 'What do you mean by weeping and breaking my heart? For I am ready not only to be bound, but also to die at Jerusalem for the name of the Lord Jesus.'"[25] The Holy Spirit had clearly directed Paul to go to Jerusalem. Agabus also was hearing right. However, the interpretation that the people made was completely wrong. Their judgment was clouded by their love for Paul and their desire to protect him.

---

25. Acts 21:13.

We must be especially careful when trying to hear God regarding strong desires of our heart. Bob Mumford, author of *Take Another Look at Guidance*, tells of a young man who desperately wanted to marry a girl named Grace. In prayer one day, he asked that God would show him if she was the right girl for him. Opening his Bible, he read Philippians 1:2, "Grace and peace from God our Father and the Lord Jesus Christ." Such a weak confirmation for such an important, life-impacting decision would not hold one through the seasons when marriage is difficult.[26]

All of us have a grid through which we see life. We cannot help it. Our families, our schooling, our environment, our personalities—they all come together to form the paradigms that govern our thinking. We have theological and political leanings. We have strong opinions, values and desires. Our safeguard against missing God is to always remain humble. As we submit to him and to his gentle teaching, he will transform our minds, making his thoughts our own. If we will be careful to learn the voice of the Holy Spirit through experience with him, compare the things we think we are hearing to the Word of God, examine the fruit that it brings in our spirits and walk together in submission to other believers, we can safely navigate the adventure of walking as Jesus walked, doing only what we see the Father doing.

In church one day, the pastor invited all the pregnant women to come forward and receive prayer. There were several expecting mothers, and he wanted to have a special time of blessing prayer for them. My friend was one of the women who went forward, and I joined the crowd of friends and husbands who gathered around to lay hands on the women. As we prayed, I heard the Holy Spirit speak one word, "Twins."

When the prayer time was over, I excitedly told my friend what I had heard. Tears came to her eyes, as she then related some passages of Scripture that had stood out to her in the last couple of months. They all had something to do with twins. Over those last months of her pregnancy, her belly and our friendship grew, as we anticipated the arrival of her two babies.

---

26. Mumford, Bob. *Take Another Look at Guidance* (Logos International, 1971) p. 73.

When the day of her delivery came, I was there with her in labor, praying for her and reminding her to breathe. She labored long and hard, and when the baby arrived, it was the only one—a large boy. I was devastated. I was sure that God had spoken "twins" to me. Where had I gone wrong?

I spiraled into a spiritual freefall. If I had made a mistake on this, what about other things I thought that God had said? If God did not speak this to me, then perhaps the things I thought I had been hearing all along were not him either. All those healing words he had spoken to my emotions—maybe I had just been deluding myself. I began to question whether God really exists at all.

I stopped having quiet times. I quit reading my Bible. How could I? It was marked in the margins with promises that I thought God had given to me. Verses I once had considered precious to me were now up for question. I walked in darkness and confusion for several months.

I knew I could not continue this way, and I longed for the experiences of sweet fellowship I had experienced with Jesus before. I finally got alone and began to cry out to him, "Where are you? Where did I go wrong? Will you please show me what is true and what is not?"

As I waited in defeated silence, revelation began to flood my soul. It was not as though God was speaking words and sentences to me, but more like a sudden awareness, an understanding, a knowing of what he had meant.

John's and my ministry is about raising up missionaries to go to the unreached. We had been traveling and speaking, mobilizing churches and college students to consider God's call, often to see only blank looks in many of their eyes. Many times it felt like banging our heads against a brick wall.

My friend and her husband also had a ministry of their own. They are lovers of the great revivals that God has brought throughout church history. They also were traveling and speaking in churches and to college students, but calling upon them to pray and seek God for an outpouring of his Spirit that would return the church to a passionate pursuit of Jesus.

During the months of my friend's pregnancy, friendship, admiration and respect for one another's ministries had been growing between us. God was uniting us in a two-fold message for the church. Christians will never respond to the call of missions until they return to connection with God in repentance and fellowship—close enough to hear the cry of the unreached in his heart.

Revival and missions go hand in hand. Every great move of God in history has resulted in a wave of missionaries taking the gospel to the ends of the earth. God had not been speaking to me of physical twins, but of embracing the ministry of the woman I had been praying for— that she was my twin, her ministry was the other half of my own!

I learned a valuable lesson from this emotionally disastrous mistake. Often God speaks to us in imagery or symbols. Jesus loved to tell the secrets of the kingdom in a parable. At times, even the disciples did not understand what he was meaning and had to ask.

When you have heard from God, there are three questions you need to ask him:

1. **What are you saying?**
    He will often repeat his word to you. Sometimes he will make it more clear or expound upon what he first said.

2. **What do you mean?**
    Just like the disciples, ask him what he means. If I had stopped to ask this question, I may have saved myself months of grief.

3. **What do you want me to do with this?**
    Do not presume that you are to immediately act or tell others what you have heard. Sometimes, God only wants a friend to share the secrets of his heart. Other times, he will clearly say, "Go and...."

Foolproof

Hearing from God cannot be quantified with a formula. There are no guarantees against mistakes or misinterpretations. This is just the reality of walking as humans filled by the Holy Spirit. In reality, it can be a scary prospect. Yet, if we are going to live in relationship with him, walking as Jesus walked, we must take the risk.[27]

James 1:5 says,

> If any of you lacks wisdom, let him ask of God, who gives to all liberally and without reproach, and it will be given to him.

It really is that simple. All we need to do is ask him, and he will show us his will. I love this verse because it also indicates that God is not frustrated with us when we ask him for guidance. He really wants to show us his will.

Will called our office one morning. He had picked up some HGM literature at a conference and had been praying about coming to Boot Camp. He felt that God had given him very clear direction that he was to come for training. However, as the time was drawing closer, now he wasn't sure. He thought that God had spoken, but maybe he had just come to this conclusion on his own. Maybe what he thought was the Holy Spirit's guidance had really just been rationalizations. How could he know for sure?

I waited for a moment, with the phone in my hand, seeking an answer from the Holy Spirit. What counsel could I give this young man? Suddenly the rest of this passage from James came to mind:

> But let him ask in faith, with no doubting, for he who doubts is like a wave of the sea driven and tossed by the wind. For let not that man suppose that he will receive anything from the Lord; he is a double-minded man, unstable in all his ways.[28]

This was exactly what Will was describing. Doubt was tossing him to and fro. Confusion had him swirling back and forth in his mind. He had heard from God, and now he had to simply believe and obey.

When we have sought the Lord for his direction, using every means we know for safety and confirmation, ultimately we must trust that God

---

27. 1 John 2:6.
28. James 1:6–8.

has given his wisdom just as he promises. We must step out in faith and do what he is telling us to do.

God's invitation for you to work with Him always leads you to a crisis of belief that requires faith and action.

Henry Blackaby

CHAPTER 14
Incoming Meteors

If I could leave behind only one piece of wisdom, it would be to echo the words of Jesus' mother, "Whatever he says to you, do it."

In those seven simple words is the secret of a life of joy, adventure and intimate friendship with God.

Belinda Burston

There are ways that God speaks that might be put into the category of the more dramatic. Again, we must remember that all of these means by which God communicates with us must be measured by the plumb line of Scripture. God's spoken Word will not contradict what he has already told us is his will.

The Gifts of the Spirit

God is the same yesterday, today and forever. His power, presence and gifts are still available just as Scripture tells us. Prophecy, words of knowledge and wisdom, and discerning of spirits are used all throughout Scripture, and God is still using them today.[1]

When Jesus met and spoke with the woman at the well, he knew information about her that there was no human way for him to have known. He told her, "You have had five husbands, and the one whom you now have is not your husband."[2] I used to think that Jesus was

---

1. I will not go into great detail about the way the gifts of the Holy Spirit work, as there are many other good books that can help you if you are interested in learning more. I would suggest you start with Jack Deere's books *Surprised by the Voice of God* (Zondervan, 1996) and *Surprised by the Power of the Spirit* (Zondervan, 1993).
2. John 4:18.

"calling out her sin." I imagined him with the facial expression and attitude of the bony-fingered prophet.

More recently, as God has been showing me more of his tenderness and love for people, I have seen this scene very differently. I see compassion in Jesus' eyes. He knew the deepest wounds of this woman's heart. He knew her longing to be loved, and the many ways she had tried to find it. When he spoke these words to her, she was not condemned, but she was drawn into the kindness of his eyes and the gentleness of his voice.

Remember that Jesus only said what he heard the Father saying. Though he was God, he set aside his powers and rights to live as a man, functioning by the power of the Holy Spirit—just like you and I can do.[3] The information that Jesus knew about this woman could be called a word of knowledge. Have you ever felt you knew something about someone? Perhaps God was speaking to you.

Growing up, I was not taught about these gifts of the Holy Spirit. I did not have a positive view of them. In fact, pastors and leaders around me openly mocked some of them. However, as an adult, I became introduced to some of these gifts and began to see the value of God's love and ministry to people through them.

I talked about some of my new awareness with my dad. As I shared some experiences with him, his eyes filled with tears. He said, "I may have been hearing God all those years." As a pastor, he would call people to come to the altar to pray. During those altar times, thoughts would often come to his mind about the people kneeling there. He would think that perhaps a couple had argued on their way to church, perhaps this man had a drinking problem. He thought that he was only being critical of his people, accusing and judging them in his mind. Now, he wondered if God had been showing him ways that he could have ministered to them. How many lost opportunities have there been because we have not been sensitive to the Holy Spirit's leading?

In a morning worship service, I was on the platform at my position on the keyboard when I looked out among the congregation. My eyes fell

---

3. Philippians 2:6–7.

upon a woman near the front. I did not know her well, but I heard the Holy Spirit give me something to say to her. I left my post and entered the pew next to her. I leaned forward and quietly whispered in her ear, "I believe the Lord is wanting me to tell you that Jesus is your husband, and he loves you."

In my heart, I thought this was a precious message to receive. God had so blessed me with this understanding. Immediately, the woman gathered up her purse and Bible, glared at me and stormed out the back of the sanctuary. I was bewildered.

Life went on with its busyness, and I did not think too much about what had happened after that Sunday. It was a large church, and I did not really notice when this woman and her family left our church. I was not privy to the conversations that were had with the pastor or any knowledge of their circumstances.

Several years passed. We had moved and no longer attended that church. One day, in passing, a visitor to our campus stopped me and told me that she had a message to pass on to me. It was from the woman I had spoken those words to so many years before.

Though I had not known it, this woman had been having an affair. When I spoke to her about Jesus being her husband, she thought that God had revealed her sin to me. She was ashamed and angry. When her family left the church, it was because her marriage was falling apart. She had left her husband for this other man, but now her testimony was that God had never let her forget what I had spoken to her that day. It was his kindness that drew her to repentance. She now was back with her husband. Her family was restored, and she just wanted me to know that I had been right in what I had heard—Jesus is her husband.

Sounded Like Thunder
Does God still speak out loud the way he did in Jesus' day? Haven't you ever wished that he would speak as loud and clearly as he did to Saul on the road to Damascus?

My brother-in-law Cory was going through of a difficult time in his life, questioning everything that he had been raised to believe about

Jesus. He wanted God to be real in his life. In desperation, he took a walk by himself out along a bike path. He began calling out to God, "If you are there, will you please speak to me?" What happened next sealed Cory in his faith for the rest of his life. He very distinctly heard God say to his soul, "Cory, I love you."

Wouldn't it be the greatest experience of your life to hear what Jesus did: "This is My beloved Son"?[4] If Jesus needed to hear God say it to him, how much more do we need to hear our Father's love and admiration, whether it is with our physical ears or the ears of our soul? He still speaks:

> "I have loved you with an everlasting love; I have drawn you with lovingkindness."[5]

Visions and Dreams

"Have you ever had an abortion?" a Boot Camp student asked me. I immediately responded that I haven't. He went on to tell me that perhaps he was mistaken, but he felt that God had given him something to say to me. I asked him to share it with me, and maybe it would make sense to me when I heard it.

He had been praying for me that morning and had seen a picture of Jesus holding a little girl. She had blonde, curly hair and was wearing a pretty little dress. Jesus had told him to tell me, "You are forgiven. Your baby is with me, and I am taking care of her."

When I left the hospital after attempting suicide, the last thing the doctor told me was, "We don't know if you were pregnant. There were too many drugs in your bloodstream to get an accurate test. However, if you were, you killed the baby."

All these years, I had lived with guilt over the possibility that I had killed a baby. Though I had never considered it "abortion," it really was. I had even hoped the baby would die. Now God, through this willing and open vessel, was giving to me his forgiveness, comfort and

---

4. Matthew 3:17.
5. Jeremiah 31:3.

rest. John and I both just wept and wept, as the knowledge of God's intimate care and forgiveness for us brought healing to an old, but still sensitive, wound.

> "And it shall come to pass afterward That I will pour out My Spirit on all flesh; Your sons and your daughters shall prophesy, Your old men shall dream dreams, Your young men shall see visions. And also on My menservants and on My maidservants I will pour out My Spirit in those days."[6]

Peter quoted these verses on the day of Pentecost, when the Holy Spirit came in power.

Do you know that God speaks to you even while you are sleeping? I love this verse:

> "For God may speak in one way, or in another, yet man does not perceive it. In a dream, in a vision of the night, when deep sleep falls upon men, while slumbering on their beds, then He opens the ears of men, and seals their instruction."[7]

Our first class of missionary trainees came into Boot Camp knowing that God had called them to go to the unreached, but they did not know where. They did not have a specific people group in mind, so they were seeking God's direction all throughout their training.

They first determined that they felt God was calling them to serve together as a team. There were two families and one single young man. Together they began to ask God to show them the people to whom they were called.

One of the men on the team had a dream in which he was standing on a rock, preaching to a crowd of people. In the dream he could clearly see their faces, their skin color, the several types of clothing they wore, particular headdresses, and so on. The team together began combing through past issues of *National Geographic* to see if they could find people who looked like those in his dream.[8]

---

6. Joel 2:28, 29.
7. Job 33:14–16.
8. This was before the days of the internet!

One of the women on the team had a dream in which she saw very clearly the terrain of the area to which they were called. It was mountainous—very tall mountains—with particularly distinctive valleys of grasslands. This became another piece of their puzzle.

The very first day of class, the young single man had come to John and asked him, "Where is the most unreached place in the world?" John had spoken to him about North India, because there were more people groups without the gospel there than any other single geographical area. He responded, "I want to go there!" The team began to wonder if maybe the desire of his heart had come from God himself.

Over a weekend, the women on the team attended a women's retreat held in Dallas, Texas. They did not know any of the other people at the retreat, but had just gone to receive teaching and ministry. During one of the main sessions, a man came down the aisle and tapped one of our team members' shoulders. She was surprised to see a man at a women's event, but quickly rose and followed him out the back door of the meeting room.

He began by asking her if she was called to be a missionary. She responded, "Yes," and that, in fact, she was in training to go to the mission field. He said, "I believe I have a message from God for you. It is only one word. Are you going to Africa?" She told him that she didn't think so, that it seemed that God might be leading them to northern India. He paused for a moment, and then said, "Well, I thought it sounded like an African word. The word is 'Menali.' Does that mean anything to you?" She said, "No, I'm sorry. I have never heard that word before." The man really had thought it was from the Lord and suggested that she write it down just in case it was to become clearer in the future. She thanked him politely, but went back to the retreat a bit confused by this encounter.

Upon graduation from Boot Camp, the team decided that the men would all take a trip together to North India to explore and see if God would confirm for them that they were to all move there and begin planting God's kingdom in that place. They had five cities that they were to visit. When they reached the city of Shimla, in the northern state of Himachal Pradesh, they discovered that it looked very much like the dreams they'd had. The people were the same, and the city was high in the mountains. In fact, this was a location that many wealthy Indians often visited for tourism. And there was a ski resort near there that was called, "Menali"! They returned home with the news that this was where they would be moving!

Sometimes it feels as though being led by the Spirit is like following breadcrumbs, much like Hansel and Gretel attempted to do in their fairy tale—an impossible trail of tiny clues. God, however, is not playing games with us. He truly does want us to know and do his will.

God gives us clues, hints, dreams and confirmations. Rarely do we get everything via one method or at one time. I believe he does it this way because it keeps us tightly connected to him. Would you appreciate it if God just clearly laid out the plan of your life for the next twenty years? Sometimes I think I would too! Except that I know my own heart—that I would take the plan and run off, leaving him in the dust. He does not want to just give us the plan. He wants to walk with us, as we discover his plan and accomplish his will together *with him*. He is Emmanuel—God with us. He made us for relationship with him, and it's quite an adventure!

Angels

We were ministering in Taiwan among the formerly headhunting tribe of Paiwanese, where John's parents had been missionaries for many years. God had been moving in miraculous ways, and we were there merely to see this revival and to offer any help that we could.

The temperatures in southern Taiwan were above 100 degrees with nearly 100 percent humidity, and I was 5 months pregnant with our second baby. We had been traveling for a couple of weeks, and I was exhausted. We awoke one morning to a day fully scheduled with activity. Noticing that I was physically worn out, John suggested that I stay and rest in bed for a few hours while he went out. Before he left, he prayed for me—that I would receive good rest, and that God would send ministering angels, as he did for Jesus in the wilderness, to comfort and refresh my body.

I slept soundly for several hours. When I awoke, I thought it was because John had returned. Something had awakened me. Out of the corner of my eye, I saw a person standing near me. When I turned to greet John, the person was gone.

I don't know why John decided to pray that way. He had never prayed for angels to do anything before. I don't know exactly what I saw that day in my room, but I know that I had most definitely been refreshed. When John returned, I was rested and ready to continue with the ministry activities that we had planned. Angels are still ministering and messaging, just as they were in Scripture.

There are many New Testament examples of angels delivering messages for God. The most profound, perhaps, were the angels surrounding the event of Jesus' birth. Zacharias encountered an angel in the Holy of Holies, telling him that his wife would give birth to John the Baptist. Gabriel appeared to Mary with the news that she would become the mother of God's own Son. Joseph also had an angel appear to him in a dream, affirming for him that Mary truly was having a supernatural experience.[9]

Angels appeared to the women at the tomb to deliver the news that Jesus was not there. In the days of the early church, an angel told Peter to get up and put on his sandals, and then led him right out the front gates of a locked prison.[10] But the question is, do angels still deliver messages for God today?

Bearing Gifts
Our second Boot Camp class included families with children. When we have families come through training, we offer a Children's Boot Camp to prepare the children for what they will face on the mission field as well. It is our hope that they will become excited about the adventure that God has called their family to, rather than feeling that Mom and Dad are dragging them away from the things they love to the other side of the planet.

During one of the afternoon classes, the children were given some time to play freely outside, while their parents were still in class. Our

9. Luke 1:5–25; Luke 1:26–38; Matthew 1:18–25.
10. Luke 24:1–8; Acts 12:1–19.

daughter Jessi was six years old at that time. She wandered off by herself for a time to the front of the property, where she saw a large angel standing on a picnic table. She told us later that the angel was very tall and wearing a suit of armor.

She was terrified, so she ran back to the dorm room where our family was living at the time. When she entered the room, the angel was standing there inside the room! With no adults around at the moment, she went to one of the older children and told her about this angel she had seen. Michelle, who was eleven years old and wise beyond her years, said, "Jessi, if it's an angel then you don't need to be afraid."

She went with Jessi back to the original place where she had seen the angel. Michelle could not see anything there, but she stood with Jessi, as Jess slowly raised her hands and took something from the giant angel. It was a small suit of armor. Jessi told us later that the angel did not say anything to her. He just held out this armor for Jessi to take.

As soon as class was over, Michelle brought Jessi to me to explain what had happened. Jessi was still shaking with adrenaline from the whole experience. I did not know what to think—angels handing suits of armor to little girls. This was not in my religious training. I had no theology for it!

All I could think was that it might be important for me to do a study with my children on the armor of God. I had begun homeschooling Jess, so we commenced studying together each one of the pieces of the armor described for us in Ephesians 6—on a six-year-old level, of course.

When this Boot Camp class graduated, it was part of our job description at that time to travel with those who were eventually heading into China and take them to Taiwan to get set up in Mandarin language study there. We were spending six months of the year stateside and six months in Taiwan every year.

While we were there in Taiwan, a 7.6 earthquake hit our part of the island. Many buildings fell, crushing thousands of people. Some Chinese friends had asked Jessi to spend the night at their home that evening. They lived just down the street from us. They were an idol-worshiping family, and we were concerned about leaving Jessi with them overnight, but after praying about it felt that God would have us allow the relationship that Jessi had with them to grow.

When the earthquake struck in the middle of the night, it was an absolutely terrifying experience. We could hear the sound of it, long before the building began to shake, as vibrations like waves moved across the ground in our direction. Immediately, the electricity went out.

We jumped out of bed, trying to find our other two children in the dark, as the floor rose and fell and the building swayed and jumped. We were living on the second floor of a three-story building. After the initial quake, we worked our way down the stairs in the dark and made our way outside the building to an open field nearby.

None of the buildings on our street had fallen, but John began to run up and down the street, calling out to our neighbors to see if they were all right. When he came to the home where Jessi was staying, he was able to hear them from a window. Everyone was okay, but because there was no power, the electric gate that served as the front door of the home was impossible to open. They were all trapped inside the building. It took some time to get them out through the back entrance and down a sewer alley. Jessi was shaken, to say the least.

It is hard to describe what the next few weeks were like. The next morning, at the fire station, we all watched with terror the news reports on the generator-powered television—reports of the damage, scenes of bodies crushed by buildings, weeping and wailing families.

Our village of 30,000 people was paralyzed with fear. Many times a day, aftershocks of 6.0 and above rocked the buildings, threatening to go ahead and bring them down. Many would not sleep in their homes, but slept in their cars or out in the streets. Jessi lived in constant fear, holding on to one or the other of us at all times. The slightest movement or loud sound would send her into frantic crying.

Firm Foundation

Several days after the earthquake, we awoke to the sound of people banging on our downstairs door. The earthquake had destroyed the dam over the water reservoir that served our part of the island. The reserve tanks of water over our neighbors' homes had run out of water, and here they were, loudly asking us for water from our well.

We did not even know that our home had a well! A couple of years earlier, we had clearly sensed the Holy Spirit leading us to this particular building, even though it was in an area of town that we personally would not have chosen. Out of obedience we had rented this building and turned it into our Heart of God Ministries base—and now they were telling us we had a well?

It was the only well in that village. The line extended way out into the street, people standing with buckets, pots and pans—whatever they could fill. This was a missionary's greatest dream! A captive audience, all standing around a well! Let's see… what do you think the topic of the sermon should be? Our job became visiting with people all day long about Jesus, the Living Water!

Through the tragedy of the earthquake in Taiwan, God brought to salvation the first fruit of our ministry on that street. It was an elderly couple who were attracted to the gospel through the water that we gave. The man died within a few short months after receiving Christ. God's timing is perfect.

But Jessi, our daughter, was traumatized.

We hoped that Jessi would improve when we got back to the States, perhaps to more secure and familiar surroundings. But her fears only got worse, more irrational, more out of control. She became so paralyzed by fear that she would not go anywhere by herself. Loud noises frightened her into a weeping puddle on the ground. We knew we had to do something to help her.

Marsha McAlister is a wonderful counselor who is associated with our ministry. She teaches classes in Boot Camp, as well as provides counseling for our missionaries. She had been specially trained to provide trauma counseling for children in Oklahoma City public schools, after a tornado tore through a large section of the metro area.

Marsha was ideal. She prayed with Jessi. She asked her questions. She had her draw pictures of the things she had experienced in Taiwan. It was only then that we realized that Jessi's trauma had been magnified by the pictures she had seen on that television at the fire station. In our own shock and trauma, we had not protected her from uncensored, bloody scenes that now filled her mind with fear.

Counseling helped to give us some tools. It helped us find out what was really going on in her mind and in her emotions. But Jessi had a battle to fight. We truly believed that she was being attacked by a demonic spirit of fear.[11]

I reviewed the teaching we had studied on the armor of God with her, and we realized that the armor only includes one offensive weapon. Everything else is protective or defensive. The only thing we have to fight with is the sword of the Spirit, which is the Word of God. We began to see what the Bible has to say about fear.

> When I am afraid, I will trust in You, in God, whose word I praise, in God I trust; I will not be afraid.[12]

She memorized this verse put to a tune by Steve Green and sang it to herself:

> For God has not given us a spirit of fear, but of power and of love and of a sound mind.[13]

I love this version, because when we become afraid, we totally lose our sound mind. Isn't that right? Our thoughts start running, we start hearing sounds that aren't there, we think we see things that aren't there. Really, we can go absolutely crazy in fear. But God's Word tells us that he has not given us a spirit of fear, but of power (over this enemy!), and of love (from him), and of a *sound mind*!

I remember waking in the middle of the night and hearing Jessi up in the loft that was her bedroom. She was quoting this verse quietly out

---

11. That is what Scripture calls it in 2 Timothy 1:7. It is not just "fear," but a "spirit of fear." Fear is not of God. It is of the devil himself.

12. Psalm 56:3, 4a (NIV).

13. 2 Timothy 1:7.

loud, "God has not given me a spirit of fear! God has not given me a spirit of fear! But of power and of love and of a sound mind! God has not given me a spirit of fear! Fear, you have to leave in Jesus' name." Jessi was using the sword of the Spirit to defeat the enemy of fear in her life, and she fought with everything in her!

Jessi had improved dramatically. No longer was she crying all the time. She could play outside without us being right there with her. We were much relieved, but as the time drew closer for us to return to Taiwan, the "scene of crime," I began to wonder. How would she do? Would all the fear return? Could she hold on to the freedom that she had attained?

Airplanes and Vomit
We awoke early in the morning to leave for the airport. Jessi came down the stairs in tears, saying that she'd had a nightmare. Frustrated because this was causing a time delay, I tried to hurry her through telling me what it was. In her dream, she had been sleeping in her bed. A snake came and started biting her. She called out for her Baba (John), and he came and knelt beside her bed to pray. He prayed and prayed, until finally the snake left. But soon another snake would come and begin biting her. This happened over and over in her dream.

As she related the details of the dream, John raised his eyebrows at me over her head. I sat down with Jessi and explained that Satan did not want her to go back to Taiwan. You see, Jessi was not just our six-year-old daughter there, but really she was an evangelist in her own right. In the home where she had been sleeping that night of the earthquake was a woman who was absolutely taken with her cuteness. She would invite Jessi over for sweet coffee and treats. She wanted to learn English, so Jess would take her children's Bible and use it to teach from.

Before she would go to this woman's home, she had me help her find the verses that talk about idols—you know, the ones that say how stupid the idols are, how they don't have eyes or ears, how they can't even hear your prayers.[14] These were the passages that Jessi used for English lessons! Inevitably, conversations between Jess and this Chinese lady were filled with questions and answers about idols versus Jesus. John

---

14. Psalm 115:3–8; Jeremiah 10:1–10.

and I, as adults, could never have talked so openly, but because she was only six, Jessi could get away with being so direct—and the woman kept inviting her back!

I talked to Jessi about her ministry in Taiwan and how the enemy would love to keep her so bound in fear that she would not return, or if she did, to keep her so paralyzed that she could not function. He wanted to steal her ability to witness to the Chinese. We prayed together, and Jessi was determined to not let Satan win.

Our flight was uneventful, until we were thirty thousand feet over the Pacific Ocean. The children had gone to sleep, two of them lying on the seats, Jessi stretched out on the floor at John's feet. I was in the chair across the aisle, leaning back in my seat to prepare for a long sleep, when Jessi began to vomit. She did not even wake from her sleep, but began to vomit all over herself and the carry-on bag of the woman in front of her!

Embarrassed, we got her up to clean up the mess and found that she was burning up with fever. I took her to the bathroom to wash her clothes and her hair. You know how small those sinks are in airport bathrooms—it was a nightmare! After cleaning everything the best we could and apologizing to everyone around us, we lay her back down on the floor.

In about half an hour, she again began to vomit in her sleep, and we went through the whole process a second time. This happened again and again, about every half hour or so. I started to experience that spirit of fear. John could feel it too, and he began to pray. My mother's heart began to meditate on her fever and how high it seemed. *Something must be dreadfully wrong with my child. We are thirty thousand feet in the air, with no doctor. What if she dies up here?*

I was so tired. My body only wanted to sleep. I could barely keep my eyes open, but I turned to John and asked him if he wanted me to take a turn sitting with her. He said, "No. I think I am supposed to continue praying for her." Suddenly, I heard the Holy Spirit say, "There were seven snakes." I began to count and realized that Jessi had vomited six times. I turned to John and told him, "I don't understand this, but

I think she is going to vomit one more time, and then it will be over. Keep praying."

Sure enough, like clockwork, here it came—with Jessi not even waking enough from her sleep to know that she was doing it. Then, when she was finished, she sat straight up and said, "Mama, I'm hungry." The fever was gone. She was absolutely fine, not a trace of sickness.

When we arrived at the base in Taiwan, it was early morning, and I knew I needed to get some breakfast ready. Since no one had been living there, the cabinets were not stocked. I told the children that I was going to go right next door and buy some sugar and rice cereal. I would be right back. Jessi came running to me and said, "No, Mama. I will go." I responded, "Jessi, I'm just going right next door. I'll be right back." She grabbed my arm and fervently said again, "No, Mama. Give me the money. I will buy them. If I don't do this, I will be stuck in this house the whole time we are here!" I put the money in her hand.

In a few minutes, Jessi returned with the items we needed, and she has never had a struggle with fear again! She fought this enemy and she won! Jess is one of the bravest people I know, and it all started with an angel delivering a small suit of armor to a six-year-old girl.

PART 3
Bearing Fruit

I am the vine; you are the branches. Those who remain in me, and I in them, will produce much fruit.

Jesus

CHAPTER 15
Plastic Produce

Love is a fruit in season at all times, and within the reach of every hand.
Mother Teresa of Calcutta

One must ask children and birds how cherries and strawberries taste.
Johann Wolfgang von Goethe

We were eating at a nice Indian restaurant—one of my favorites! It had a large buffet, so our children were all getting their own food and would meet us back at the table in a few minutes. Finally, we were all gathered, ready to eat our delicious mountains of curry and rice, only Jael was not yet with us. Looking toward the buffet, we tried to spot her little blonde head among the carts of food. There she was, looking frustrated, trying to pluck one of the plastic grapes from the decorative centerpiece. We all watched in amusement for a few moments before John finally sent Josiah to tell her that the grapes were fake.

> Then God said, "Let the earth bring forth grass, the herb that yields seed, and the fruit tree that yields fruit according to its kind, whose seed is in itself, on the earth"; and it was so.[1]

Embedded deep in the DNA of every element of creation is this created purpose to reproduce itself. Plants and animals of every kind are continually in the process of reproduction. They can't not reproduce. God made them with this purpose.

---

1. Genesis 1:11.

In more Victorian times, the illustration of the "birds and bees" perfectly described for young people what God has designed for human beings. God spoke to Adam and Eve, giving the first command of all of Scripture:

> "Be fruitful and multiply; fill the earth and subdue it; have dominion over the fish of the sea, over the birds of the air, and over every living thing that moves on the earth."[2]

This has not been a difficult task for the girls in my family. We merely have to think about new babies and.... One of my sisters has five children, another seven, and I have five of my own!

This imagery of fruitfulness is found throughout all of Scripture.

> He shall be like a tree planted by the rivers of water, that brings forth its fruit in its season, whose leaf also shall not wither; and whatever he does shall prosper.[3]

> "For he shall be like a tree planted by the waters, which spreads out its roots by the river, and will not fear when heat comes; but its leaf will be green, and will not be anxious in the year of drought, nor will it cease from yielding fruit."[4]

The tree flourishes with its roots extended deep into the water of the river. Jesus is our source of life. As we press into relationship with him, we receive the life-giving power of his Spirit in us to begin bearing fruit.

Jesus used this imagery of fruit to describe what is to come from intimacy with him:

> "I am the true vine, and My Father is the vinedresser. Every branch in Me that does not bear fruit He takes away; and every branch that bears fruit He prunes, that it may bear more fruit. You are already clean because of the word which I have spoken to you. Abide in Me, and I in you. As the branch

2. Genesis 1:28.
3. Psalm 1:3.
4. Jeremiah 17:8.

cannot bear fruit of itself, unless it abides in the vine, neither can you, unless you abide in Me. I am the vine, you are the branches. He who abides in Me, and I in him, bears much fruit; for without Me you can do nothing. If anyone does not abide in Me, he is cast out as a branch and is withered; and they gather them and throw them into the fire, and they are burned. If you abide in Me, and My words abide in you, you will ask what you desire, and it shall be done for you. By this My Father is glorified, that you bear much fruit; so you will be My disciples."[5]

Jesus told parables that illustrated the kingdom of God by describing soil, seed and fruit, and said that we would be recognized by our fruit.[6]

Paul picked up this imagery when he wrote to the Romans:

> Therefore, my brethren, you also have become dead to the law through the body of Christ, that you may be married to another—to Him who was raised from the dead, that we should bear fruit to God.[7]

Jesus is the bridegroom and we are his bride. Naturally, spiritual fruit should come from intimate relationship with him.

Again Paul writes to the Colossians:

> For this reason we also, since the day we heard it, do not cease to pray for you, and to ask that you may be filled with the knowledge of His will in all wisdom and spiritual understanding; that you may walk worthy of the Lord, fully *pleasing Him, being fruitful* in every good work and increasing in the *knowledge of God*.[8]

This verse is rich with Paul's understanding of intimate relationship with Jesus! Remember that pleasing God means that by believing

---

5. John 15:1–8.
6. Mark 4:20; Matthew 7:16–20.
7. Romans 7:4.
8. Colossians 1:9, 10, emphasis mine.

and trusting him, we allow him to enjoy intimate friendship with us.[9] We looked at this word "knowledge"—to know. It means intimate fellowship with God. Paul's prayer for the Colossians is that the expected outcome of fruit would become a reality in their lives!

The Book of Revelation ends with a beautiful picture of the kingdom of God—a tree:

> And he showed me a pure river of water of life, clear as crystal, proceeding from the throne of God and of the Lamb. In the middle of its street, and on either side of the river, was the tree of life, which bore twelve fruits, each tree yielding its fruit every month. The leaves of the tree were for the healing of the nations.[10]

Just as Jesus described in Matthew 13, the kingdom of God becomes a tree in which all the peoples of the earth can find their home.

This is not an exhaustive list of "fruit" verses, but merely a sampling to show you how central this theme of bearing fruit is throughout the whole of Scripture. It is God's design, as seen in nature, for our spiritual lives in the kingdom of God.

So what are we talking about? What does it mean to bear fruit? What kind of fruit should we expect from intimate relationship with God?

Two Become One

I have many commentaries on the Song of Solomon—they fill a whole shelf in my office. Over the years, John has picked them up for me at used bookstores. Some are new and many of them are written by saints who, throughout the generations, have been blessed by the divine love story contained in it.

Because the Song of Solomon is an allegory, each person might be ministered to in different ways through its symbolism. This becomes clear when you look through the different commentaries. The Holy

---

9. For more about pleasing God, refer back to chapter 9.
10. Revelation 22:1, 2.

Spirit highlights different elements of the parable to illustrate aspects of relationship with Jesus.

As I mentioned before, the book goes back and forth from the voice of the bridegroom to that of the bride. The section headings in your Bible designating the different speakers were not there in the original Hebrew text. These have been added for our benefit in understanding the story. However, you will find that different versions of the Bible have titled these sections differently.

In the beginning chapters, it is quite obvious who is speaking, as male and female aspects of relationship are described. However, most commentators agree that as you read through the later chapters, it becomes increasingly difficult to designate which of the two is speaking, the bride or the bridegroom.

What a wonderful illustration for us is this most precious of books! Isn't that the way that husband and wife are to be? We are to become one. By the end of the story, the bride has so taken on the character of her husband, that no longer can you tell the difference between her and him. They look the same. They sound the same. They act the same.

Jesus modeled this for us when he said, "He who has seen Me has seen the Father," and "The Son can do nothing of Himself, but what He sees the Father do."[11] He was in perfect union with the Father, perfect fellowship, perfect relationship, and the fruit of his life looked just like the Father.

Scripture lays out for us, in very specific terms, what kind of fruit should become evident in our character if we are experiencing intimate relationship with Jesus:

> But now having been set free from sin, and having become slaves of God, you have your fruit to *holiness*, and the end, everlasting life.[12]

---

11. John 14:9; 5:19.
12. Romans 6:22, emphasis mine.

Now no chastening seems to be joyful for the present, but painful; nevertheless, afterward it yields the peaceable fruit of *righteousness* to those who have been trained by it.[13]

I grew up in a holiness denomination and then spent many years of my adult life pursuing together with a body of believers purity, righteousness and holiness. These I thought I clearly understood, however, many of us in that camp were completely lacking in the most basic of fruit that Scripture describes:

The fruit of the Spirit is *love, joy, peace, longsuffering, kindness, goodness, faithfulness, gentleness, self-control.*[14]

In our attempt to define and hold others to our understood standards of holiness and purity of doctrine, I am ashamed to say that we, in the holiness camp, have often been guilty of meanness instead of kindness; hatred instead of love; strife instead of peace; harshness instead of gentleness; cutting off of relationship with other believers instead of longsuffering; and even loss of control in expression of intense emotion instead of self-control.

Pastor Hal Perkins described it this way: He likened people to vessels that hold liquid. Every time someone "bumps" us, something spills out. Will it be ugliness or will it be the sweet, refreshing Spirit of Christ? The "bumping" is the test of what is truly inside.

We must examine the fruit being produced by our internal attitudes, and if we find that we see and smell little or nothing of the character of Jesus, our bridegroom, then we must return to intimate fellowship with him.[15] There, he can begin to transform our nature and begin to produce the fruit of true righteousness and holiness—that of the fruit of the Spirit.

---

13. Hebrews 12:11, emphasis mine.

14. Galatians 5:22, 23, emphasis mine.

15. I am talking about repentance. Repentance is returning to intimate fellowship with Jesus! It means that we were walking our own direction, doing our own thing, but we turned around and began walking with him—in relationship with him. Yes, it means our behaviors change, but that is because we are now walking with someone we love! We begin to find out the things he likes and doesn't like. We begin to see things the way he sees them, and we begin to say and do things the way that he says and does them. We begin to look like Jesus!

Birthing Fruit

When a woman is birthing a baby, it hurts. I can tell you from experience five times over. I'm going to use this illustration of birth to help you understand how God produces fruit of character in us. I will try not to be too graphic for you guys, but I've got to use what I know. Consider it a science lesson.

When the time comes for a baby to be born, the mother begins experiencing pains. These pains are called contractions for a very good reason, because that is exactly what is going on. The great big muscle called a uterus is contracting, just like your biceps do when you lift weights. The reason that it is contracting is to widen the opening called the cervix at the bottom of the womb. The cervix has to open in order for the baby to pass through. And these contractions hurt.

Now, what is our normal response to pain? We don't like it. When something hurts us, we resist it. In labor, women often fight the pain of contractions by tensing up their muscles. This is the opposite of what we need to do, because it prevents the uterus muscle from doing what it needs to do. In order for it to contract like it should, we need to relax and go with the process. Often when we resist the pain, it lengthens the labor and ultimately makes it more painful.

Okay, enough of the science lesson. What is my point? Look at Romans 5:

> And not only that, but we also glory in tribulations, knowing that tribulation produces perseverance; and perseverance, character; and character, hope.[16]

What is it that produces character in us? It's tribulations. It's painful circumstances and experiences. The Greek definition of that word, "tribulation," actually means "pressure."[17] Just like a grape has to be squeezed in order to produce wine, we must experience tribulations in order to bear the fruit of the Spirit.[18]

---

16. Romans 5:3, 4.
17. All of my Greek and Hebrew word meanings come from Strong's Concordance and the New American Standard Lexicon found online at www.biblestudytools.net.
18. Okay, I know I'm mixing metaphors, but hang with me.

When a physical baby is ready to be born, there really is not anything you can do to prevent it. It is going to come. However, when God is trying to birth the fruit of good character in us, we can abort the baby, so to speak. It is not automatically produced. Sometimes we abort it by running away from the people or circumstances that are producing the pressure in our lives. We quit jobs that are unpleasant. We take ourselves out of painful relationships. We leave churches that we don't like.

If we don't physically leave, then sometimes we just emotionally check out. We avoid certain topics. We distance ourselves. We put up those walls. And when we do these things, the fruit that God is trying to birth in our character is not produced. We remain the same, looking like our old selves, rather than looking like Jesus.

Just as in physical labor, we must surrender to the contractions. We must relax and submit to the Holy Spirit and his work in our lives. If we fight with him, it only produces more pain for us. Madame Guyon wrote of this pain:

> All of our troubles spring from our resistance; and our resistance comes from our attachment to things. The more you torment yourself over your suffering, the sharper that suffering becomes. But if you surrender yourself to the suffering, more each time, and you allow the crucifying process to go on undisturbed, the suffering is used more effectively.[19]

If we will allow him to work through the difficult circumstances of our lives, we will no longer "be conformed to this world, but we will be transformed by the renewing of our mind, that we may prove what is that good and acceptable and perfect will of God."[20]

Every one of my physical labors has been characterized by a raging battle in my mind. The very first contraction brings a flood of fear, as I begin to think about how much more painful it will become and how long it will last. Fear can overwhelm you, if you don't take your thoughts captive.

---

19. Guyon, Jeanne. *Final Steps in Christian Maturity* (SeedSowers Publishing House, 1985) p. 49.
20. Romans 12:2.

I have delivered my babies at home with a midwife. I have a group of
girlfriends who come to help me during labor, and one of their primary
jobs—besides giving me drinks, reminding me to breathe and rubbing
my back—is to help me take these fearful thoughts captive. We have
created a "rule" for labor: they never allow me to say, "I can't do it."
Instead, every time I feel fearful and think I can't go on, I must say,
"Jesus, help me." Instantly, I remember who is my source.

Spiritual birth is the same for us. Sometimes we begin to meditate on
the pain of the sacrifices that God is asking of us. We begin to resent
the trials that he has allowed to press us. We start thinking about how
long we are going to have to endure this tribulation, and we begin to
fear that we are incapable of fulfilling the call that God has given to us.

In difficult times of spiritual birth, we must not isolate ourselves or
withdraw from fellowship with other believers. Just as in physical
labor, in humility, we must allow others around us to help us. They are
"midwives," so to speak—good leaders, wiser, older in Jesus. Perhaps
they have delivered lots of "babies" in their own lives. We can trust
their counsel and guidance.

Then we must choose to surrender to the "contractions" and breathe.
We focus only on the present, not meditating on how much is yet before
us. We must take our fearful thoughts captive, choosing faith instead.
We cry out, "Jesus, help me." Resisting the thoughts that we cannot do
it, we must remember that we can do all things through Christ, "being
confident of this, that He who began a good work in you will carry it on
to completion until the day of Christ Jesus."[21]

Wholiness unto the Lord
For many of the years that I spent in holiness churches, I was very
aware of my shortcomings. I saw how far away I was from looking like
Jesus, and it only produced in me a sense of guilt and shame. Each time
I failed, I tried harder, only to find myself failing again or failing in
another area.

---

21. Philippians 1:6. I am grateful to my friend, Lucretia Smithers, for helping me deliver
my babies and for teaching this spiritual concept to me.

Looking back now, I can imagine myself as a tree. I would scrunch up my eyes, shrug my shoulders, grunt a little and push really hard—and then look out at empty branches (or limbs, as the case may be), only to see that no apples had appeared. Even if I could show any fruit for my efforts, it was usually shriveled up raisins, instead of plump, juicy grapes! Just like Jael trying to pick that plastic produce, if you looked too closely, my fruit was fake.

The Holy Spirit has since given me a picture of what the "plant" of my life looked like in those days. I was a very broken person. Each wound that I had received growing up, each pain of rejection and betrayal, each broken relationship, had fractured the main stalk of my plant. It was as though I had left pieces of myself all over the place. Some of it with the men who had abused me. Some of it with my childhood friends. Some even with my parents. I was not a whole person, but merely a fraction of the thing that God had intended.

As I began to experience the joys of intimate friendship with God, he began to prove himself trustworthy to me. I began to lower my defenses—those walls that I had put up to protect my heart from pain. I began to see the brokenness of my life and my *inability* to bear good fruit. As I began allowing the Holy Spirit to shine his light on some of the deepest places of my heart, he began to bring healing to some of those broken places. It was like putting my roots down deep into living water.

Holiness is not automatically produced in our lives simply because we have declared that we are a Christian. Rather, God desires to produce holiness in us that is the result of *wholiness*.[22] It is a natural outcome of intimate, healing experiences. Through intimate relationship with him, he brings healing to our wounds. He brings back together the many parts of our selves that we have left strewn all over the place. He makes us whole again, and we naturally begin to look like Jesus.

One Sunday morning about six years into being married to John, I had an amazing worship experience. During one of the worship songs, I wanted to express my gratefulness to Jesus. I wanted to show him how much I loved and appreciated all that he was doing in my life. I raised

22. This is my own made up word. It simply means that holiness happens in us as we allow God to make us whole.

both my hands high in front of me, as an expression of my love. As I stood in that position, singing my praises, I felt the presence of the Holy Spirit come very near to me. In my mind's eye, I imagined that in my hands, I was holding the face of Jesus, his chin resting in my palms, my fingers encircling his cheeks. He was smiling, and I could almost feel his breath upon me. It was precious and intimate. I knew that as I had drawn near to him, he had drawn near to me.[23]

On Wednesday morning of that same week, the payphone out in the hallway of our apartment building began to ring. It rang and rang, so I finally ran out and answered. The voice on the other end of the line sent shivers down my spine. The young man that I had dated back in high school was saying, "Hello," and calling me by name.

I had not seen nor heard from this guy in ten years! How did he get this number? We didn't even have a phone at the time! I had no idea how he tracked me down—calling on the payphone outside my apartment? He went on to explain to me that he had recommitted his life to Jesus, and in repenting of past sin, the Lord had convicted him to go back and apologize to people he had wounded in his past. He was asking if he could come and visit me to speak to me in person!

With the rush of adrenaline pumping through my veins and my heart beating in my ears, I paused for a moment. I didn't know what to say. How could I forgive this man who had caused so much damage in my life? Then I remembered Sunday morning. Immediately, Jesus was there with me. His presence was so near that it was almost tangible. I had held his face in my hands! He was with me!

I told him that, yes, he could come. I would like to see him, and we arranged a day and time to meet at a restaurant. He would be driving several hours just for this purpose. I was impressed with his diligence.

My parents and John went with me, and I must say that I was nervous as we waited in that Mexican restaurant for him to arrive. Would he be as large and intimidating as I remembered? Would I suddenly be transported to old memories and be unable to speak? What would he look like? How would he look at me?

---

23. James 4:8.

When he came through the door, I knew a chapter of my life was closing. None of my worst fears came to pass. We ate a meal together. We asked about one another's families. We caught up on each other's history. He told us of things that God was doing in his life. And then he asked me to forgive him for all that he had done to hurt me in high school.

I suddenly was aware that he probably didn't have any idea of the depth of the damage that he had done. How could he know the lasting effect of his words to me? He would never know. I knew that even the parts he could identify had never been intentional. I knew what Jesus meant when he said, "Father, forgive them. They know not what they do."[24] With Jesus right there by my side, I was easily able to say to him, "I forgive you."

> Grace and peace be multiplied to you in the knowledge of God and of Jesus our Lord, as His divine power has given to us all things that pertain to life and godliness, *through the knowledge of Him* who called us by glory and virtue, by which have been given to us exceedingly great and precious promises, that through these you may be *partakers of the divine nature*, having escaped the corruption that is in the world through lust.
>
> But also for this very reason, giving all diligence, add to your faith virtue, to virtue knowledge, to knowledge self-control, to self-control perseverance, to perseverance godliness, to godliness brotherly kindness, and to brotherly kindness love. For if these things are yours and abound, you will be neither *barren nor unfruitful in the knowledge of our Lord Jesus Christ*. For he who lacks these things is shortsighted, even to blindness, and has forgotten that he was cleansed from his old sins. Therefore, brethren, be even more diligent to make your call and election sure, for if you do these things you will never stumble; for so an entrance will be supplied to you abundantly into the everlasting kingdom of our Lord and Savior Jesus Christ.[25]

---

24. Luke 23:34.
25. 2 Peter 1:5–11, emphasis mine.

Peter is not speaking here of a salvation issue. He is not speaking of heaven and hell. Rather, he challenges us to choose an entrance into the kingdom of God that is characterized by an abundance of fruit! Will you allow him to heal you, to change you—to make you abundantly fruitful?

CHAPTER 16
Large Families

One cannot save and then pitchfork souls into heaven.... Souls are more or less securely fastened to their bodies...and as you cannot get the souls out and deal with them separately, you have to take them both together.

Amy Carmichael

I have discovered that the people who believe most strongly in the next life do the most good in the present one.

C.S. Lewis

Last summer I visited India, where I was privileged to speak in a church that is ministering in one of the many giant slums. There were about three hundred poor people present that morning, and I felt led to share a message about Jesus, our Good Shepherd. I talked to them about his gentleness and about what it means to be one of his lambs. I told them of his love for them and invited them to receive the tender, compassionate care of the Shepherd. At the end of the service, many came forward to receive prayer.

After the service, Irene, the pastor's wife, invited me to go with her on a tour of the slum and their ministry there. A beautiful layperson named Shanta Rani also went with us, leading the way as we entered the maze of concrete buildings. These buildings really were simple, square, box-like rooms with no doors, only openings that led to people's homes.

We first stopped at the home of a young couple. Living with them in an eight-by-eight-foot room was the young woman's thirteen-year-old sister and their daughter, who was mentally disabled. We left our shoes outside and entered this little house. Irene introduced me to each of them and went on to tell me in English that he was a rickshaw driver and she a maid. During the day, the younger sister took care of the child, having nothing to eat until the mother returned each evening to cook a simple meal of rice and vegetables.

The woman spoke to her sister, who ran out the door and down the "lane." (This is what they called the four-foot-wide mud pathways that were the maze between each row of houses.) In a few minutes, the little girl returned with three bottles of soda, one for each of us visitors. I asked Irene if I could give it to the little girl, but she told me that I must receive their hospitality. They wanted to bless me!

On the concrete wall hung a picture of Jesus alongside a painting of an idol. Shanta Rani explained that this young couple was leading a house church. Having recently accepted Jesus as Savior, they still did not understand the full implications of the gospel, but she was helping them to pass on each lesson that they learned.

When we reentered the lane, children had been playing with my shoes, and I then realized that the mud was not only mud, but also human and animal feces. As we continued down the lane, a rat darted out and ran right across the top of my right foot. The children—who were naked from the waist down and following merrily after us—laughed and shouted, much as my children would at the sight of a squirrel.

In another of these concrete homes, Irene introduced me to a woman with HIV. Her baby was very ill, but she would not take her to the doctor. She did not want to find out if the child also had the disease.

Queen of Peace
As we walked, Irene told me about the lady I was following. Shanta Rani means "Queen of Peace." As a young woman, her husband had left her with three small children and no source of income. She moved into the slum and began working as a prostitute to provide for her kids. Getting a job as a maid or nanny is not easy, and even if she did, she would have to spend half of what she made to pay for public transportation back and forth from the slum to the rich sector of the

city. Prostitution is an easy and convenient way to make money. The market is constant and never ending.

Through the church, Shanta Rani came to know Jesus. Church people helped her to get a job as a maid. Now, all her children are grown, and she spends all her time overseeing house churches and discipling young Christians all throughout the slum.

The farther we progressed into the maze, the poorer the houses became. Pretty soon they were no longer made of concrete, but were literally items of trash that had been put together to form a shelter—pieces of sheet metal, plywood, plastic tarps and old signboards. The lanes became narrower and narrower and the sewage around our feet wetter and wetter.

Finally, the houses were nothing more than shacks built about three feet above the ground. Under them was exposed, running sewage and everything you would imagine finding at the dump—old plastic bags, leftover food scraps, broken toys, pieces of old clothing—now soaked in muck. I cannot describe the stench. My stomach twisted and turned as I endeavored to continue smiling at the people who slept a few feet above the foul refuse.

I followed Shanta Rani up a rickety ladder that had been made from random pieces of trash into a tiny "home" where a teenage girl met us. She and her husband lived there with their little baby. Irene told me that the baby is constantly sick with fever. The young father was away attempting to earn some money driving a rickshaw. Another house church met in this little home, and Shanta Rani was teaching these young people what it means to follow Jesus.

Good Shepherd

When we climbed up into another dwelling, I was told that this was a rental house. It was a "second story apartment," created from trash, and it creaked like it just might not hold our weight. About the size of a twin bed, a young woman lived there with her daughter, sleeping together end to end on the floor.

Irene began to tell me the events of this woman's life that had led her to be living in such a condition, and as I listened to the list of hardships, my eyes began to fill with tears. This young woman knew some English, so I turned to her and began to apologize. I told her that I was sorry that so many terrible things had happened to her and that her life was so filled with pain.

Immediately, the young woman stopped me. She said, "No! My life is not terrible. Didn't you tell me this morning in church that Jesus is my Good Shepherd, that he is taking care of me?" I was overcome with emotion and began to weep convulsively. How could the gospel apply in these conditions? If I had known what their homes looked like before I had spoken that morning, could I have been so confident of Jesus' love and concern for them? She asked me to pray for her, and I could barely find words to form a prayer—I felt that I was the one who needed her prayers!

Yes, the gospel was breaking forth in this very dark and needy place. Jesus had come to the slum in the form of Shanta Rani, the "Queen of Peace." He was feeding the poor, healing the sick, teaching the children—and they could feel his gentle arms of love around them.

The Glory of the Lord

There is a lot of talk of the "glory of God" in the church today. We talk about doing things for the "glory of God." We talk about world evangelization really being about "God's glory." But sometimes "glory" is left a very nebulous idea. What is his glory? Is it a bright light that surrounds him? Is it his shininess?

Moses asked God to show him his glory. So God hid Moses in the cleft of a rock and told him that he was going to make all his *goodness* pass before him. As God passed by, he proclaimed to Moses all that his glory entails:

> "The Lord, the Lord God, compassionate and gracious, longsuffering, and abounding in goodness and truth, keeping mercy for thousands, forgiving iniquity and transgression and sin, by no means clearing the guilty, visiting the iniquity of

the fathers upon the children and the children's children to the third and the fourth generation."[1]

God's glory is his character, which is good. In fact, his character is love. God is love. Everything that comes from God, including his laws, comes out of his good and loving character.

When Moses came down from the mountain, his face shone so brightly with God's glory that he wore a veil. The people were afraid of him. He came away from an intimate encounter with the Living God and he looked different. Some of God's "character" had rubbed off on him.

As we become intimate with Jesus, God's character begins to flow through us. As we get in touch with the Father's heart, we begin to care about the things that he cares about. We become concerned about his concerns. We think like he thinks. His desires become our desires. And our actions become the actions of God establishing his kingdom here on the earth.

Jesus told us that when we see him, we see the Father.[2] In fact, Hebrews tells us that this brightness or shininess of God's glory is defined in Jesus:

> [God] has in these last days spoken to us by His Son, whom He has appointed heir of all things, through whom also He made the worlds; who being the *brightness* of His glory and the express image of His person....[3]

The New Living Translation says it this way:

> The Son reflects God's own glory, and everything about him represents God exactly.

If we want to see what God is like, what his character is like—and thus what we are to be like—all we need to do is look at the life and teachings of Jesus. Most simply put, Jesus' life and ministry was

---

1. Exodus 34:6–7.
2. John 14:19.
3. Hebrews 1:3, emphasis mine.

characterized by the job description for the Messiah that's quoted in Luke 4 from Isaiah 61:

> "The Spirit of the Lord is upon me, for he has appointed me to preach Good News to the poor. He has sent me to proclaim that captives will be released, that the blind will see, that the downtrodden will be freed from their oppressors, and that the time of the Lord's favor has come."[4]

Poor Jesus

Jesus focused his ministry upon the poor, the rejected, the marginalized of society—his heart went out to them in compassion. As he fed the hungry, healed the sick and cast out demons, Jesus was not exhibiting a new emphasis in God's ministry on the earth. God has always been about the poor and needy. The Old Testament is full of God's heart for them:

> "No, the kind of fasting I want calls you to free those who are wrongly imprisoned and to stop oppressing those who work for you. Treat them fairly and give them what they earn. I want you to share your food with the hungry and to welcome poor wanderers into your homes. Give clothes to those who need them, and do not hide from relatives who need your help.

> "If you do these things, your salvation will come like the dawn. Yes, your healing will come quickly. Your godliness will lead you forward, and the glory of the Lord will protect you from behind. Then when you call, the Lord will answer. 'Yes, I am here,' he will quickly reply.

> "Stop oppressing the helpless and stop making false accusations and spreading vicious rumors! Feed the hungry and help those in trouble. Then your light will shine out from the darkness, and the darkness around you will be as bright as day."[5]

---

4. Luke 4:18, 19 (NLT).
5. Isaiah 58:6–10 (NLT).

"Learn to do good. Seek justice. Help the oppressed. Defend the orphan. Fight for the rights of widows."[6]

"Give fair judgment to the poor and the orphan; uphold the rights of the oppressed and the destitute. Rescue the poor and helpless; deliver them from the grasp of evil people."[7]

"But a beautiful palace does not make a great king! Why did your father, Josiah, reign so long? Because he was just and right in all his dealings. That is why God blessed him. He made sure that justice and help were given to the poor and needy, and everything went well for him. *"Isn't that what it means to know me?"* asks the Lord.[8]

True Revival

For fifteen years, my heart has burned with a desire to see revival in the church in America. I have prayed fervently in my own times with the Lord, started corporate prayer meetings for revival, attended other prayer meetings, read books on the subject, studied Scripture, and received countless promises from God for his church.

My understanding of revival has evolved over the years. David Smithers, who is a scholar and revival historian, has defined revival as the manifest presence of God here on the earth. I have heard him teach many times on the Lord's Prayer—that we are to pray that God's will is done on earth as it is in heaven.

I began to pray for revival with an understanding that God's manifest presence would make his church holy—that when he comes in power, there will be a massive move of repentance among believers. I saw in my mind's eye waves of people with faces on the ground weeping over their sin, one at a time standing to make public confession and commitment to live for God. I prayed with these pictures in mind.

When I became exposed to spiritual gifts and the more supernatural workings of the Holy Spirit, I began to include miracles in my desire

6. Isaiah 1:17 (NLT).
7. Psalm 82:3–4 (NLT).
8. Jeremiah 22:15–16, emphasis mine (NLT).

for revival. I read of past revivals where God manifested himself in power, and I longed to see a move of God that would heal the sick, cast out demons and glorify God through supernatural displays of his power. This became the theme of my prayers.

Incidentally, over the years I have seen both of these kinds of outpourings, on an individual level, a local church level and in larger mass movements of the Spirit that touched hundreds and thousands of lives. However, the longing in my heart has not been quenched. I have yet to see a move of God that transforms whole communities and literally brings the kingdom of God to this earth in a dramatic and life-changing way.

Recently, I believe that the Holy Spirit has brought new understanding for me as to what he desires to do. I believe that he is both gently rebuking me and faithfully encouraging me by pointing out to me that "revival" has already come—in the person Jesus! If David Smithers' definition is correct, and I believe it is, then the manifest presence of God has already come to this earth. Not only did he come in the form of a man, but he sent his Holy Spirit (the Spirit of Christ) to dwell in and live through his people.

Are you getting this simple truth? As we, his people, do the ministry of Jesus—as we help the poor, feed the hungry, heal the sick, take care of the widow—we are bringing revival! The manifest presence of Jesus comes through us, bringing the kingdom of God. His will is done on earth as it is in heaven.

John Wesley said,

> The Gospel of Christ knows no religion but social, no holiness but social holiness. You cannot be holy except as you are engaged in making the world a better place. You do not become holy by keeping yourself pure and clean from the world but by plunging into ministry on behalf of the world's hurting ones.

Billy Graham has said,

I can no longer proclaim the Cross and the Resurrection without proclaiming the whole message of the Kingdom which is justice for all.[9]

The Sin of Sodom

Some of God's greatest judgments upon his people have been the result of not caring for the poor and needy.

> "Woe to those who decree unrighteous decrees, who write misfortune, which they have prescribed to rob the needy of justice, and to take what is right from the poor of My people, that widows may be their prey, and that they may rob the fatherless. What will you do in the day of punishment, and in the desolation which will come from afar? To whom will you flee for help? And where will you leave your glory? Without Me they shall bow down among the prisoners, and they shall fall among the slain. For all this His anger is not turned away, but His hand is stretched out still."[10]

> Then the word of the Lord came to Zechariah, saying, "Thus says the Lord of hosts: 'Execute true justice, show mercy and compassion everyone to his brother. Do not oppress the widow or the fatherless, the alien or the poor. Let none of you plan evil in his heart against his brother.'" But they refused to heed, shrugged their shoulders, and stopped their ears so that they could not hear. Yes, they made their hearts like flint, refusing to hear the law and the words which the Lord of hosts had sent by His Spirit through the former prophets. Thus great wrath came from the Lord of hosts.[11]

Zechariah says that this sin of not caring for the poor and needy is the reason that God scattered Israel among the nations. Even the reason for God's judgment of Sodom and Gomorrah—which the church has traditionally labeled as the sin of homosexuality—is clearly stated:

---

9. Graham, Billy. *Approaching Hoofbeats* (Hodder & Stoughton, 1984).

10. Isaiah 10:1–4.

11. Zechariah 7:8–12.

"Look, this was the iniquity of your sister Sodom: She and her daughter had pride, fullness of food, and abundance of idleness; neither did she strengthen the hand of the poor and needy."[12]

My desire for holiness in the church is found not only in her freedom from sin, but in her reflection of God's heart for the poor and needy. My desire to see miracles of healing and deliverance is not found merely in the supernatural activity of God's Spirit, but in the practical ministry of the Holy Spirit through us, as we reach out to those in need.

I have also noticed that many of the Old Testament passages that I claimed as promises of revival are attached to this call to care for the poor. Just as Jesus taught us to pray, I now desire to see God's kingdom come on earth, which means all that Jesus quoted from Isaiah 61:

"The Spirit of the Lord God is upon Me, because the Lord has anointed Me to preach good tidings to the poor; He has sent Me to heal the brokenhearted, to proclaim liberty to the captives, and the opening of the prison to those who are bound; to proclaim the acceptable year of the Lord."[13]

God Loves Raymond

Two years ago, John and I and a small group of friends decided to put these thoughts to the test. We opened a coffeehouse in Valley Brook, a poor community in the heart of Oklahoma City. This area of town is well known for its "famous" strip clubs, high crime rate, drug addiction and poverty. We wanted to see if God would help us take the kingdom of light into a place where darkness has reigned for many years.

Right next to Valley of the Dolls, one of the favorite strip clubs on the block, sits our little coffee shop called Joe's Addiction. Our dream was that the place would become like the old TV sitcom *Cheers*—where everybody knows your name. God has blessed it, and now, an eclectic group of bikers, homosexuals, drug addicts, prostitutes and computer programmers all consider one another friends, and they hang out

12. Ezekiel 16:49.
13. Isaiah 61:1–3.

drinking coffee with us. Through Joe's we have been able to feed hungry people, help find jobs for the poor, provide social and medical help to the mentally challenged and befriend the broken and needy.

During the daylight hours, the neighborhood is relatively safe, so our daughter Jessi began working at Joe's when she was fourteen. One afternoon, during a lull in business, she was sitting on the couch, crocheting beanies for her friends. An openly homosexual man in his fifties named Raymond came in to order coffee. He noticed Jessi's crochet and excitedly announced, "I love to crochet!" He immediately ran home to get his yarn and hook.

He and Jessi spent countless hours visiting with one another while they crocheted hats and scarves or played Skip-Bo, his favorite card game. As weeks passed, he began to tell Jessi about his life. He talked about his family, about his lifestyle, about the rejection that he had received from some who disapproved. He even identified some of the wounds that he believed had caused him to be attracted to men. She talked with him about how much Jesus loves him.

Jessi finally suggested that Raymond come to church with her on Sunday. He protested, saying that he wasn't sure that church was the place for him—that he would feel really uncomfortable. Jess assured him that if he would come, she would sit by him, and he wouldn't have to feel like he was all alone. He finally agreed to come and visit.

When Raymond arrived, Jess was watching for him. She met him at the door with a hug and began introducing him to other people in our church, who welcomed him with smiles and handshakes. He recognized people who he had seen at Joe's. Then Jessi led him down the aisle to sit with her in the second row! There was no hiding. He was right down front in the middle of the action.

The moment the band struck the first chord, Raymond began to weep. Big tears poured down his face through every worship song we sang. When my husband John stood to preach his sermon, Raymond continued to weep. He cried through the whole thing. He even cried through the offering! I'm not sure that he even knew what he was crying about—only that his emotions had been deeply touched, and he would be coming back.

The next week, Raymond sat with Jessi on the front row, and again he wept through the whole service. John's message that morning was about the love of God. He spoke about God's very personal love for each one of us, and Raymond just couldn't stop crying. At the end of the sermon, John invited anyone who would like to receive prayer to come forward. A team of ministers was waiting who would be happy to pray for them.

Raymond did not move. In fact, there were a few awkward moments, as it looked like no one would respond to the invitation. But Kevin, who was serving on the ministry team that morning, noticed Raymond weeping on the front row and decided that he was not going to wait for him to come. Kevin went to him and asked if it would be okay to pray for him. Before the question was out of his mouth, Raymond threw his arms around Kevin's shoulders and began to sob loudly.

Several other men gathered around Raymond as the Holy Spirit began to minister. They each prayed precious prayers that Raymond might know and experience how much God loves him, how special he is to God. Several of them had prophetic words that they gave to Raymond—God speaking to the deepest places of wounding in his heart—to which Raymond began crying out in a loud voice, "God is here! Can you feel that? I feel him! God is here!" And he raised both of his hands in open worship of the one who loved him more than anyone ever had in his life.

Raymond is a changed life! God has delivered him from homosexuality and, perhaps even more difficult, has changed him from the dour, depressed, rather grumpy old man he was into a joyful, kind and gentle beacon of light in the community. Heaven came to earth in Raymond's life!

Over these last two years, we have seen prostitutes, drug addicts, thieves, sex offenders and strippers come to know and love and follow Jesus. Light is breaking through the darkness. The kingdom of God is coming to Valley Brook! It has not been through violent revolution, in the form of picketing the strip clubs or even street evangelism. Nor has it been through endless hours of prayer meetings—although many prayers have been prayed.

The kingdom of God is coming to Valley Brook as we feed the poor, help get medicine for the sick, drink coffee with the outcasts—much in the same way that Jesus did it. I have never had so much fun in the kingdom of God in my life! This is what Jesus loved to do when he walked here on earth, and it's what he still loves to do—only he has to do it through us, with us! Intimacy will produce fruit! Big fruit!

I do not believe that all those years of prayer were wasted, but I do believe that God was saying, "Yes. Okay. Let's do it. I'm ready. Let's go." Prayer accomplishes nothing without us stepping out to be his hands and feet. He is God with us.

Look at Them

Still overwhelmed by all that I had seen in the slum in India, I went to speak at a women's retreat at a church in the same city. In attendance were two hundred young Christian Indian women, whose church leaders felt that they would be the next generation of leadership in their denomination. At the retreat, I shared my testimony and the lessons I have learned from the life of Mary of Bethany. As I came to the example of Mary's open grief and anger, I could hear quiet weeping around the room.

During the breaks, girls came to me, one after another, to ask me to pray with them. Without exception, each one of them started her conversation with these words: "I have never told anyone this before…" And then she would go on to tell me of some horrible abuse that she had suffered, some at the hands of fathers, some from boyfriends and husbands.

On Sunday morning, the last service of the weekend, Dwayne Weehunt, the director of Sower of Seeds International, spoke to the girls about the father heart of God. He told the story of Jesus healing the woman with the issue of blood and pointed out that Jesus called her "daughter." He spoke about God's love for these girls and his affirmation of each one of them.

Dwayne then brought his own daughters onto the stage and began to speak to them in front of the Indian girls. He told them how much he loves them, how beautiful they are and how proud he is of each of their unique personalities and giftings. These Indian girls had never heard anyone say these things, much less their own father. We could tell that the Holy Spirit was moving deeply in their hearts.

When Dwayne finished, we waited to see what the Holy Spirit wanted to do. In the silence, we could hear quiet weeping from several places in the room. After a few minutes, a leader in the denomination stood and addressed the girls. He affirmed what Dwayne had said and began to pray for the girls.

In mid-sentence, the man stopped and said, "Girls, you need to know that it is okay for you to weep. Go ahead." When this permission was given, it was as though a dam had been released. Weeping broke out all over the room. It soon became wailing, as years of pent-up pain and anguish of soul came pouring out at the feet of Jesus.

Dwayne instructed several of us ministers to move to the front to be available to pray for the girls one at a time. He gave us instructions to say to them three things from the Father: "I love you, I'm proud of you, and my heart is filled with joy every time I look at you." He told us not to take a long time praying for each one, as there were two hundred of them, and they would surely all desire prayer. We did not have long, but he wanted to be sure that each one of them at least heard these three affirmations.

The girls lined up, and I began praying over them one at a time, being careful to include the three things Dwayne had instructed us to deliver. As I went to lay hands upon the shoulders of the girl in front of me, I heard the Holy Spirit say, "Look at her." I paused. "Look at her." Her head was bowed, so I took her chin and raised her eyes up to mine. They were dark and beautiful.

Suddenly, my heart was overwhelmed with compassion and my eyes were full of tears. I knew what I was to pray and how to pray it. I put my arms around her and began to whisper in her ear the precious words from God: "I love you. I am so proud of you. I want you to know how beautiful you are to me." Her knees buckled, and she began to sob, as the beautiful grace of God began to wash away her pain. Similar things were happening all around the room, as God brought a deep, healing work to this new generation of leaders.

Again and again all throughout the Gospels, we see Jesus modeling this kind of ministry for us. He looked at the multitude, his heart was moved with compassion and then he fed them. He looked at the sick, his heart was moved with compassion and then he healed them. He looked at the multitude, his heart was moved with compassion and then he sent his disciples—us—out into the harvest fields.[14]

Antoine de Saint-Exupéry once said,

> Love does not consist in gazing at each other, but in looking outward together in the same direction.[15]

Jesus is calling us, in intimacy with him, to look. Look at the poor, the sick, the needy, the marginalized, and join him in the tender heart of God. Jesus wants a bride who will walk with him among the poor and needy, touch the lepers, feed the hungry, care for the those in need— and thus bring to earth the very kingdom of God itself! Proverbs 31 is the description of the perfect bride:

> She extends her hand to the poor, Yes, she reaches out her hands to the needy.[16]

Faith without works is dead.
James 2:20

---

14. Matthew 15:32; 14:14; 20:34; Mark 1:41; Matthew 9:36.
15. As quoted in *Beyond the Veil* by Alice Smith (Regal Books, 1996) p. 131.
16. Proverbs 31:20.

CHAPTER 17
Out on a Limb

Why not go out on a limb? Isn't that where the fruit is?

Frank Scully

I first came to know my friend Rikki shortly before her marriage to Tom. We lived with them in a church-owned house, as we all served on the church staff together. Rikki had dreamed her whole life of becoming a wife and mother. She had no other goals, no other ambitions, but to have some children and enjoy raising them. So Tom and Rikki began trying to have a baby shortly after they were married. But before too long, it became apparent that reaching her goal was not going to be an easy task.

Other young women around Rikki—her friends—began to declare their own news of a baby on the way, unintentionally inflicting pain with each announcement. As often is the case when you desperately desire something, it seemed that everyone around her was getting her heart's desire, while month after month, she was left more and more depressed.

Rikki attended the baby showers of her friends, trying to smile and rejoice with their blessings. Then she'd quickly return to the privacy of her bedroom, where she unleashed her pain, sobbing out her questions to God there on her bed. She could not understand why he would withhold from her this one desire. It was a good desire, a godly desire. Why had he chosen her to experience this trial?

But rather than retreat into her pain and anguish, I watched as Rikki poured out her anguish in vulnerable, Mary-of-Bethany-type intimacy with Jesus, and there she made a choice. God showed her, through observing another barren woman's demeanor, that she could live in either bitterness or acceptance of her circumstances. She very clearly could see in the lines of this other woman's face, in her relationships with others, that a life of bitterness was not the path she wanted to take. So Rikki surrendered to Jesus, in acceptance of his will for her life, no matter how painful it might be.

Surrender did not mean that her desire disappeared, and nearly daily she had to die to her dreams, making the decision to accept whatever Jesus had for her. I watched my friend, again and again, lay her hopes and dreams for children on the altar.

A group of our friends began praying on Sunday evenings in our living room. Some of my most precious memories were formed in the special times we had together as we worshipped, prayed and ministered to one another, sometimes late into the night. Some evenings, one or another of those friends would share a message that God had laid upon his or her heart. We enjoyed the simplicity of fellowship in God's Spirit.

During one of these gatherings, Kris, a very quiet, reserved friend of ours, felt that God was stirring her to pray for Rikki that God might give her a baby. Kris approached Lucretia, another friend of ours, and whispered this desire into her ear. Lucretia told her to just go ahead, but Kris said, "No, I have to be loud...."

Lucretia and Kris grabbed me and we went to get Rikki. She had been sitting on the floor for some time, so when she tried to stand, her legs crumpled beneath her. They had completely fallen asleep. So the three of us took Rikki by the arms and practically carried her back to our laundry room, where we would be able to pray without disturbing the meeting that was continuing in the living room. Much like the men who brought their paralyzed friend on a mat to Jesus, we brought Rikki to him.

That little laundry room became an "upper room" that night, as we felt the Holy Spirit's presence descend upon us, leading us to pray. Typically quiet and shy Kris became a shouting prayer warrior, as she pled with God to give Rikki a baby. The Holy Spirit led us to the story of Mary and her simple faith, as she simply accepted God's will for her life, and we affirmed the fruit of character that we saw so clearly in

Rikki's life—in her surrender to him, in her patience, in her kindness to others who had received her heart's desire.

Then Kris, anointed by the Holy Spirit, began to shout all the more. She was filled with faith and believed without a shadow of doubt that God was going to give Rikki a baby. The four of us sobbed with joy, as our hearts soared with the gift of faith that God was giving to us all. Rikki raised her hands in worship and began to sing her praises, just like young Mary who had received the promise of child:

> I bow my knee. I bow my heart.
> I bow my life before Your throne.
> I lift my hands. I lift my eyes.
> I lift my voice to You in song.
>
> O mighty King, almighty King.
> I pledge my loyalty to Your highest royalty.
> O mighty King, almighty King.
> I surrender all of me to Your full authority.
> Almighty King.[1]

When we emerged from that laundry room, the four of us were floating with excitement about what God had just done. We quietly crept back into the living room, where David Smithers was sharing a message with the group. As we seated ourselves again on the floor, we looked at one another in amazement. David was preaching straight from the story of Mary, talking about her acceptance of God's will and her willingness to become the vessel that would deliver the manifest presence of God to earth! How could we doubt God's word to us now?

Faith Rollercoasters

Over the next months, we waited for the news from Rikki. We decided to pray for her and Tom at every weekly gathering. The ladies in our group also began to meet weekly for a women's prayer time, and Rikki's need became a regular topic there as well. Many Scriptures were given as promises from the Lord. Many prayers were prayed, as the Holy Spirit led us to hold Rikki up before him.

1. McGuire, Dony and Reba Rambo. "Almighty King." (New Kingdom Music, 1984–1985).

Not only did months pass, but years. I watched Rikki ride the rollercoaster of faith, and took many rides with her myself. Some days we'd be sure we had heard another confirmation from the Lord, and other days we thought that perhaps we had made up the whole experience. Kris's faith never waned, however. She had heard God so clearly in that laundry room that she was a rock of faith whenever Rikki doubted.

Each time we heard from God, we recognized the fruit that he gave — fruit of encouragement, peace, joy, hope and faith. Even though Rikki had not yet seen the answer to her prayers, her heart overflowed with gratitude — gratitude that God had spoken, gratitude that he saw her and knew her, that he knew her greatest desire and her greatest wound. Many times those prayer meetings turned into a precious time of worship, as we thanked God for all that he was doing for Rikki.

One such confirmation came when we took a group of missionary students to a prayer conference in Colorado. During one of the main sessions, the speaker asked for all the barren women in the audience to stand. He felt that God was prompting him to pray that their wombs would be opened. Besides Rikki, there were several other women who stood and received prayer. Once again, Rikki raised her hands in simple surrender to God's plan for her life.

When that service was over, she began to gather her purse and Bible, and she noticed at her feet an envelope that someone had dropped. She picked it up and began asking those seated around her if it might be theirs. No one claimed it, so she opened it, thinking she might be able to discover whose it was. Inside was a baby dedication card.

Startled, Rikki examined the card carefully. There was no handwriting on it. No name. Instead, she found that several of the verses that God had given to her as promises — her verses — were there inside this card. She looked closely and discovered that the publication date on the card was the exact date of her own birth. This card was for her!

We all encouraged Tom and Rikki to hurry away to the hotel to take advantage of God's anointing! We were sure that they would be pregnant the very next day!

However, more years passed. One summer, Rikki accompanied me on a trip to Taiwan. While we were there, the Chinese ladies we met asked her why she did not have any children. They felt sad and compassionate toward her when they learned that she and Tom had been married for several years. They began to encourage her to come to Taiwan for in vitro fertilization. It was much cheaper there, and they were sure she could get pregnant.

Rikki felt that God was prompting her to share her story with a woman named Rongro. Rongro is one of the sisters in the family who owned the *bing* shop (who rescued me from the spiderhouse). Over the years, she and I'd had many conversations about Jesus, but Rongro and her family still did not believe. They were idol worshipers.

What if God did not come through? What if we had all made a mistake? What if we had just wished our own desires to be true and made them God's promises? How could Rikki be sure? But she could not escape the conviction that she was to testify to Rongro.

In the setting of a beautiful little teashop, Rikki told Rongro the history of God's promises to her. She explained that she would not be using in vitro fertilization because she believed that God had told her he would give her a baby. Tears began to fill Rongro's eyes as she saw the intensity of Rikki's faith.

As Rikki finished her story, another woman who was drinking tea with us pointed out the wall hangings all around us. Each one of them was a promise from the Bible! This was not a Christian teashop. The owners merely thought the blessings were neat. With the red lights of idol shelves glowing from the windows of every home around us, somehow we had ended up in a teashop that was decorated with Scripture!

Again, years went by and still no baby. Another opportunity came for Tom and Rikki to visit Taiwan with us, and as the time for the trip drew near, Rikki's anxiety grew. Would Rongro remember her story? She still did not have a baby. What could she say?

Risky Faith
Just as she feared, at the first opportunity, Rongro asked Rikki about her baby. Before Rikki could come up with an answer, Tom quickly

responded, "I believe that God is going to give us a baby before this year is over." Rikki was shocked! Oh, no, Tom! Now he had put a timetable on God. If Rikki had learned anything over these last few years, it was that you could not tell God the best time. There had been many times that she had thought the timing was perfect, only to be disappointed. What was Tom thinking?

Later that year, Rongro and her family made a trip to America. They wanted to visit us and to do some sightseeing. We picked them up in California and decided to make the long drive to our home in Oklahoma so that they could see some of the beauty of our country. Coming from a crowded little island, they could not believe the vast, open territories where nobody lived! It was fun to see their response to American hotels, wide highways and fast food. They couldn't believe the all-you-can-drink soda pop!

While we were on our way to Oklahoma with Rongro, Rikki was driving home to the HGM campus and received a call on her cell phone. It was her doctor. He had taken a blood sample from her earlier in the week, and he was calling to say that the tests had come back positive! Rikki was pregnant! She immediately called Tom, who said, "Don't tell anybody until I get there!"

Many of the ladies who had prayed for Rikki all these years, including Kris, who had originally heard the promise from the Lord, were gathering that day with their children to do a work project at HGM. Rikki knew that some of them would already be there when she arrived. How could she keep it a secret from them? How could she keep her secret from showing on her face?

As Rikki had expected, Lucretia was there when she pulled in at HGM, so after she had gathered herself, she got out of the car to greet her friend. Just then, in a cloud of dust, Tom came racing up the drive. He jumped out of the car and ran over to where the two women stood. Lucretia said, "What? What's going on?" Then she took one look at Rikki's face, and she began to shout at the top of her lungs. She began jumping up and down, twirling, laughing and crying all at the same time.

Kris and the other women began arriving, and the news quickly spread.
Then, in the most miraculous of timing, just as the celebration was
breaking out, we arrived with Rongro and her family. As Rongro got
out of the car, Rikki ran down the drive to meet her with the news.
Jesus had given her a baby. The news had come just that hour—just for
Rongro—to prove his existence and his love for her! After nine years of
waiting, his timing was perfect.

> I give my praise. I give my love.
> I give my soul and vow to serve.
> I'll take Thy Word. I'll take Thy will.
> I'll take Thy Name to all the earth.
>
> O mighty King, almighty King
> I pledge my loyalty to the highest royalty.
> O mighty King, almighty King
> I surrender all of me to Thy full authority.
> Almighty King.[2]

Lest I Die

The Old Testament tells the story of several barren women. In fact, the
first three generations of our faith were barren until God performed a
miracle on their behalf. Sarah finally conceived Isaac when she was
long past childbearing age. Isaac prayed for Rebekah and God opened
her womb. After watching Leah, her sister, bear several children for
Jacob, God blessed Rachel with children of her own.[3]

For each of these women, barrenness was a humiliation, a reproach.
In Jewish culture, bearing children was part of a woman's purpose,
her identity. The commission to be "fruitful" had been successfully
passed down from the first time God gave it to Adam and Eve. It was a
woman's aim to be married and give children to her husband.

Hannah was so distraught at her own barrenness that she could not eat.
Her husband, Elkanah, who loved her dearly, became worried for her

---

2. McGuire, Dony and Reba Rambo. "Almighty King." (New Kingdom Music,
1984–1985).
3. Sarah—Genesis 21:1, 2; Rebekah—Genesis 25:21; Rachel—Genesis 30:22.

and tried to comfort her by asking, "Isn't my love for you enough to satisfy?" Really, he said, "Am I not better to you than ten sons?"[4]

The passion that led these Old Testament women to pray, "Give me children, lest I die," is somewhat foreign to most Christians in America. In fact, Christian couples in America are averaging 1.2 children per household. By choice, we are not even breaking even in reproducing ourselves, so it is difficult for us to relate to the desperation that these women felt.

Similarly, it is often difficult for us to experience the desperation of spiritual barrenness. Is it enough for you to be called a Christian? Perhaps you prayed a sinner's prayer some years ago. Perhaps you go to church regularly and give your tithe. Maybe you have learned to resist the temptation to participate in worldly pleasures. But are you bearing fruit? Do you have any children in the kingdom of God?

Intimacy with Jesus should equal having his heart. If our heart does not burn with a passion for souls, then we do not have the heart of God. David Smithers wrote:

> The Church has been sanctified and set apart for holy union with Jesus Christ. A primary purpose of this intimate union is the reproduction of Christ-like character in our individual lives and the lives of others around us. The Father longs for Christ to bring forth fruit through us, the Bride of Christ. He desires for heirs who bear His Name unto His glory. We have been both created and commanded to reproduce after our own kind.[5]

I have heard many arguments and justifications for lack of fruit over the years. Many of them have come from my own heart:

> "My calling is to minister to the Church—the Bride."

> But the Good Shepherd leaves the ninety-nine and goes after the one lost sheep.

---

4. 1 Samuel 1:8.

5. You can listen to David Smithers' sermon, "Barrenness," online at www.sermonindex. net.

"My focus is on mobilizing others to become missionaries."

But God is not willing that any should perish.

"My gifting is worship leading."

But he desires worship from every tongue, tribe and nation.

If we think that we know Jesus, and yet our heart, our mind, our energy, our money does not run after those who do not know him—many of whom have never even heard of him—then we do not truly know him. We are those who say, "Lord, Lord...."

Hannah was not satisfied even with intimate relationship with her husband. She wanted children! If we find that we are spiritually barren—we have no spiritual children that we have birthed into the kingdom of God—then our heart cry should be the same as these women of the Old Testament: "Give me children, lest I die!" We should beg God to do whatever it takes in us, in our character, in our schedule, in our location, even in our personality, to make us spiritually fertile!

Grandchildren

I was on a journey through China with three of our missionaries. They had been studying Mandarin in Taiwan and were nearing the time when they would be ready to transition to working among an unreached people group in China. John and I agreed to accompany them on an exploratory, fact-finding and prayer-walking tour of several unreached groups.

In late November, we ventured into a Tibetan region where there is a monastery that serves as a pilgrimage site to thousands of nomadic Amdo Tibetans who live out on the grasslands. Once a year, they bring their herds of goats and sheep to town to trade, and they stay, paying homage to the gods in the monastery until their money is spent.

Although strikingly beautiful, most of Amdo Tibetans were absolutely filthy. We were told that many of these nomads only bathe three times in their entire life—once when they are born, once when they get married, and then their body is washed after they die. I believe I discovered the reason why they bathe so infrequently. It is freezing cold there up in the ten-thousand-foot altitude! I had seven layers of clothing on and hot water bottles in my pockets, and I was still cold! No one wants to take off their clothes to take a bath!

As our group of five stood outside our hotel building, we watched long-haired, wild-eyed men come riding into town on yaks. They carried long knives in their belts, and upon seeing us foreigners, they stuck out their tongues at us! So we, in turn, stuck out ours at them! This is their greeting. They believe that if a person has a demon, his tongue will be black. They were showing us that their tongues were pink—they were safe—and they wanted to see our tongues in return.

The women were dressed in brightly-colored layers of wool clothing and wove thick ribbons in their black braids. Many of them had on heavy jewelry made of colored stones. Their cheeks were always bright red, some of them even appearing bruised by the cold and high altitude. Most of the girls smiled brightly at us and giggled among themselves.

King of Hell
There is much about Tibetan Buddhism in the news these days, and many in Hollywood have brought attention to the plight of its adherents, as the Chinese government has oppressed and, in some locations, even eliminated their culture. The impression one might get from Hollywood is that Tibetan Buddhism is a peaceful, meditative religion that brings happiness and enlightenment to its followers.

I went into this monastery and observed the worship of the main god, Yama, who is called "the king of hell." He looks very much like a monster in a nightmare, with hair made of human skulls, three eyes in his forehead, teeth like fangs and humans in his mouth. Blood is dripping off of his chin as he chews on his followers.

Yama's clothes are made from human skins, and their skulls make up his belt. Underneath his feet are worshippers who have their hands raised, begging for mercy, but Yama is crushing the life out of them. If his physical description weren't enough, every depiction we saw of him, whether in a carving or a painting, Yama was either raping a woman or forcing a bull to rape a woman.

At the heart of Tibetan Buddhism is an ancient shamanistic and animistic religion called Bon. It is demonically dark and mirrors the violence and perversity found in Aztec and Mayan cultures in the west, including demon worship and human sacrifice.

The average life expectancy of an Amdo Tibetan is forty-five years old. Life is hard on these nomads. The altitude takes its toll on their bodies. Their diet is often lacking in nutrition. They are not trained in clean sanitation, and the cold often leaves them frostbitten and exhausted.

The Tibetan religion itself contributes to their fatigue, as they are required to fulfill many rites and rituals to gain merit, in hopes of being reincarnated into a better life after they die. Most of these nomads are illiterate, yet they are required to read the Buddhist scriptures. We saw many of them taking a two-kilometer hike around the monastery, spinning large and small prayer wheels that contain the written scriptures inside. Each time they spin a wheel, they receive the merit of having read that portion of scripture.

Some of these pilgrims would take a few steps, kneel down, and then lay down flat, putting their foreheads to the ground, then go back to kneeling again, and then stand to take a few steps and do it all again. We asked a guide why some of them were prostrating themselves this way, and she told us that these pilgrims were trying to receive forgiveness for their sins. They must do one hundred thousand prostrations in order to be forgiven for one sin—and this must be done within four months' time. However, there is no guarantee that they will receive forgiveness because Yama is not a god of mercy. They can only hope that their rituals will earn his favor and give them a better life in their next cycle.

The first day that we were in this town, I fell in love with these precious people. Their bright smiles with golden teeth, their embarrassed giggles and their bright red cheeks—oh, their cheeks. I wanted so badly to reach out and touch those beautiful cheeks. Of course, I did not know how culturally appropriate that would be, and those men had such long knives on their belts…

As we were going to bed, I couldn't stop thinking about those beautiful cheeks. I was surprised by my desire to touch them because I am not usually a very physically affectionate personality. This desire made me wonder if the Lord might be doing something in my heart. I laid out my "fleece," and asked Jesus: "If this desire is really from you, will you give me a clear opportunity? If you give me the chance to touch their cheeks, I will take it."

Youth Group

Early the next morning, our group again began to walk around the monastery. We spent the morning praying that God's kingdom would come to this place, that one day the name of Yama would no longer be remembered and that the worship of Jesus would reign.

Walking and praying quietly, our group spread out, and I found myself alone. I sat down on some steps to watch and pray for the pilgrims. A few minutes later, a group of about twenty Tibetan young people started up the hill toward the monastery. They were dressed in bright colors, chattering loudly, pushing and shoving one another—generally having a good time, like young people do together.

As they passed the steps where I was sitting, they noticed me there, and suddenly the whole group ran directly toward me! My first emotion was fear, as I again took note of those long knives. But as they came closer to me, I could see that they were all smiling. They were yelling greetings at me in Tibetan.

When they came to the steps, they all sat down around me—the girls on my left and the boys on my right. The girl on my left took my arm and put hers through mine, snuggling up close to me. The boy on my right put his arm around my shoulder! He looked to be about sixteen years old. Besides the gold on his front teeth, he wore giant earrings in his ears and kept pointing to them and chattering a hundred miles an hour to me in Tibetan. I could not understand a thing!

Girls came close and sat at my feet. They began pointing at the bright ribbons in their dark black hair and touching my very different brown hair, also chattering in Tibetan that I could not understand. I looked at their shiny hair. I looked at their dark eyes and their beautiful red cheeks, and my heart was overwhelmed with compassion. Here was my opportunity!

No one—no Christian—had ever prayed for *these* young people before. I laid my hands on them, one at a time, and prayed that each would come to know Jesus! I took their lovely cheeks in my hands and held their faces up to mine and prayed that someone would come here, would learn their culture and take the time to learn their language, so that they would hear of the God who loves them, who wants to rescue them from the oppression of Yama, the king of hell!

I touched them, every one that was within my reach. They continued to talk and point at my cheeks as tears poured down my face. How God's heart aches for these precious Tibetans to know of his saving love for them! I couldn't communicate anything to them, only my smiles and my touches, which I hoped told them that I loved them with all my heart.

After they sat with me for about ten minutes, they all got up and waved to me as they headed back down the hill away from the monastery. I sat there for a few moments, stunned by the experience that God had just allowed me to have. I knew that I had somehow entered into his heart for these who had never heard of Jesus.

In my mind, I looked back over my life, reflecting on the plans I had made for myself. If I had decided to pursue my own dreams, I would have become a music teacher in some small town in Washington State. That was as big as I could dream. It would have been a fine life—maybe even God's life—for someone else. But God had much bigger dreams for me. I could never have even imagined what I had just experienced.

Remembering the size of my fears (those giant spiders!) I knew that if I had made the decisions for my life, my fears would have cornered me into an existence that was the size of those fears—a spider-sized life—instead of the whole-world-sized life that God had planned for me.

I can testify to you that when you are standing on this side of the line, deciding whether to step over into complete surrender to God, the future is a terrifying prospect. I know. My knuckles were white as I gripped that pew. However, I want you to know that the blessings of life on the other side of that line are beyond anything you could have ever dreamed.

As I sat there contemplating it all, I heard the Holy Spirit speak to my heart: "You will have grandchildren among the Tibetans." I knew that he was encouraging me to continue in the calling that he had given to me. If I could choose any place to be on the earth, I would live among the beautiful Amdo Tibetan nomads. I would be freezing cold! But they are burned deep into my heart.

God does not have John and I overseas in this season of our life. He has called us to train others, to multiply ourselves. We are aiming at a goal of training six hundred lifetime (long-term) missionaries through our program called Beautiful Feet Boot Camp. Perhaps then he will allow us to go ourselves. So as I watched those Tibetan teenagers walk away, I knew that God was encouraging me that some of those who we have trained would go to these precious people, and that there would be Tibetans who come into the kingdom of God because of them—and that I can claim them as my grandchildren—my fruit!

Ask of Me and I will give You the nations for Your inheritance. Psalm 2:8.

CHAPTER 18

Giant Grapes

When we understand His character, we find ourselves willing, ready and longing to go...on the greatest adventure ever made possible to man—TO KNOW GOD AND TO MAKE HIM KNOWN.

Joy Dawson

Both of my sisters and their families had come to Oklahoma, and we were all together with my parents for Christmas—a rare occasion, as we're often spread all over the earth. The pastor at my parents' church was offering special individual communion services for the season, and we signed our family up to celebrate Jesus' birth by taking communion together.

As we all knelt at the altar—my parents, my sisters, their husbands and the eleven grandchildren—the pastor asked each of us to say something that we were thankful to God for this Christmas. The answers went down the line, as each parent or child expressed their gratitude during this season.

When it came time for Dad to give his answer, he said, "My three girls. If I had known they all would grow up to serve the Lord, I would have had many more children." My mother let out a little gasp and began to weep. I knew that she had desired to have more children, but Dad had told her three was enough. She must have been sad to hear that now he too wished he had let her have more.

John and I had three children then and had talked many times about whether or not we should have any more. We weren't sensing any clear leading from the Lord, and I had not been experiencing that feeling rise up in me when I held other people's babies.

Each time I thought about having another baby, I couldn't help but sigh. The morning sickness, the sleepless nights with a giant belly, the long labor, the colicky crying in the night, the inconvenience of constant nursing. Having a baby was so much work, and I was beginning to enjoy the freedoms that came with my children becoming more independent.

That spring, I read a book called *The Marechale*. It is about Katie Booth, a daughter of William and Catherine Booth, founders of the Salvation Army. In 1880, at the age of twenty-two, she went as a missionary to France. In relating the difficulties she experienced on the mission field and the corresponding result of people who came to know Jesus, she stated a principle: There is no fruit without sacrifice.

Shortly after finishing this book, I read the autobiography of Rosalind Goforth called *Climbing*. She and her husband, Jonathan, had eleven children while missionaries in China from 1888-1935. They lost five of them on the mission field. She tells of the trials they experienced—sicknesses and deaths, communists beating and chasing them out of the country—and the fruit of widespread revival that came to the Chinese during their ministry there. In her book, she points out the principle found in 2 Corinthians 9:6:

> He who sows sparingly will also reap sparingly, and he who sows bountifully will also reap bountifully.

Two of my friends have brought many people into the kingdom of God. For many years, I had just thought that perhaps it was because they were particularly gifted as evangelists. They would often strike up conversations with strangers and end up leading them to the Lord.

My personality was very different. I was shy, socially backward and generally very task oriented. When I went to the store, I went there to buy my groceries, not to visit with the checkout lady. I had used these personality traits to justify the fact that I did not bear as much fruit as they did. However, the Holy Spirit began convicting me that it really had nothing to do with personality. It was a matter of percentages.

These two friends of mine were "sowing" all the time. Naturally, they would have more fruit. I began to wonder if God might even be able to change my personality.

How Many Children?

John and I take every class of Boot Camp students to Mexico to put into practice all that they have been learning. That year, as I was processing this idea of sowing and reaping, Raul Gomez, the pastor of the local church that helps us with this immersion phase, came to us when we arrived with the students and announced that he believed that God wanted us to help him start another Boot Camp there in Mexico. This one would be for Spanish-speaking Christians who hear God calling them to go as missionaries to the unreached.

John did not give an immediate answer, but told Raul that he would pray about it. That was a Saturday evening. John did not sleep all night. I remember getting up several times in the night to find him sitting in the chair in the living room, thinking and wrestling in prayer.

The next morning he told me, "Jamie, I don't know if I want to do this all over again." He was remembering all the effort that went into starting our first Boot Camp class—the hours of preparing curriculum, finding teachers, scheduling classes, recruiting students. And this time it would all have to be done in Spanish—a language that neither of us speaks well!

We joined the worship service that Sunday morning with a heavy heart. Our friends in this Mexican church love to worship God. They sing loudly at the top of their voices, clap and raise their hands, and nearly raise the roof. But John and I were preoccupied with our thoughts and, honestly, a bit distracted, even though the crowd around us was enjoying their raucous praise.

Suddenly, I heard the Holy Spirit say to me, "You can have as much fruit as you want—as you are willing to sacrifice for." I quickly reached for something to write this down, as I knew John would never be able to hear me if I tried to whisper it in his ear. All I could find was a gum wrapper. I wrote it down and passed it to him.

I knew that God was challenging us with a question. *How much fruit do you want?* This was not a salvation question. It was not even a question of obedience. He was not commanding us to do anything. He was giving us the choice. We could have more fruit in the kingdom of God, if we were willing to make the sacrifice. We could choose to bear thirty-, sixty- or even one-hundred-fold![1] It was up to us.

I thought about my dad's comment the Christmas before. If only he had known.... What if many more could come to the saving knowledge of Jesus? Would we be willing?

We decided to have both another spiritual baby, the Mexican Boot Camp, as well as another physical baby! I still carry that gum wrapper in my Bible next to Psalm 127:

> Behold, children are a heritage from the Lord. The fruit of the womb is a reward. Like arrows in the hand of a warrior, so are the children of one's youth. Happy is the man who has his quiver full of them; they shall not be ashamed, but shall speak with their enemies in the gate.[2]

Dreams

Kelly came to Boot Camp not sure where she was going. She knew that God had called her to be a missionary. There was no mistaking that. She had left college with confirmation from her parents to come to training. She entered Boot Camp with a good friend of hers, a handsome young man, who she secretly hoped might become her husband. He, too, was sure of his calling and was headed to China.

Kelly longed to be married. It was the deepest desire of her heart, and she feared that if she went to the mission field unmarried she might never find a husband. She began to believe that God was telling her that this young man was the one for her. She had a number of confirmations from godly counselors, as well as Scripture and personal experiences in prayer.

---

1. Matthew 13:23.
2. Psalm 127:3–5.

Upon graduation, they both joined a church-planting team that was heading to Taiwan to begin Mandarin language study. The team was to meet up in Los Angeles and fly together to Asia from there. There was bad weather in Denver, and some of the team were unable to make their connection to L.A. Kelly boarded the plane alone. Her greatest fear, that of going to the mission field alone, seemed to stare her right in the face.

As she took her seat, it became apparent that no one would be sitting next to her. Even worse, she was most certainly completely alone, headed off to the other side of the world, without a mate, and without anyone to even accompany her. But then the Holy Spirit began to speak to her heart: "I am in this seat next to you. You are not alone. I am your husband. We will go together." Once again, Kelly surrendered to God's call upon her life.

During her time in Taiwan, she dreamed of the day this young man would realize that he was madly in love with her. She was convinced that one day they would be married and enter China together as a couple. So it was a devastating blow when he announced that he was in love with another girl and had asked her to marry him. He had not chosen Kelly.

Kelly nearly self-destructed. John and I were with her in Taiwan as she tried to process her confusion, anger and grief. I think that Kelly would agree that insanity did not seem very far away. Doubt ruled supreme. Everything was up for question. If she had heard God wrong on this issue, what else had she heard incorrectly? Perhaps she had merely followed this young man to the mission field. Maybe God hadn't called her after all. Was there even really a God who loved her at all?

John and I prayed with her and gave her counsel, but nothing seemed to bring her any comfort. We were at a loss to know how to help her. This was a private, personal battle that Kelly had to win. We knew that if we sent her home, the likelihood that she would ever return to the mission field was slim to none. We did not want to see her derail God's plan for her life, so we began to desperately seek God for a plan to rescue her.

During our morning quiet time, John was lying in the bathtub (in cool water—Taiwan is hot!) and I was sitting in our living room at the base.

Both of us agreed to ask God to give us an alternative. Kelly could not stay where she was. She would have to daily interact with this young man and his new fiancée. That was impossible. And we didn't want to send her home. Surely there must be another way.

When we came together, God had spoken the same idea to both of us separately. We were to send Kelly to the other side of the island to an orphanage for a few months. There, a wonderful older couple who ran the orphanage would care for her soul and put her to work at the same time. Perhaps she would come out of her cycle of depression as she loved and cared for babies around the clock.

God's plans are always the best. Kelly received our counsel, and slowly but surely, he began to bring healing to her heart. Once again, she surrendered to God's plan for her life—even if it meant that she would be single. She would follow him.

Kelly was with us on that exploratory journey through China, when I first experienced God's heart for the Amdo, and she, too, fell in love with a half-blind old Tibetan woman who would not let go of her hand. She was determined to take the gospel to these precious people who only know the worship of Yama, the king of hell.

Boy Meets Girl

Kelly's grandfather was very ill, so she returned to the States to see him before he died. While she was home, John asked her to come and share with the current Boot Camp class some of the experiences she'd had on the mission field and some of the things God had taught her.

In that class of missionary students was a young man who had grown up on the border of Texas and Mexico. He had a desire to go to Tibet. As Kelly talked about her experiences with the Tibetans and her plans to move into China, Josh's heart began to soar. Here was a woman who was already out there ahead of him. She was doing what he wanted to be doing—studying the language, learning the culture, living in difficult conditions—and was called to the people who were also on his heart.

Later, Kelly told us that when Josh would raise his hand to ask a question, she would think to herself, *Oh, he is so cute. Don't even look*

at him It's me and Jesus; I've already settled this issue! She would
answer without even looking his direction.

Josh and Kelly spent a total of six hours together that day, always
with the whole group of students, eating a meal, asking questions,
fellowshipping together. Then she went back to Taiwan.

Soon after they met, Josh came to John and I to inform us that he
thought God would have him marry Kelly. We have a "no-dating
policy" during Boot Camp to try to help the students focus on their
studies. But, in all honesty, what can you do? Pre-field training is a
hotbed of missionary romance! These are all passionate people headed
out to the ends of the earth!

John asked Josh to try to focus and wait until the end of Boot Camp to
pursue this question about Kelly further. So over the next few months,
they communicated by email and internet chat, as friends, getting
to know one another. By the time Boot Camp was over, Josh was
convinced.

Now, this was not a naturally easy match. Kelly's father was a Southern
Baptist pastor. Josh's family was energetically Pentecostal. During their
first meeting, Josh asked Kelly's dad what he thought about casting
out demons! Josh's family is of Hispanic origin and grew up along the
southern border of Texas; Kelly is white and from the Midwest.

However, when Josh asked Kelly's parents for her hand in marriage,
they—being godly people—earnestly sought God's will. They were
convinced God was putting these two together. Josh's parents felt
the same thing. Josh also asked Kelly's team leaders on the field to pray
with him about it. They, too, were certain God was creating a match
made in heaven.

Josh asked Kelly to marry him and they spent one month together
before their wedding. Then, after six weeks of honeymoon and rest,
they returned to Taiwan for Josh to learn Mandarin.

Happily Ever After
Josh and Kelly are now living among the Amdo Tibetan people. Their
life there has not been an easy one. The winters are cold. The food took

some getting used to. Kelly is a very social person, and for two years, she was the only woman on their team. She was terribly lonely.

During pregnancy, Kelly was ill with dysentery and became extremely dehydrated. She called from China on Christmas Eve, asking for prayer. She and the baby both improved.

They had their first baby, and he began to show signs of health problems. He was not growing. He would not gain weight and his heart showed signs of stress. For a couple of months, Kelly feared that she, like Rosalind Goforth, might lose a child in China. Doctors finally determined that the altitude was preventing him from growing and recommended that they move at least a few hundred feet lower in the mountains. God directed them to a new location and the baby began to improve immediately.

Josh and Kelly have experienced spiritual warfare like nothing we see here in the States. Demon possession as Jesus encountered in the New Testament is commonplace. Nightmares and apparitions have plagued them at times, to be fought off only by intense seasons of fasting and prayer.

Despite all of this, Kelly felt that God was calling her to deliver her second baby in China. She recommends that no one do it unless they know that God is calling them to. It was a very frightening experience, as the hospital was not even sanitary, much less equipped with modern technology in case of an emergency. But Kelly felt that God wanted her Tibetan friends to see that she was willing to live with them, like them, not running away to the safety of America when they do not have that option.

Josh and Kelly now have three little ones, their third also born in China. This last Christmas, they received a gift to come home for a visit so their families could meet their newest baby. After spending just a few weeks in the States, they hurried back to their Tibetan friends and the ministry that needed their attention.

I want you to read in Kelly's own words what they found when they returned:

We arrived in our little village yesterday only to find things so much worse then we could have thought. Our house, while we were away, was completely taken over, infested, you name it, by rats and all their little mice buddies too. I am going to share details because we really want your prayers.

All of our beds (including the sweet baby crib with new bedding) were completely covered in rat droppings and little yellow spots (hmm…). Little Monkey was waiting for Baby Eli to return… Well, he became a casualty; his face was gone, leaving only cotton all over the bed. Not only did they get the monkey on the bed, along with the sheets, but they actually ate through the bassinet, leaving rat-sized holes. They ate through everything from clothes to food to blankets. Our house is covered with the markings of these nasty rodents.

Along with the Ratatouille episode, our pipes, which run heat through our house, busted, and the ceiling in our bathroom came down.

So how are we? Well, to be honest, yesterday, when we saw the place, began 4–5 hours of tears and feelings of being absolutely overwhelmed. Today, we are standing in the presence of Jesus and trusting in Him only. What I realized today as I woke up is the same realization we face all the time out here… We have a real enemy that hates that we have come in the name of King Jesus, savior of the people of Tibet. Some of you may have your own conclusions on what is going on out here, but for us it is black and white.

We write you not to say, "Please feel sorry for us," not to ask you to help us replace anything lost, but to realize that we are in a fight, and we need the Body to stand with us. Pray. Yes, we still feel pretty discouraged and a bit overwhelmed at times throughout the day as we are trying to figure out how to make the house livable again. Yesterday all I wanted to do was pack it up and head back to the States. (This is me, Kelly, not my husband's feelings.)

This morning I really woke up feeling the same way but a song came on by Rita Springer, which put everything in perspective for me. She simply sang, "I don't understand your ways, but I will give you my song, give you all of my praise....with it you are pulling me closer into your ways...the sight of your face is all that I am needing, it's gonna be worth it, gonna be worth it, gonna be worth it all...YOU are worth it, You are worth it all."[3] I asked myself as I listened, "Do you believe this? Is it gonna be worth it? He is either worth it or He is not." My answer was quickly, "I believe it and yes, You are worth it all."

Frankincense and Myrrh

In the beautiful romance of Song of Solomon, we find the bridegroom inviting his bride to go with him to the mountains. He tells her that he will go to the "mountain of myrrh" and the "hill of frankincense." At first reading, you might sigh. It sounds so romantic...until you recognize the symbolism of frankincense and myrrh.

Frankincense was used in temple sacrifice. God commanded that with every burnt offering, the Israelites must throw a handful of frankincense into the fire. This turned every offering into a sweet-smelling sacrifice of worship to God.

Myrrh was used as an embalming ointment. When a person died, the body was first anointed with myrrh and other fragrant spices to cover over the smell of death. Then it was wrapped in linen cloths.

Okay, not so romantic. Sacrifice and death. The bridegroom is being slightly morbid here!

Mountains also regularly symbolize something in the Scriptures. The high places, or mountains, were the location of highest worship. Throughout the Old Testament, we see the high places either being used for worship of the one true God or as a pagan location for idol worship. Josiah was a great and godly king, for not only did he remove the

3. Springer, Rita. "Worth it All" (Floodgate Records, 2007).

idols from God's holy temple, but he tore down the idols from every mountain in the nation.

Isaiah's declaration is reminiscent of the bridegroom's invitation:

> How beautiful upon the mountains are the feet of him who brings good news, who proclaims peace, who brings glad tidings of good things, who proclaims salvation, who says to Zion, "Your God reigns!"[4]

And then Paul echoes this in the form of an appeal for missionaries to take the gospel to those who have never heard:

> How then shall they call on Him in whom they have not believed? And how shall they believe in Him of whom they have not heard? And how shall they hear without a preacher? And how shall they preach unless they are sent? As it is written: "How beautiful are the feet of those who preach the gospel of peace, who bring glad tidings of good things!"[5]

Sacrifice and death is what it will require if we are to go to those dark locations where the worship of other gods has existed for thousands of years. In the midst of this most passionate of love stories lies a deeper understanding of relationship—a deeper understanding of *passion*.

One of the definitions of passion is: suffering. That is why we call the crucifixion scene in the Gospels the "passion of the Christ." Are we so passionate about Jesus that we are willing to run with him on these mountains? Are we so filled with a passion for souls that we are willing to suffer in order to see them brought into the kingdom of God?

Jesus said,

> When He had called the people to Himself, with His disciples also, He said to them, "Whoever desires to come after Me, let him deny himself, and take up his cross, and follow Me. For

---

4. Isaiah 52:7.
5. Romans 10:14–15.

whoever desires to save his life will lose it, but whoever loses
his life for My sake and the gospel's will save it."[6]

His disciples understood that he was calling them to become martyrs.
There was no other explanation for a cross. It was not a piece of
jewelry, as it is to us today. Rather, they knew that he was saying, if you
follow me, you will lose your life—and he was asking them to lose it
willingly.

J. Oswald Sanders speaks of this:

> Our Lord made it unequivocally clear that fruitfulness in
> service was inevitably linked with a cross: "Truly, truly, I say
> to you, unless a grain of wheat falls into the earth and dies,
> it remains by itself alone; but if it dies, it bears much fruit"
> (John 12:24). In that indisputable fact lies the explanation of
> the fruitfulness or unfruitfulness of our lives. To the extent in
> which the cross is operative in our lives, will we live again in
> other lives. Did not the one kernel of wheat that fell into the
> ground at Calvary live again in three thousand lives on the day
> of Pentecost?[7]

As I write this, I'm sitting on the campus of El Oasis, our Hispanic
missionary training school in Mexico. Tall green mountains paint a
picturesque backdrop, and in the foreground of this magnificent vista
is a tree. It is not an apple tree; it is a grapefruit tree. All around, on the
ground below it, lie deliciously ripe grapefruits that were so heavy they
no longer could resist gravity's pull, and the tree itself bows low under
the weight of dozens more that are waiting to be harvested.

The amount of fruit that comes from our lives is up to us. Remember
Peter exhorted us to make our call and election sure by entering into
the kingdom of God with an abundance of fruit.[8] We can *choose to*
bear a thirty-, sixty- or one-hundred-fold harvest from our lives.[9] When
the Israelites finally went into the promised land, they faced a host
of giants. It was a difficult fight, and they were willing to die. But in

---

6. Mark 8:34–35.
7. Sanders, J. Oswald. *Enjoying Intimacy With God* (Discovery House, 1980) p. 118.
8. 2 Peter 1:10–11.
9. Matthew 13:23.

the end, they inherited a land that consisted of milk, honey and *giant grapes*!

A Crown of Jewels

When John and I finally decided to have a fourth baby, the whole time I was pregnant, I was searching for a name for her. God had either directly told us or led us to the names of our first three children, and I fully expected him to give us a name for this one. The first three names all represented the season of our spiritual life that we'd been in—what it was that we'd been learning with him.

Jessi means "The Lord Exists," and she was born while we were discovering a living, active relationship with Jesus. Josiah came from the story of King Josiah, who destroyed the idols in Israel, bringing revival to God's people. He was born as we were understanding the need for the church to first surrender to Jesus as king, before they would even hear the call of the unreached. And I already told you the story of Jael's name.

The lesson of the season of my fourth pregnancy was that of sacrifice in order to bear more fruit, so I searched the baby name books for any name that might mean sacrifice or suffering. (Morbid, I know.) Fortunately, I found none. I then pondered the people in the Bible. Was there one who represented this lesson? (Of course, I was looking for "J" names, since we already had that pattern established.) Nothing stood out to me.

Sometime in the middle of that pregnancy, John and I took a trip to Taiwan to minister to our missionary team there. We spent time meeting with each one of them, listening to their questions and struggles, counseling and praying with them. We also took time to teach the team the latest lessons that God was laying upon our hearts.

As I was sharing my newfound understanding that we can have as much fruit as we are willing to sacrifice for, I was thinking of the baby in my womb. In mid-sentence, I heard the Holy Spirit speak to me. He said, "You are meditating on the wrong thing! You are not to meditate on the sacrifice, but on the reward that will be yours on the other side!"[10]

In *Hinds Feet On High Places*, one of my favorite books, a woman named Much Afraid journeys to the high places of surrender, maturity and intimacy with the Good Shepherd. Much like *Pilgrim's Progress*, I believe it is an anointed allegory that helps us understand the lifelong walk of following Jesus. In the end, the ugly little rocks that Much Afraid has gathered along the long and difficult way up the mountains—each of them representing an altar of surrender to the Good Shepherd—are turned into the very jewels that adorn her crown once she reaches her destination. Instantly, I knew this baby's name. She would be called Jewel—the reward for our suffering!

> "Except it fall into the ground and die..."
> Can "much fruit" come alone at such a cost?
> Must seed corn be buried in the earth,
> All summer joy and glory seemingly lost?
>
> "Except it fall into the ground and die..."
> But what a harvest in the days to come;
> When fields stand thick with golden sheaves of corn
> And you are sharing in the Harvest Home.
>
> To you who "lose your life," and let it die,
> Yet in the losing find your life anew,
> Christ evermore unveils His lovely face,
> And thus His mirrored glory rest on you.[11]

Kelly and Josh's life is not merely a life of pain and suffering. Yes, they have made the choice to sacrifice much for Jesus, but they also have big fruit—spiritual babies in the kingdom of God! I wish I could introduce you to my first Tibetan grandchild. His name is Wandee.

This is what Kelly was talking about. It is worth it! He is worth it! The precious Tibetan people who he loves with all his heart are worth it!

---

10. Hebrews 12:2.

11. Anonymous. As reprinted in *Enjoying Intimacy With God* by J. Oswald Sanders (Discovery House, 1980) p. 118.

Jesus said that he endured the cross for the joy that was set before him—the joy of people from every tongue, tribe and nation coming into intimate friendship with him—the fulfillment of his simple obsession.

> After this I saw a vast crowd, too great to count, from every nation and tribe and people and language, standing in front of the throne and before the Lamb. They were clothed in white and held palm branches in their hands.[12]

May the Lamb receive the reward of his suffering!

---

12. Revelation 7:9 (NLT).

EPILOGUE

As there really are no formulas in forming relationship, my intention
in writing this book is not to give you a particular list of how-to's.
However, I'd like to leave you with a few reminders of some practical
things that you can do to cultivate the development of your own simple
obsession.

Remember that Jesus is a person! Do the things that you
would do when trying to get to know a new person in your
life, or when trying to get to know someone better. Get to
know him as your friend, your father, your lover.

Spend time with Jesus. Set aside time regularly for just being
with him. Take a date night with him! Treasure your time with
him! It is not just a task you must accomplish in order to be
a good Christian. You are getting to know the one who loves
you deeply!

Read the Bible—especially the Gospels! Look at Jesus as
you read them. Look at how he interacts with people, how he
speaks to people, how he treats them. Learn what this amazing
person is really like!

Make sure that in your time with Jesus you take some time to
be quiet. Listen to him. Don't get frustrated if you don't hear
words. Pay attention to what you are feeling, what you are
sensing, impressions that come to mind, etc.

Have pen and paper ready (or your computer). Anticipate that
Jesus will speak to you, that he will share with you the things
that are in his heart. Return to Chapter 8 for more practical
suggestions like this about how to spend time with Jesus.

In your time with Jesus, be vulnerable. Remember that he
already knows the darkest parts of your heart. Talk to him

about them. He will meet you in the places of your deepest
need.

Be ready to obey anything Jesus shows you. As you develop
trust in your relationship with him, it will become easier and
easier to simply say "yes" to his plans, because you know that
he has your best interest in mind.

It is my hope for you that as you spend time with him, you will
discover how wonderful our amazing God truly is, that you will
experience his deep and tender affection for you, that your relationship
with him will become the most valuable thing you possess, and that as
your heart becomes one with his, you will reflect the affection that he
has for you and begin to love others the way that he loves you.

OTHER BOOKS BY HGM PUBLISHING

PASSION FOR THE HEART OF GOD:
MAKING HIS HEART COMPLETELY YOURS
John W. Zumwalt

"Today a revolution is needed; a revolution that needs to take place in the Church, not only in America, but around the world; a revolution that gets people's focus off of themselves and on to God and His glory; a revolution where once again, man will serve God, not God serve man; a revolution that will move the Church to take our Father's glory to all of the nations on the face of the earth. In John's insightful book, Passion for the Heart of God, John gives a creative challenge to the Church to pursue God's heart to the ends of the earth. His stories are fresh, energizing and easy to read, but best of all, he holds nothing back. John challenges us all to become a part of the needed revolution. I highly encourage anyone in the Body of Christ to read this book."

— Bob Sjogren, president, UnveilinGLORY and author, Unveiled at Last

COMPLETE IN HIM TO COMPLETE THE TASK
James Lee West

"How can we ever hope to have a passion for the lost if there is no passion for Jesus that causes us to leave behind everything that would compete for love and loyalty? The call of Jesus is that we follow Him completely. Unless we are complete in Him, the very idea of completing the commission to go into all the world and make disciples will always remain a mythical part of mere Christian teaching."

— from Complete in Him

OTHER BOOKS BY HGM PUBLISHING

PRAYER AS A PLACE
SPIRITUALITY THAT TRANSFORMS
Charles Bello

Prayer as a Place is an invitation to partner with Christ as he leads
the believer into the dark places of his or her own heart. The purpose
of this journey is to bring holiness and wholeness to the child of God.
With candor and brutal honesty, pastor Charles Bello shares his own
reluctance, and then resolve, to follow Christ on this inward journey.
In sharing his story, readers gain insight into what their own personal
journeys may look like. Prayer as a Place reads like a roadmap as it
explores the contemporary use of contemplative prayer as a means of
following Christ inward.

SIMPLE OBSESSION

$15   SUGGESTED DONATION

Books & resources from HGM Publishing are sold for whatever you can afford.

TO PLACE AN ORDER

Visit the online bookstore   www.heartofgod.com

Call or email Heart of God Ministries   405 - 737 - 9446
                                              resources@heartofgod.com

Or mail the form below to   Heart of God Ministries
                                              ATTN: HGM Publishing
                                              3720 S. Hiwassee Rd.
                                              Choctaw, OK 73020

- -

☐   Please send me _____ copies of *Simple Obsession*
    at US $_____ each.

☐   Please send me more information about
    Beautiful Feet Boot Camp missionary training.

Name _____

Address _____

City _____ State _____ Zip Code _____

Country _____ Telephone _____

Email _____

Total Payment Enclosed $_____
          Please make checks payable to Heart of God Ministries.